Empowerment for Ministry

*A Complete Manual on Diocesan Faculties
for Priests, Deacons, and Lay Ministers*

Empowerment for Ministry

*A Complete Manual on Diocesan Faculties
for Priests, Deacons, and Lay Ministers*

John M. Huels, J.C.D.

PAULIST PRESS

New York/Mahwah, N.J.

Cover design by Lynn Else

Book design by Celine Allen

Copyright © 2003 by John M. Huels

Library of Congress Cataloging-in-Publication Data

Huels, John M.
  Empowerment for ministry : a complete manual on diocesan faculties for priests,
deacons, and lay ministers / John M. Huels.
      p.   cm.
   ISBN 0-8091-4126-4
  1. Dioceses (Canon law) I. Title
   KBU2835 .H84 2003
   262.9'4—dc21

2003010258

Published by Paulist Press
997 Macarthur Boulevard
Mahwah, New Jersey 07430

www.paulistpress.com

Printed and bound in the
United States of America

Contents

APPENDICES

INDICES

ABBREVIATIONS

The *editio typica* of a liturgical rite is cited in this work only when the adapted English version used in the United States and/or Canada is numbered differently, or when the English version is not yet published. The Canadian and American versions of a liturgical book are both given if the two differ; the ICEL text is given if either the Canadian or American versions include adaptations not found in the original ICEL version. '

AAS   *Acta Apostolicae Sedis*

Au   Authorization (a non-jurisdictional faculty)

BB   *Book of Blessings*, 1987 (ICEL), 1989 (USA)

c.   canon

cc.   canons

CCCB   Canadian Conference of Catholic Bishops

CCLA   *Code of Canon Law Annotated*, ed. E. Caparros, M. Thériault, and J. Thorn

CCEO   *Code of Canons of the Eastern Churches (Codex Canonum Ecclesiarum orientalium)*

CDF   Congregation for the Doctrine of the Faith

Chpl   Chaplain (indicates a faculty appropriate for all chaplains)

CLD   *Canon Law Digest*

CLS   Canon Law Studies

CLSA   Canon Law Society of America

DAPNE   Directory for the Application of the Principles and Norms on Ecumenism (Pontifical Council for Promoting Christian Unity), 1993

DB   *Rituale Romanum: De Benedictionibus, editio typica*, 1984

DSCAP   Directory for Sunday Celebrations in the Absence of a Priest (Congregation for Divine Worship), June 2, 1988

EDM   *Ecclesiae de mysterio*, Instruction on Certain Questions Concerning the Cooperation of the Lay Faithful in the Ministry of Priests (Congregation for the Clergy et al.), August 15, 1997

ELB   Emendations in the Liturgical Books Following upon the New Code of Canon Law (Sacred Congregation for the Sacraments and Divine Worship, 1983; ICEL, 1984)

EP   Executive power of governance (cited at the beginning of a commentary to indicate a jurisdictional faculty)

ExM   Extraordinary ministry (indicates a faculty that may be exercised by a lay person when clergy are lacking)

GILH   General Instruction of the Liturgy of the Hours, 1971

GIRM   General Instruction of the Roman Missal, 3rd edition, 2000

HCWE   Rite of Holy Communion and Worship of the Eucharist Outside Mass, 1973

ICEL   International Commission on English in the Liturgy, Washington, DC

NCCB   National Conference of Catholic Bishops of the United States of America (as of 1 July 2001, the United States Conference of Catholic Bishops)

OA   *Ordo admissionis valide iam baptizatorum in plenam communionem Ecclesiae catholicae, editio typica*, 1972 (RCIA USA, nn. 473 ff.; Canada, nn. 387 ff.)

OCF   *Order of Christian Funerals*, 1985 (ICEL), 1986 (Canada), and 1989 (USA)

OCM   *Ordo celebrandi Matrimonium, editio typica altera*, 1990

OE   *Ordo exsequiarum, editio typica*, 1969

OICA	*Ordo initiationis christianae adultorum, editio typica*, 1972
OUI	*Ordo unctionis infirmorum eorumque pastoralis curae, editio typica*, 1972
PC	Pastoral commentary (intended for those receiving the faculties, to be included on the *pagella*, if desired)
PCS	Pastoral Care of the Sick: Rites of Anointing and Viaticum, 1983
PV	Parochial vicar (indicates a faculty of a pastor that is also appropriately delegated to a parochial vicar, or is a faculty of a parochial vicar by law)
R	Rectors of churches (indicates a faculty of a pastor that is also appropriately delegated to a rector of a church)
RBC	Rite of Baptism of Children, 2nd ed., 1973
RC	Rite of Confirmation, 1971
RCIA	Rite of Christian Initiation of Adults, 1988 (USA) and 1987 (Canada)
RP	Rite of Penance, 1973
SDO	*Sacrum Diaconatus Ordinem*, the apostolic letter *motu proprio* of Pope Paul VI restoring the permanent diaconate, June 18, 1967
SPCU	Secretariat for Promoting Christian Unity
TC	Technical commentary intended for canonists and diocesan officials
USCCB	United States Conference of Catholic Bishops
VG, EV	Vicar general, episcopal vicar (indicates a faculty that the vicar general and episcopal vicar have by law as local ordinaries, used only in Chapter Eight)

General Introduction

The Second Vatican Council and the 1983 Code of Canon Law both affirm that all the faithful participate in the mission of the Church in virtue of their baptism. All the baptized have their own share in the sanctifying, teaching, and ruling functions of the Church.[1] However, public ministries exercised *in the name of the Church* require additional empowerment beyond baptism. The principal sources of this additional empowerment are the sacrament of holy orders, the canonical faculties attached by law to pastoral or administrative offices and functions, and the faculties granted by ecclesiastical authority for specific acts and duties. This work is concerned with all three sources, but especially the third—the faculties granted by the diocesan bishop to those who minister within the local church.

Public, ecclesial ministries are exercised, for the most part, within the *local church* headed by the diocesan bishop. Priests, deacons, and designated religious and lay persons are the bishop's close collaborators in the Church's apostolic mission. An important means by which they are empowered for ecclesial ministry is the grant of faculties by the bishop. Such faculties allow them to perform specific acts of ministry or administration that they could not lawfully—and often not even validly—perform without the faculties.

---

1. *Lumen gentium*, 31; *Apostolicam actuositatem*, 2; c. 204, §1.

Diocesan faculties are the legal powers and authorizations granted by the bishop to his collaborators in the ministry for specific liturgical and other ministerial acts as well as for acts of parochial or diocesan administration. Traditionally, diocesan faculties have been granted only to priests, but now they are also being granted to deacons and increasingly also to lay ministers, especially those who serve in full-time pastoral positions such as chaplains, pastoral associates, those who participate in the pastoral care of a parish without a resident pastor, and lay officials who serve in the diocesan curia and tribunal.

The aims of this book are both theoretical and practical, serving both the science of canon law as well as church administration and pastoral ministry. It seeks: (1) to develop a coherent theory of the juridical nature and the delegation of faculties, one that is rooted in the 1983 Code of Canon Law and the practice of the Church; (2) to identify and organize the pertinent rules of canon law and the canonical tradition on the grant, supply, use, and cessation of diocesan faculties; and (3) to provide model faculties and commentaries on them for clergy, lay ministers, and chancery officials.

Given these aims, both scholarly and pastoral, a broad audience may benefit from using this book: (1) diocesan leaders and those who advise them in the preparation and updating of diocesan faculties; (2) canonists and students of canon law; (3) priests, deacons, and lay ministers who have faculties by law and/or delegation; and (4) those preparing for ecclesial ministries–seminarians, deacon candidates, and lay ministers in formation.

The body of the book is divided into two parts and eight chapters. Part I, "Theory and Rules," presents a comprehensive treatment of diocesan faculties and all the canonical rules applicable to their initial grant, their use, delegation, subdelegation, and cessation. Part II, "Model Faculties and Commentaries," offers lists of faculties and commentaries on them for priests and deacons, pastors, parochial vicars, those who share in the pastoral care of parishes without a resident pastor (c. 517, §2), chaplains, and chancery officials. The appendices provide further information pertinent to diocesan faculties and the use of this book. Among these is a glossary of canonical terms used in this work.

Why This Book?

Besides assisting ministers and church administrators to understand the nature of diocesan faculties and the canonical rules for their use, the need is equally great to educate canonists, students of canon law, bishops, and chancery officials about this fundamental canonical institute. The subject is complex, and good studies are lacking. Over the course of my career as a canonist, I have had occasion to review numerous diocesan *pagellae* (lists of faculties) and have noted some consistent problems with them.

On all the *pagellae* I have seen, the most common weakness is their inattention to the liturgical books and other sources of law apart from the Code of Canon Law. Faculties are given exclusively, or nearly exclusively, on the basis of the laws in the code. However, there are scores of additional possibilities for diocesan faculties to be found in the liturgical books, the Directory for the Application of the Principles and Norms on Ecumenism, and several other documents. The norms in these texts typically require the diocesan bishop's or local ordinary's permission for some act, for example, celebrating the Eucharist at a mixed marriage. Many of these are matters that ought to be in a diocesan *pagella* for the good order of diocesan practice and to ensure that the universal law is observed both in letter and in spirit.

A second problem with most diocesan *pagellae* is that they do not establish any conditions for the use of certain faculties. The reason the bishop's or local ordinary's permission is required for many acts is the need for him to judge whether it is suitable in the circumstances to perform the act in question. If the faculty to grant such permissions is routinely delegated to priests (and deacons, when applicable) without any conditions or explanations, then priests and other ministers are left without any guidance about when an act is suitable and when it is not. Each minister is left to his or her own devices, and improper and unfortunate pastoral choices are sometimes made. There are times and circumstances when permissions should not be automatically granted for certain acts that would be routine under other conditions. By establishing the acceptable conditions on the list of faculties, the local ordinary's explicit permission would only be necessary in individual cases that are not among those expressly stated.

A third problem with many diocesan *pagellae* is the lack of clarity between faculties given by law and faculties granted by delegation. The two are often interspersed, and on some *pagellae* it looks like the bishop is granting a faculty that is already given by universal law. This is particularly true of lists of faculties for deacons. The few lists I have seen contain only faculties by law, yet it appears as if the bishop is granting them. Some lists of faculties, especially for deacons and lay ministers, also mix faculties together with duties of office without indicating the difference. Yet, their juridical natures are completely different and different rules apply to them.

Strictly speaking, a *pagella* does not need to list any faculty by law, because its purpose is precisely to delegate faculties. However, certain faculties by law are traditionally listed (e.g., the faculty to preach), while others are listed for the information of priests so that they know they have the faculty. The main concern is always to indicate clearly which faculties are by law and which by delegation.

The confusion over the distinction between faculties given by law and those given by delegation has practical consequences. From time to time a bishop removes the faculties of a priest, instead of suspending him, or he does not grant diocesan faculties to a controversial extern priest who will be visiting the diocese. It is commonly thought that the priest without faculties cannot function at all as a priest, or that also the faculties *by law* given on the *pagella* are taken away or not granted. In my experience, the affected priest himself thinks that. However, the withdrawal or non-conferral of faculties only means that the *delegated* faculties of the diocese are withdrawn or not given. Restrictions on powers of order and the faculties given by law, such as the celebration of the public liturgy, can be imposed by particular law or by a penal action, but not by the simple removal of diocesan faculties. The bishop cannot remove a faculty he has never granted! Thus, the whole question of the removal of faculties—how it may be done, under what circumstances, the rights of the minister involved, etc.—needs closer attention by diocesan personnel and is treated in chapter 2.

A fourth problem with the lists of faculties I have seen is the indiscriminate granting of the same faculties to all priests in the diocese. Some faculties should be granted only to the pastor, others only to priests who serve in pastoral care (including parochial vicars and chaplains), while others may well be granted to all priests, including those who have no pastoral office.

A fifth problem has to do with dioceses that have no faculties for deacons who assist in parishes or for deacons and lay ministers who administer a parish that lacks a resident pastor. Since local churches have no traditions upon which to draw with respect to faculties for these ministries, models are provided in this book to help them develop *pagellae* suitable for their own situation.

A sixth problem has to do with doubts arising when the vicar general, rather than the bishop, delegates the faculties, as is done in some dioceses. Some of the faculties being delegated are reserved in law to the diocesan bishop, yet there is no evidence that the diocesan bishop has expressly mandated the vicar general to grant the faculty. If this has not been done, their delegation is invalid.

Finally, a new situation exists in dioceses today in which lay persons, lay religious, and deacons are holding positions formerly held by priests, such as chancellor, director of the tribunal, and parish director, but diocesan personnel are unsure of what faculties may properly be delegated to such officials.

To be sure, it is no easy task to compile a comprehensive diocesan *pagella*, much less to do it without any tradition upon which to draw for new ministries and for diocesan offices now being held by lay persons. In the science of canon law, very little has been written on diocesan faculties, despite their practical importance in the life of the Church at every level. This lack of attention to faculties derives in large measure, I believe, from the fact that canon law itself has no clear presentation of the matter. Diocesan faculties are governed by numerous laws of the Code of Canon Law, but nowhere in the code is there a section devoted to faculties as such. In fact, there is only one, somewhat ambiguous, reference to habitual faculties in general (c. 132, §1). Because there is no section of the code on faculties, or even a single canon explicitly devoted to diocesan faculties as such, canonical commentators for the most part ignore the subject. Students can get advanced degrees in divinity or canon law without ever learning in any systematic way what laws of the code apply to diocesan faculties or how they function within the canonical system, yet diocesan faculties are fundamental to the ministry and administration of the local churches around the world, both at the diocesan and parish levels.

It is my hope that this book will benefit canonical scholarship; augment the canonical education of canonists, students, chancery officials, and pastoral ministers; and serve as a practical guide for devising and revising the diocesan faculties needed in today's Church. I thank my colleagues at Saint Paul University, Professors Augustine Mendonça and Frank Morrisey, O.M.I., for their insights and suggestions, and Judge Amy Jill Strickland of the Boston Metropolitan Tribunal for editorial assistance. I am also grateful to Saint Paul University, which granted me a six-month sabbatical in 2001 to prepare this work.

PART I
THEORY AND RULES

INTRODUCTION TO PART I

This introduction first gives an overview of the three chapters that constitute Part I. Following this are four sections of a technical nature that provide: a brief account of the evolution of the law and practice concerning faculties from the 1917 Code of Canon Law to the code of 1983; an explanation of the category of faculties called "authorizations"; an analysis of whether "favors" should be retained as a category of faculties; and the rationale for determining the canonical rules that govern faculties.

Overview of Part I

Part I, "Theory and Rules," presents a theory of diocesan faculties rooted in the 1983 code and the practice of the Church, and it fleshes out the canonical rules applicable to faculties. The core of the theory is that all diocesan faculties can be divided into two kinds—those that are for acts of the power of governance and those that are authorizations for other acts.

Chapter 1 treats fundamental matters necessary for understanding faculties and how they function in the canonical system: their purposes, sources, juridic nature, and the ways they may be categorized. Chapter 2 treats the grant of diocesan faculties by the diocesan bishop and their revocation by him, as well as the supply of faculties by the law (c. 144). This is the most technical chapter, of greater concern to canonists and diocesan officials than to other readers. Chapter 3 is on the use of faculties, their delegation and subdelegation, and their cessation, matters that directly affect those who have faculties or who may be receiving them in the future.

Before commencing our investigation, we need clarity on what is meant by a "faculty." Sometimes the law explicitly uses the word "faculty" for a specific act, such as the faculty to hear confessions, the faculty to preach, or the faculty to assist at marriages. The term also has a broader, generic meaning in canon law. For example, canon 566, §1 speaks of the chaplain being provided "with all the faculties that proper pastoral care requires." This refers not only to what is called a "faculty" in canon law, but to all necessary powers and authorizations. Therefore, a faculty rightly refers to any power or authorization necessary to perform an act lawfully. It need not specifically be called a "faculty" in the law.

Canon law does not use a uniform vocabulary for the faculties for different ministries, even at times for the very same function. For example, the code speaks of presbyters and deacons having the "faculty" to preach (c. 764) and lay persons being "admitted" to preach (c. 766). Nevertheless, it is correct to speak of any of these ministers, when lawfully authorized, as having the "faculty" to preach, in that they have been lawfully empowered to preach, whether by the law or by a mandate of the bishop. With respect to the lay preacher, the "admission" to preach is an authorization to preach. Therefore, it fits the definition of a faculty, as we shall see in chapter 1.

Given the past practice of granting diocesan faculties only to priests, some diocesan personnel have been reluctant to say that lay ministers can have faculties. However, this caution has no foundation in the law. The universal legislator shows no hesitation in speaking of lay persons being granted a faculty. Some examples are the 1990 Rite of Marriage (OCM 119), the *Book of Blessings* (BB/DB 18d), and the 1997 Instruction on Certain Questions Concerning the Collaboration of the Lay Faithful in the Ministry of Priests (EDM art. 10, §3). It is necessary to check the original Latin texts, since translators, particularly non-canonists, frequently render *facultas* by a word other than "faculty."

The remainder of this introduction to Part I is directed mainly to canonists, students of canon law, and others interested in canonical theory. First, it sketches the theory and practice of habitual faculties in the system of the 1917 code and shows the ways in which this changed at Vatican II and in the 1983 code. Next, it explains the basis for dividing diocesan faculties into two categories—those that are authorizations and those that grant executive power of governance. It concludes by identifying the canonical rules that govern habitual faculties. Given the technical nature of this subject, some readers may wish to move directly to chapter 1. Before doing so, readers may find it helpful to glance at some faculties in Part II to get a practical idea of what is treated theoretically in Part I.

From the 1917 Code to the 1983 Code

The practice of the Church concerning faculties in some respects is the same and in other respects is significantly different under the system of the 1983 Code of Canon Law than it was under the first code of 1917. To understand these differences, as well as to see the basic continuity between the two systems, it will be helpful to explain the treatment and practice of faculties under the system of the 1917 code and to point out the changes that came about at the time of Vatican II and its aftermath.[1]

In the canonical doctrine (the writing of scholars) on the 1917 code, faculties were categorized according to their source as *apostolic* or *episcopal*.[2] Apostolic faculties were those granted by the Apostolic See to diocesan bishops and other ordinaries. Quinquennial faculties were granted to diocesan bishops every five years at the time of the

---

1. For historical treatment of faculties preceding the 1917 code, see George Eagleton, *The Diocesan Quinquennial Faculties Formula IV*, CLS 248 (Washington: The Catholic University of America, 1948) 1–33; A. J. Quinn, "Faculties (canon law)," *New Catholic Encyclopedia*, ed. William J. McDonald et al. (New York: McGraw Hill, 1967) 5:786–787; Raoul Naz, "Facultés apostoliques," in *Dictionnaire de Droit Canonique* 5:802–807.

2. A third category consisted of *regular* faculties. These were faculties granted by superiors of exempt religious orders to their priests. Such priests were called "regular" because they were subject to their order's rule *(regula)*. The faculties given by religious superiors are not the concern of this work.

bishops' quinquennial report to the Holy See (1917 c. 340). The Sacred Congregation for the Propagation of the Faith granted decennial faculties, valid for ten years, to ordinaries in mission territories. Some of the quinquennial and decennial faculties could be subdelegated to priests in the diocese. This practice contributed to a "pyramidal" ecclesiology, in which it was thought that all powers in the Church come from God and are given to the pope, who in turn apportions some of them to the bishops, who in their turn subdelegate some of them to priests to be used on behalf of those at the bottom of the pyramid, the laity.

However, the significance of this distorted pyramidal ecclesiology should not be exaggerated. Even under the 1917 code, the bishop had many powers in law and by holy orders that did not need to be delegated by the Holy See. In fact, most faculties granted to priests on the diocesan *pagellae* of the time were not received from the Holy See and then subdelegated by the bishop. Instead, they were "episcopal faculties," ones that the bishop could grant on his own authority.

In the canonical doctrine on the 1917 code, faculties were also divided according to their extent as *actual* or *habitual* faculties.[3] An actual faculty was limited to a specified case or several specified cases. Habitual faculties were granted for use on an ongoing basis, not for a specified act or acts.[4] The faculties granted by the Apostolic See to bishops and other ordinaries were habitual faculties. Diocesan faculties granted by the bishop to priests were also habitual faculties, as they were given for repeated use and not for individual instances. Thus, habitual faculties could be either apostolic or episcopal, and the canonical rules governing habitual faculties were applied to both diocesan faculties and apostolic faculties.[5] In the 1917 code (c. 66,

---

3. Edward G. Roelker, *Principles of Privilege According to the Code of Canon Law*, CLS 35 (Washington: The Catholic University of America, 1926) 141.

4. Habitual faculties were granted in perpetuity, for a specific period of time, or for a certain number of cases (1917 c. 66, §1). However, even if granted for a certain number of cases, they were still indeterminate in that the precise cases were not specified, just their number.

5. Hubert L. Motry, *Diocesan Faculties According to the Code of Canon Law*, CLS 16 (Washington: The Catholic University of America, 1922) 24.

§1), a habitual faculty was considered a kind of privilege. Since the rules on rescripts also applied to privileges (1917 c. 62),[6] the applicable canons on both rescripts and privileges regulated habitual faculties (1917 cc. 36–79).

Commentators on the former law also categorized faculties according to their nature. The two major categories were *jurisdictional* faculties and *non-jurisdictional* faculties. Jurisdictional faculties were mainly for acts of what is now called the executive power of governance (granting dispensations, permissions, sanations, etc.). The faculty for hearing confessions was also considered jurisdictional in the system of the 1917 code, but not in the 1983 code. Now, this faculty is understood as an authorization that enables the priest validly to use a power of order.

In the canonical doctrine on the 1917 code, non-jurisdictional faculties were divided into authorizations *(licentiae),* favors *(gratiae),* and precautionary grants *(concessiones ad cautelam).*[7] For example, decennial faculties granted by the Sacred Congregation for the Propagation of the Faith to missionary ordinaries contained mostly jurisdictional faculties, some authorizations, and a few favors. Precautionary grants were not genuine faculties. They simply advised the recipient that he already had the faculties. They would have been real faculties only if the recipient did not actually have the faculties that he was thought to have had.

The most significant developments to affect the law and practice on faculties resulted from decisions of Vatican II, Pope Paul VI, and the first Synod of Bishops in 1967. Already in 1963, before the council had yet completed any major documents, Paul VI promulgated a new law by which many faculties of diocesan bishops, formerly

---

6. A habitual faculty was considered to be like a privilege *apart* from the law *(praeter ius),* not a privilege against the law *(contra ius).*

7. See Peter B. Chyang, *Decennial Faculties for Ordinaries in Quasi-Dioceses,* CLS 402 (Washington: The Catholic University of America, 1961) 35. For an informative treatment on the nature of a faculty, see Juan González Ayesta, "La noción jurídica de «facultad» en los comentadores del Código de 1917," *Ius Canonicum* 40 (2000) 99–123. This study also looks at the nature of faculties in the 1983 code.

granted to them by the Apostolic See, would henceforth belong to them in virtue of their office.[8] Paul VI acted in response to developments occurring at the council that would result in major shifts in ecclesiology and changes in canon law.

Vatican II reversed the distorted pyramidal model of the Church and recovered a more ancient ecclesiology that shows more clearly the Church's true nature. In its presentation on those who make up the Church, the council began with the people of God—all the baptized believers in Christ—before it took up the hierarchical constitution of the Church.[9] The council retrieved the ancient but long neglected notion of the Church as a communion of churches, each with a bishop at its head in communion with all the other Catholic churches and with the see of Rome.[10] The council fathers taught that episcopal ordination was a sacrament, that bishops are the vicars and legates of Christ, and that they are not to be regarded as vicars of the pope. They exercise their sacred power directly in the name of Christ. This power is proper, ordinary, and immediate, although the supreme authority of the Church may regulate its exercise and place limitations on it.[11] Furthermore, the council decreed that diocesan bishops have the power to dispense from universal laws.[12] This would eliminate the need to get apostolic faculties for dispensations.

In 1967, the first Synod of Bishops issued ten principles to guide the reform of canon law in line with the decrees of Vatican II.[13] The fourth principle held that faculties, previously granted by the Apostolic See to bishops and other ordinaries, were to be incorporated in the Code of Canon Law. The synod said the code was to be revised to rec-

---

8. Apostolic letter *motu proprio*, *Pastorale munus*, November 30, 1963, AAS 56 (1963) 5–12.

9. *Lumen gentium*, chapters 2 and 3.

10. *Lumen gentium*, 13, 23, 26.

11. *Lumen gentium*, 27; *Christus Dominus*, 11. The supreme authority of the Church is the pope or the college of bishops acting collegially with the pope.

12. *Christus Dominus*, 8b.

13. *Communicationes* 2 (1969) 77–85; English translation in Jordan Hite and Daniel J. Ward, *Readings, Cases, Materials in Canon Law: A Textbook for Ministerial Students*, rev. ed. (Collegeville: The Liturgical Press, 1990) 84–92.

ognize the governance and dispensing powers of bishops as decreed at Vatican II. Henceforth, the presumption of canon law would be that diocesan bishops have all the faculties they need to govern their dioceses; a reservation of any matter to the Holy See must be explicitly stated in the law or by decree of the pope. Already by the late 1960s, the Apostolic See had ceased to grant quinquennial and decennial faculties. These faculties were no longer necessary, as diocesan bishops now had all their necessary powers in virtue of episcopal ordination and in virtue of their office, not by delegation from the Holy See.

The revised Code of Canon Law of 1983 incorporated the changes begun with Paul VI and Vatican II and it implemented the fourth principle of the 1967 Synod of Bishops. Canon 381 of the revised code says that the diocesan bishop has all ordinary, proper, and immediate power required for the exercise of his pastoral office, except for cases that by a law or decree of the pope are reserved to another ecclesiastical authority. The provision of Vatican II on the bishop's dispensing power was codified in canon 87, §1, which says the diocesan bishop may dispense the faithful from all disciplinary laws, including universal laws, except those laws whose dispensation is reserved to the Apostolic See.

In the revised code, apostolic faculties have a much more limited function than they formerly had. Now, they are usually granted only in extraordinary cases, such as that of a coadjutor or another auxiliary bishop endowed with special faculties to resolve serious difficulties that the bishop himself is unable to resolve (cf. c. 403, §§ 2, 3). Consequently, habitual faculties are no longer routinely granted from outside the diocese by the Apostolic See but are given by the bishop himself from *within* the diocese. Habitual faculties today are mainly *episcopal*, not apostolic faculties. These are the habitual faculties that are the subject of this book, the diocesan faculties given by the bishop to diocesan officials and to those who exercise the ministry within the diocese—priests, deacons, and some lay ministers.

Besides reflecting these major shifts in the practice of faculties, the 1983 code also has a different understanding of the nature of habitual faculties from that of the 1917 code. Unlike the 1917 code, habitual faculties are no longer considered a kind of privilege. The canon on habitual faculties in the revised code (c. 132) is found among the canons on the power of governance, not among the canons on privileges. Moving the canon out of the context of privileges was a positive development because it acknowledges the reality that faculties are not true privileges. Still, situating the canon on habitual faculties in the title on power of governance is not without its own difficulties, since not all the canons on delegated power apply to authorizations.[14]

Authorizations

We have seen that faculties were traditionally divided into jurisdictional faculties (mostly for acts of executive power of governance) and non-jurisdictional faculties (all other faculties). Non-jurisdictional faculties were further distinguished as authorizations, favors, and precautionary grants. Canonists recognized that precautionary grants were not true faculties; in any case, they are no longer given, so this category is obsolete. The subcategory of "favors" will be treated below.

The category of "executive power" is well known to canonists, since the code treats it explicitly (cc. 134, §3; 135, §§ 1, 4; 136–144). The category of "authorizations" may be unfamiliar, since the code has no parallel treatment of it, so some initial remarks are necessary to explain it. In this work, "authorization" is used in its traditional sense as a non-jurisdictional faculty, except it is now the exclusive category for any faculty other than a faculty for the exercise of the power of governance. In other words, all non-jurisdictional faculties (those that are true faculties) are authorizations.

---

14. Canon 132, §1 says that habitual faculties are governed by the rules for delegated (executive) power. The choice of this context may have been influenced by the fact that most habitual apostolic faculties granted (what the 1983 code calls) executive power of governance. However, not all apostolic faculties granted power of governance; some were non-jurisdictional. As for episcopal faculties, authorizations make up a sizeable portion, oftentimes the majority, of the faculties granted on diocesan *pagellae*.

The chief problem is c. 137, which gives rules for the delegation and subdelegation of executive power. The problem is that authorizations cannot be delegated or subdelegated unless this power is expressly granted by law or delegation. Thus, the rules on executive power apply to authorizations, but not completely.

The Latin word for authorization, in the doctrine on the 1917 code, was *licentia*. Is this use of *licentia* as a non-jurisdictional faculty identical with the use of the word *licentia* in canon law today? The answer is both yes and no. Many *licentiae* in the code are true faculties, but some are not. Likewise, many non-jurisdictional faculties have the same nature as *licentiae* but are called something else.

The 1983 code uses the word *licentia* about sixty-five times in the sense of a permission or authorization. In about two-thirds of these instances, the *licentiae* have the nature of non-jurisdictional faculties. The *licentiae* that are true faculties authorize a person to perform an act of ministry or administration *in the name of the Church*, while the *licentiae* that are not faculties permit persons to perform acts *in their own name*.[15]

The code contains only one general norm governing *licentiae*, namely, canon 59, §2: "The rules on rescripts, unless otherwise established, also apply to the grant of an authorization *(licentia)* and the oral granting of favors." This rule applies to all *licentiae*, both those that authorize acts to be performed in the name of the Church (faculties) and permissions for acts to be performed in one's own name. Moreover, this rule applies not only to laws in which the precise word *licentia* is used, but also to laws using other terms that have the same meaning as "permission" or that indicate a non-jurisdictional faculty.

In a study for a canonical journal, I analyzed the juridical nature of a *licentia* as used in the Latin and Eastern codes, and I compiled a list of terms that are equivalent to *licentia*, both in its sense as a permission for an act done in one's own name and in the sense of a non-jurisdictional faculty that authorizes a person to act in the name of the Church.[16] The code uses the word *licentia* as both genus and species.

---

15. As we shall see in chapter 1, an essential feature of a ministerial faculty is that it enables a person to act *in the name of the Church*. The word *licentia* appears frequently in the 1983 code, but it does not always have the meaning of a non-jurisdictional faculty, that is, an authorization for a ministerial act or an act of administration done in the name of the Church. For example, transferring from one's church *sui iuris* to another, for which a *licentia* is needed (c. 112, §1, 1°), is not a ministerial faculty but is an act performed in one's own name.

16. John M. Huels, "Permissions, Authorizations, and Faculties in Canon Law," *Studia Canonica* 36 (2002) 25–58. The equivalent terms are published in vol. 37 (2003).

The *licentia* of canon 59, §2 is the genus; elsewhere in the law, it is used as the species. The genus, or category, of *licentia* consists of any singular administrative act that may be used in a sense equivalent to a permission or a non-jurisdictional faculty (*concessio, concedere; permissio, permittere; delegatio, delegare; venia; facultas; licentia* [used as the species], etc.). Appendix I lists various terms that may indicate a faculty that is an authorization, depending on the context in which the terms are used in the law. This is not a taxative list but includes only those words taken from laws used for faculties in this book.

The *licentia* of canon 59, §2 functions as a generic category that includes a variety of words indicating an act that has the same nature and function as a *licentia*. By an analogy of law *(anologia legis),* the rule of canon 59, §2 should be applied to these differently named acts that have the same nature and function as a *licentia*. This conclusion is the only reasonable interpretation of the law, and rationality, or reasonableness, is at the heart of the canonical system.[17] It would be unreasonable to conclude that the legislator intended the rules on rescripts to apply only when the law specifically mentions a *licentia* but not when it uses equivalent terminology for acts that have the same nature and function as granting a *licentia*. In other words, the norm of canon 59, §2—that the rules on rescripts are applicable to the granting of a *licentia* —applies to any act that has the nature of a *licentia*, no matter what it is called. For example, canon 905, §2 says that, if there is a shortage of priests, the local ordinary can grant *(concedere)* that priests may binate for a just cause or trinate on Sundays and holy days of obligation in cases of pastoral necessity. Instead of *concedere*, the legislator could have said *permittere, dare licentiam, conferre facultatem*, or something similar, and the meaning of the law and the juridic nature of the administrative act of granting or permitting would have been the same. Consequently, all *licentiae* and equivalent acts, including faculties that are authorizations, are governed by the rules for rescripts. Other canonists,

---

17. Thomas Aquinas defined law as an "ordinance of reason for the common good promulgated by one who has the care of the community." See *Summa Theologiae,* I–II, q. 90, a. 4. That a canonical norm be reasonable (*rationabilis*) is explicitly required for a custom to attain the force of law (c. 24, §2).

albeit with differing approaches, have also concluded that the *licentia* of canon 59, §2 functions as a category.[18]

Favors

On the list of quinquennial faculties in use up to Vatican II, none was a favor, and only a few of the decennial faculties were favors. With these lists obsolete for many years, we can reassess the need for favors as a subcategory of faculties.

In the broad sense of the word "favor" *(gratia),* all faculties are favors, because they enhance the juridic condition of the recipients by enabling them to act lawfully in ways that heretofore they could not.[19] In the strict sense of the word, a favor is a benefit granted by the com-

---

18. See, e.g., Francesco D'Ostilio, "Tipologia ed esecuzione degli atti amministrativi," *Apollinaris* 45 (1972) 268; *idem, Il diritto amministrativo della Chiesa,* Studi Giuridici, no. 37 (Città del Vaticano: Libreria Editrice Vaticana, 1995) 325; Eduardo Labandeira, "Naturaleza jurídica del poder de absolver los pecados desde la perspectiva del Vatican II y del nuevo Código," in *Reconciliación y penitencia: V simposio internacional de teología de la Universidad de Navarra,* ed. Jesús Sancho et al. (Pamplona: Universidad de Navarra, 1983) 957–981, esp. p. 976; *idem, Cuestiones de derecho administrativo canónico* (Pamplona: Universidad de Navarra, 1992) 238–246; and Javier Canosa, "De rescriptis," in *Comentario exegético al Código de Derecho Canónico,* ed. Angel Marzoa, Jorge Mira, and Rafael Rodríguez-Ocaña (Pamplona: EUNSA, 1996) 598.

19. The commission *(coetus)* on general norms in the code revision process, according to the statement of its adjunct secretary, appeared to employ a broad understanding of a favor as "any favorable concession for the benefit of someone." (See *Communicationes* 22 [1990] 304.) This broad notion enables the rules on rescripts to be applied to those authorizations *(licentiae)* and other favorable matters that are not strictly favors. In an earlier draft of Book I, rescripts were said to grant "a privilege, a dispensation, or another favor, or an authorization *(licentia).* (See ibid.) The promulgated text did not say that rescripts grant authorizations, but only that they are subject to the rules on rescripts (c. 59, §2). Interestingly, the Eastern Code returns to the earlier notion in the draft of the Latin code and says that rescripts grant authorizations (CCEO, c. 1510, §2, 3°).

Javier Canosa understands a rescript, which by definition grants a favor (c. 59, §1), as any favorable grant that "broadens the sphere of faculties and rights of a person." See "De rescriptis," p. 594.

petent authority to an individual person (physical or juridic), which the person is free to accept or not and is free to use or not (cf. c. 71).[20] However, a faculty given by a hierarchical superior cannot be refused and must be used on behalf of the community for which it was granted. This point will be discussed in chapter 3.

A faculty, as the word is commonly used in the law and the practice of the Church, is a power or authorization needed for a person to perform some act of ministry or administration lawfully (validly and/or licitly) in the name of the Church.[21] Faculties are granted primarily for the benefit of the community. Favors, such as, for example, a dispensation, commutation, privilege, remission of a penalty, sanation, indult, etc., grant a benefit to an individual physical or juridic person. Such favors benefit someone personally; they are not an empowerment to act for the community, as a faculty is. Therefore, faculties are not usually favors in the strict sense, although they are favor*able* to persons in that they give them a new power or ability to perform some act lawfully that previously they could not lawfully perform.

Rarely, a faculty is granted for a person's own benefit. For example, the bishop may grant clerics the power to dispense themselves from the daytime offices when they are prevented from celebrating an hour at its proper time due to the demands of the apostolate. Although this faculty is truly a favor, there is no need for a separate category of faculty called "favors," since this is the delegation of executive power, which already is a category. Another example is the faculty given to binate. This faculty is ordinarily used for the benefit of the faithful, but it could be used when the priest wants to concelebrate a second Mass on the same day for a just cause. This use of the faculty is a favor because the priest is not required to concelebrate for the

---

20. Canon 71 says that no one is obliged to use a rescript granted only in one's own favor unless bound to do so by some other canonical obligation. If someone is bound to use a rescript, the content of that rescript is not a true favor, because a favor always is voluntary in nature. Such a rescript could contain a faculty, however, which the recipient is bound to use on behalf of the community for which it was given.

21. This understanding of "faculty" pertains to its usual meaning in the law, but the code sometimes uses the word *facultas* in other ways. See González Ayesta, "La noción jurídica de «facultad» en los comentadores del Código de 1917," 120–121.

benefit of the faithful. However, the faculty itself is still an authorization. No separate category is necessary simply because this faculty is used as a favor. Indeed, most favors that are not faculties (dispensations, commutations, etc.) should *not* be given on a list of faculties. Such favors are not habitual faculties for regular and repeated use, but should only be granted in individual instances when they are justified by the circumstances. If such a favor were to be included on a *pagella*, it would retain its nature as a favor; its inclusion on the *pagella* would not make it a faculty. Thus, two categories of faculties suffice in the canonical system today—authorizations and the grant of power of governance. All the faculties listed in Part II of this work pertain to one of these two categories.

The Rules Applicable to Faculties

In chapters 2 and 3, we shall examine the canonical rules that apply to faculties. These are primarily the rules on executive power of governance, singular administrative acts, and rescripts. We shall now briefly explain why these rules are applicable.

1) The *rules on executive power* are applicable due to canon 132, §1, which says that the norms for delegated power—namely, canons 133 and 136–144—govern habitual faculties. All these canons apply to faculties granting executive power of governance, since they treat executive power. Most of them apply also to authorizations or, if they do not, the canons themselves have excepting clauses acknowledging that a rule does not always apply. In this latter case, it is possible to exclude, within the terms of the law itself, the provisions that do not apply to authorizations.[22] However, canon 137 contains provisions on

---

22. For example, c. 136 says, in part, that executive power [and habitual faculties] can be exercised over one's subjects even *outside* one's territory, *unless the nature of the matter or a prescript of law (ius) establishes otherwise* [italics mine]. Unlike executive power, faculties that are authorizations may not ordinarily be used outside one's territory. However, this fact does not conflict with c. 136, since it is clear that the law, sometimes explicitly and sometimes implicitly, excludes the use of authorizations outside one's territory without the necessary

the delegation and subdelegation of executive power which, for the most part, do not apply to faculties that are authorizations. It is clear from both practice and law that most authorizations cannot be delegated and subdelegated unless the power to delegate and subdelegate itself is granted, or unless delegation and subdelegation are permitted by law, as with the faculty to assist at marriage.[23] The law does not permit most other authorizations to be delegated and subdelegated.[24] For example, a presbyter who has been authorized to confirm cannot subdelegate this faculty to allow another priest to substitute for him; or a lay person who has been authorized to preach cannot subdelegate this faculty to another lay person. We can conclude, therefore, that the canons on delegated power apply to all faculties that grant executive power as well as to authorizations, with the notable exception of canon 137, which does not apply to most authorizations.

2) The *rules for singular administrative acts* (cc. 35–47) are also applicable to faculties. It is clear, both from the nature of the act and from the common opinion of the authors on the 1983 code, that the grant of a faculty is a singular administrative act. It follows that the general norms on singular administrative acts must be taken into account in the grant, use, interpretation, and revocation of habitual faculties.

3) We have seen above that authorizations, in keeping with canon 59, §2, are governed by the *rules for rescripts*. However, in the system of the 1917 code, *all* habitual faculties were governed by the applicable canons on rescripts, including jurisdictional faculties. Is

---

permission. See, e.g., cc. 561; 764 (if particular law requires permission to preach); 886, §2; 888; 1115; 1118.

23. Even among the decennial and quinquennial faculties, relatively few, e.g., only twenty of the sixty-eight decennial faculties, could be subdelegated. Under the former law, habitual faculties could be subdelegated only when this was expressly permitted.

24. Besides marriage, another authorization that can be delegated and subdelegated is a faculty to make contracts in the name of an ecclesiastical juridic person. For example, the pastor can give a general delegation to a parish employee to purchase supplies. As well, the employee must have this authority in the civil law, e.g., by being able to sign checks, use a parish credit card, place orders with certain suppliers, or the like. The ability to delegate and subdelegate the authority to make contracts is a universal and immemorial custom.

this still true in the law of the 1983 code? Canon 6, §2 requires that the canons of the code be assessed in light of the canonical tradition insofar as they refer to matters in the old law. The canons on rescripts provide helpful rules that were developed over centuries, rules that have application not only to the grant of favors in the strict sense but also to related singular administrative acts that grant something favorable or advantageous.[25] In keeping with the canonical tradition, the applicable canons on rescripts should be observed in the grant and interpretation of all faculties. In chapters 2 and 3, we shall see how these canons are pertinent.

Summary

The granting of habitual faculties, both apostolic and episcopal, was routine under the system of the 1917 code. With ecclesiological developments at Vatican II and changes in law in the 1960s, the routine issuance of apostolic faculties to diocesan bishops and other ordinaries was discontinued; these faculties are now granted to diocesan bishops by law in virtue of their office. The practice of granting episcopal (diocesan) faculties was unaffected by these developments. Diocesan faculties are habitual faculties granted by the bishop to priests, deacons, and lay ministers for regular use on an ongoing basis. Two categories of diocesan faculties are viable today—those that grant executive power of governance and those that are authorizations. Habitual faculties that grant executive power are subject to the rules on delegated power of governance; habitual faculties that grant authorizations are subject to most, but not all, of these rules. The rules on singular administrative acts and several of the rules on rescripts are applicable to all habitual faculties. These rules will be explained in chapters 2 and 3, but first we must attend to more fundamental matters regarding faculties, which is the subject of chapter 1.

---

25. This is also the view of Javier Canosa, who gives a sizeable list of acts, other than favors, that are subject to the norms on rescripts. See "De rescriptis," pp. 591–592. Canosa attributes this position also to R. Entrena Cuesta, *Curso de Derecho Administrativo* (Madrid: 1982) 189.

CHAPTER ONE

The Fundamentals of Faculties

This chapter explores fundamental matters related to diocesan faculties, such as the purposes of diocesan faculties, their sources, the juridic nature of faculties, and some ways in which they may be categorized. Understanding these fundamental matters will help those who give or have faculties of different kinds. This basic information is also necessary background for the more technical material in chapters 2 and 3, and it serves to assist ministers in seeing how their faculties function in the canonical system and in the pastoral life and administration of the Church.

In this chapter and the next, many concepts are introduced that may be unfamiliar to readers who lack in-depth knowledge of canon law. Additionally, some words have a technical meaning in canon law that they do not have in common English speech, such as, for example, the word "priest" *(sacerdos),* which means either a presbyter or a bishop. These words are defined in the glossary, Appendix III.

1. Purposes of Faculties

The overall purpose of diocesan faculties is to empower persons for ministry and administration within the diocese. Faculties are a juridical means to link the bishop, who is responsible for overseeing all ministries in the local church, and those who collaborate with him in the ministry. Diocesan faculties are intended to be used for the spiritual benefit of the faithful and the common good of the Church. Beyond these broad values and ends, diocesan faculties have three specific purposes: (1) to ensure that only qualified persons are assigned to perform certain acts of the ministry or administration; (2) to facilitate diocesan and/or parochial administration and the pastoral ministry; and, rarely, (3) to benefit the Church's ministers personally.

1.1 Ensuring Qualified Ministers and Administrators

For the Church's mission to be served well, its ministers and administrators must be qualified and competent. Since a faculty enables a person to function in the name of the Church, those who are given faculties should be in full communion with the Catholic Church. They must also be "in good standing" in the Church, to use the colloquial term popular in the English-speaking world. Above all, this means that no imposed or declared penalty bars them from exercising faculties, as discussed in chapter 2. If they are clerics, they must be subject to the authority of their ordinary (cc. 134, 273, 283, §1). If they are lay people, they should live worthy lives and have a good reputation, and their family situation should conform to the teachings of the Church (EDM art. 13). If they are members of religious institutes or societies of apostolic life, they should have the permission of their superiors to hold the office or perform the ministry for which the faculties are being given (cc. 678, 682, 738).

Faculties also serve to assure that individuals chosen for a specific function have the formation and personal endowments necessary to perform it well, or at least properly. Many faculties are equivalent to a license or authorization for performing certain liturgical or ministerial acts or various acts of administration. The bishop grants such faculties only to those who have had the necessary formation, are legally capable of performing the act, and have the personal characteristics or experience that may be desirable for a certain act. Such faculties include those for preaching, hearing confessions, and assisting at marriages.

1.2 Facilitation of Administration and the Ministry

Many faculties are granted to facilitate diocesan and parish administration or pastoral ministry, especially when an act is commonplace.
In many dioceses, the bishop delegates pastors, or even all priests and
deacons in parishes, the faculty to permit mixed marriages. The delegation of the faculty to grant the permission for a mixed marriage
frees the local ordinary from responding to numerous requests for a
routine permission, and it frees the pastors and other ministers from
the burden of repeatedly making these requests.

1.3 Personal Benefit of Ministers

Faculties are given for the good of the church community, but in rare
instances a faculty is given that benefits the minister personally. For
example, the local ordinary could delegate to priests the power to
grant another priest the faculty to hear their confession. This enables
priests to choose any validly ordained priest in full communion with
the Church to hear their confessions, even if the priest lacks the faculty by law or from the ordinary.

Sometimes a faculty might be both a benefit for the community
and for the minister personally, depending on the circumstances. A
routine diocesan faculty given to priests is the faculty to celebrate or
concelebrate the Eucharist twice in one day (c. 905, §2). To grant the
faculty, the local ordinary must verify that there is a lack of sufficient
priests in the diocese such that the priests would generally need the
faculty. Once he gives the faculty, the priest may use it for a just
cause. This ordinarily would be due to the needs of the apostolate, for
example, to celebrate a weekday Mass for the parishioners and a
funeral Mass later that day. In this case, the faculty is used for the
benefit of the community. Sometimes, however, the faculty may be
used for the personal benefit of the priest. For example, he celebrates
Mass for the parishioners in the morning, and he concelebrates at a
Mass later in the day at a gathering of priests. His pastoral duties do
not require him to concelebrate at the gathering of priests. In this

instance, he is using the faculty as a favor. The just cause for binating might simply be to show solidarity with his brother priests and to participate in the Eucharist in a ministerial role.

2. Sources of Faculties

There are two sources of diocesan faculties. They may be given by the law itself *(a iure)* or by delegation from a person *(ab homine)* competent to grant the faculty. Moreover, faculties by law may be divided according to whether they are granted at ordination, by provision of an office, or apart from an office. We shall first look at the three categories of faculties granted by law, then at faculties granted by personal delegation. Under the heading of "personal delegation" is also a brief explanation of the diocesan *pagella* and the term "habitual faculties," since the three are closely related. Diocesan faculties are habitual faculties, listed on the diocesan *pagella*, which the bishop delegates personally.

2.1 Faculties Granted by Law at Ordination

Deacons, presbyters, and bishops receive many faculties at ordination. These are so closely connected with the cleric's order that the Church determines that every deacon, presbyter, or bishop is to have them from ordination. For example, in virtue of his ordination, a deacon may preach in churches and oratories, baptize infants, read the gospel and assist at Mass in other ways distinctive of a deacon, and give holy communion, especially ministering the chalice; he may preside at the liturgy of the hours, give numerous blessings, celebrate eucharistic benediction, preside at penitential services and funeral rites, etc. The bishop does not grant the deacon these faculties; they come to the deacon from the law itself when he is ordained. Moreover, the bishop cannot restrict or remove faculties granted at ordination, unless permitted by the law, for example, with respect to preaching (c. 764). The bishop could suspend the exercise of the faculties as a penalty, but only after a penal process that determined the cleric to be guilty of a canonical crime. This will be discussed in chapter 2.

The Power of Order

Traditionally, the power of order is divided into the power of order of the divine law and the power of order of the ecclesiastical law.[1] Very few powers of order are of the divine law. They are the power to celebrate the sacraments of confirmation, the Eucharist, penance, possibly the anointing of the sick (a disputed question), and holy orders. All other powers of order are powers of the ecclesiastical law, that is, the Church itself determines that certain powers (which rightly may be called "faculties") are appropriate to the order of deacon, presbyter, or bishop and that these faculties are granted at ordination. In this work, powers of order of the divine law are called not "faculties," but simply "powers of order." Powers of order of ecclesiastical law are called "faculties granted by law at ordination," as in the paragraph above. This makes it clearer that the real origin of such faculties is the universal law of the Church, not the sacrament of holy orders itself.

Using the term "faculties granted by the law at ordination" makes it clearer that the supreme authority of the Church has control over these faculties. He can change them, add new faculties, and remove obsolete ones. For example, in the 1917 code (c. 1337), the faculty to preach was not granted at ordination but had to be delegated to clerics individually by the local ordinary. The faculty could be used only within the diocese. Every time a priest was going to preach in another diocese, he needed the faculty from the local ordinary there. In the 1983 code, the supreme legislator (the pope) determined that this faculty was to be granted when a man is ordained a deacon, in accord with canon 764.

The celebration of two sacraments requires both the power of order and a canonical faculty. For a presbyter validly to confirm in the Latin church, he not only must be ordained but he must also have the faculty by law or delegation. Likewise, for a presbyter or bishop to celebrate the sacrament of penance, he must have the faculty to hear

---

1. Raoul Naz, "Le pouvoir d'ordre," *Dictionnaire de droit canonique* (Paris: Librairie Letouzey et Ané, 1957) 6:1148.

confessions. In both cases, the faculty is required for the validity of the sacrament. In virtue of his presbyteral ordination, the priest has the power to celebrate the sacraments of confirmation and reconciliation, but before that power can be activated, he needs the faculty, whether by law or by delegation from the competent authority.

In the former law, the faculty to hear confessions was called "jurisdiction" for hearing confessions. In the 1983 code, the use of the term "faculty" instead of "jurisdiction" shows a change in approach. The celebration of the sacrament of penance is an act of the sanctifying function of the Church, not the ruling function; therefore, it is not an act of the power of governance, or jurisdiction. The faculty is an authorization to use the power of order the priest received at ordination.[2]

2.2 Faculties Granted by Law to Officeholders

Ecclesiastical offices have faculties attached to them by the law itself. Among the faculties of the pastor, for example, are those of hearing confessions, assisting at marriages, confirming those who are no longer infants[3] and are being baptized or received into the full communion of the Catholic Church, and dispensing from the obligations of feast days and days of penance. The pastor has these faculties in virtue of his office; they are granted by the universal law when the priest takes office as pastor (cc. 968, §1; 1108, §1; 883, 2°; 1245). Like the faculties granted at ordination, the bishop cannot grant or remove these faculties, since the universal law gives them. If he wanted to restrict someone from exercising the faculties of office granted by the universal law, he would have to remove the person from office or transfer him to another office; or he or the diocesan tri-

---

2. See Eduardo Labandeira, "Naturaleza jurídica del poder de absolver los pecados desde la perspectiva del Vatican II y del nuevo Código," in *Reconciliación y penitencia: V simposio internacional de teología de la Universidad de Navarra*, ed. Jesús Sancho et al. (Pamplona: Universidad de Navarra, 1983) 957–981.

3. The expression, "those who are no longer infants," refers to those who are at least seven years old and have the use of reason. See cc. 97, §2 and 99.

bunal would have to suspend the exercise of one or more faculties by means of a canonical penalty, observing the procedural laws of an administrative or judicial penal process.[4]

Most diocesan offices are established in universal law, but the diocesan bishop is free to create new ones to serve the needs of the diocese or parish. In creating an office by means of a decree, the bishop should specify the rights and duties of the office (c. 145), which would include the faculties of the officeholder—the powers he or she may lawfully exercise. These would be faculties attached to the office by the law—by the decree creating the office.

2.3 Faculties Granted by Law Apart from an Office

Some faculties are granted by law to persons who have no office. Typically, such faculties are granted in danger of death or other urgent need. For example, in a case of necessity, the law grants the faculty to baptize to any person with the intention to do what the Church does when it baptizes (c. 861, §2). Another example is the faculty of all priests and deacons to dispense from canonical form and from most marital impediments in danger of death, in accord with the rules of canons 1079, §2 and 1116, §2. This is different from a faculty granted by law at ordination, because the cleric has this faculty from the law only when the situation required by law is verified.

2.4 Faculties Granted by Personal Delegation

The faculties of greatest interest in this work are those *delegated* from one person to another, in particular, the faculties that the diocesan bishop may grant for habitual use to priests, deacons, and lay ministers and officials of the diocese or parish. These are the only true diocesan faculties, because they are faculties that the bishop may

---

4. The removal of the faculties for preaching and hearing confessions does not require a penal process, as we shall see in chapter 2.

grant in addition to those faculties that ministers or officials have by virtue of the law. Some of these delegated faculties are routinely given to ministers in good standing. For example, the local ordinary usually grants the faculty to hear confessions to all priests of the diocese, including retired priests and others who might not be regularly involved in pastoral ministry (e.g., teachers, monks, chancery officials, etc.). Some delegated faculties are usually given only to clergy who are appointed to a parochial office; these faculties include, for example, the faculty to assist at marriages, given to parochial vicars and parish deacons (pastors have the faculty by law). The bishop may also, by personal delegation, grant certain faculties to diocesan officials in addition to those they have by universal law. For example, in a diocese where the bishop and the vicar general are too busy to respond to numerous requests for routine permissions and dispensations, the bishop could delegate this power to the chancellor or another official.

Regarding the deacon or lay person who shares in the pastoral care of a parish without a resident pastor (c. 517, §2), this is a function without a name or any faculties in the universal law, so the bishop and/or the priest who supervises the parish must delegate the faculties for these ministers. A deacon who serves in this capacity also has all the faculties given by the universal law to deacons at their ordination. (See chapter 6.) Another option would be to establish this office in the diocese by decree (c. 145), giving it a name like "parish minister of pastoral care" or "pastoral administrator." In the decree, the bishop would determine the basic faculties of this office by law, which all such parish ministers would receive upon their appointment to office. Additional faculties could be delegated according to the needs and circumstances of the parish and the qualifications of the person chosen for the office.

Many faculties are proper to the bishop or other local ordinary, and he may delegate them to other ministers and officials when appropriate, especially to help them in their ministry or to facilitate diocesan or parish administration. The bishop is free to delegate these faculties as he sees fit. A special concern of this book, especially in Part II, is to help church authorities and canonists to be aware of the possibilities in the law for delegating such optional faculties.

The Diocesan Pagella

Habitual faculties for priests and other ministers are listed in the diocesan *pagella*. The Latin word *pagella* means "a little page," which suggests that lists of faculties at one time could fit on a small page. Now, a *pagella* indicates any list of diocesan faculties, short or long. Until recently, only priests received a list of diocesan faculties, but today it is commonplace for the bishop to issue separate *pagellae* for priests, deacons, and sometimes lay ministers, especially lay directors of parishes (c. 517, §2) or lay officials of the diocesan curia.

Habitual Faculties

Faculties on the diocesan *pagella* are habitual faculties, since they are granted for general, repeated use,[5] not just for an individual instance or specified cases. A habitual faculty is sometimes called "general delegation," as in "general delegation to assist at marriages" (c. 1111, §2). For example, if the pastor gives a general delegation to the parish deacon to assist at marriages, the deacon has the habitual faculty and may validly preside at any wedding in the parish. In contrast, special delegation is given only for one or more specifically determined cases, as when the pastor delegates a visiting priest to assist at a specific marriage in the parish. If the visiting priest were to assist at any other marriage besides the one for which he was delegated, the marriage would be invalid.

Habitual faculties may be granted for a determinate or indeterminate period. For example, the local ordinary may grant an extern priest, who is a graduate student in the diocese for a two-year degree program, the faculty to hear confessions for this period. This is a determinate time, but it is still a habitual faculty because it may be used repeatedly for any celebration of the sacrament of penance. Likewise, the local ordinary may grant an indeterminate habitual faculty. He could grant the faculty *for as long as the priest remains in the diocese*, which might be longer than the anticipated two years of study.

Faculties on the diocesan *pagella* also may be granted determinately or indeterminately. If the bishop delegates faculties in virtue of

---

5. See the discussion in the introduction to Part I, pp. 6–7.

an office, then the term of the faculties should coincide with the term of office; they should be granted *determinately*. Faculties given to all priests or deacons, which are not given in virtue of an ecclesiastical office, should be given *indeterminately* to the priests and deacons domiciled in the diocese, that is, for as long as the priest or deacon continues to retain his domicile or remain incardinated in the diocese, unless the faculties are expressly revoked.

3. Nature of Faculties

Now that we have seen the purposes and sources of faculties, understanding the more abstract issue of their juridic nature will be easier. We begin this discussion with a definition of a canonical faculty. *A faculty is an ecclesiastical power or authorization necessary for performing lawfully an act of ministry or administration in the name of the Church.* The faculty is a either a *power of governance* or an *authorization*. These two terms will be explained in section 4.2. Here we will explain the other key terms of the definition.

3.1 Ecclesiastical, or Human, in Origin

In common usage, a faculty is understood as a power or authorization of only *ecclesiastical* or human origin, not of divine origin. As noted above, some powers come to presbyters and bishops by the sacrament of holy orders itself; they are not faculties assigned by the Church to those who are ordained but God-given powers that come to the cleric by ordination. One does not speak of the "faculty" of a priest to celebrate the Eucharist, since this is a divine law power of order, not a faculty of ecclesiastical law.

3.2 An Act of Ministry or Administration

A faculty is always a power or authorization *to act* lawfully. It may be given for an act of administration (e.g., granting a dispensation, approving a budget, making contracts) or a ministerial act (especially preaching and celebrating liturgical rites). Sometimes, a diocesan *pagella* may include items that do not empower a person for a distinct act of ministry or administration. For example, it may give a statement of a general policy on some matter or express an obligation of some kind. If the statement does not empower the minister or official for some act (a ministerial act, a juridic act, or a non-juridic act of administration), then it is not a real faculty.

3.3 For Validity and/or Liceity

A faculty is necessary for performing an act *lawfully*—for validity and/or liceity, depending on the nature of the act. An *invalid* act is juridically inefficacious. For example, if a presbyter in the Latin church attempts to celebrate confirmation without the necessary faculty, he acts invalidly. The confirmation is canonically null and void. An act is merely *illicit* if it is done contrary to a law that has no invalidating effects. If a lay religious preaches at a service of the word in a church or oratory without the faculty to preach (c. 766), she acts illicitly but not invalidly.[6] Preaching cannot be valid or invalid. Nevertheless, it is done licitly or illicitly, depending on whether it is done in accord with the law or not. With the faculty, the minister functions lawfully; without it, the act of ministry or administration performed would be unlawful and, often, even invalid. Moreover, without the faculty, even if the act is valid, it is not done in the name of the Church.

---

6. Canon 766 says that lay persons can be admitted *(admitti possunt)* to preach in a church or oratory if in certain circumstances it is necessary or in particular cases it would be advantageous, in accord with the norms of the conference of bishops and without prejudice to c. 767, §1. In canon law, the word *admissio* or *admittere* normally does not indicate a faculty, but it has this sense in c. 766.

The 1997 instruction, EDM art. 2, §3, says that lay preaching is not a matter of a right to preach, which is a right specific to bishops, nor is it a question of the faculty such as that enjoyed by priests and deacons. Clearly, it is not a faculty such as is enjoyed by priests and deacons; clerics have the faculty by law in virtue of their ordination. Lay persons must have the faculty granted to them *ab homine*. It is legitimate to call this a faculty, because this admission to preach empowers the lay person to preach lawfully in the name of the Church.

3.4 In the Name of the Church

When using a faculty, the ministers act *in the name of the Church*. Those who have a faculty do not act only in virtue of their baptism and the fact that they are in full communion with the Catholic Church. Their faculty is an ecclesiastical warrant to act on behalf of and in the name of the Church itself. For example, all the faithful, in virtue of their sacramental initiation in the Church, are obliged to contribute to the Church's mission of spreading the divine message of salvation to peoples of all times and places (c. 211). All the faithful must be witnesses to the good news of the Gospel by their words and deeds and the example of their Christian life (c. 759). One possible way of fulfilling this duty is by preaching. All Christians are free to preach anywhere in their own names in virtue of their baptism; they rarely do this, but they have the freedom to do it if they wish. They may preach in their homes, to their neighbors and friends, on the streets, etc.; but to preach in a Catholic church or oratory requires a faculty (c. 766). Those who have the faculty to preach in a church or oratory do so not in their own name but in the name of the Church itself.

4. Categories of Faculties

Faculties may be classified in two ways. First, they may be categorized as to whether they pertain to the sanctifying, teaching, or ruling functions of the Church. Second, they may be categorized according to whether they are faculties involving the exercise of the power of governance, traditionally called "jurisdictional faculties," or whether they are authorizations.

4.1 Sanctifying, Teaching, and Governing Faculties

Since Vatican II, and especially since the promulgation of the revised Code of Canon Law in 1983, it has been commonplace to divide the various activities of the Church into three categories of functions *(munera)*. As Christ was priest, prophet, and king, so also the functions of the Church are the sanctifying, teaching, and ruling (or governing) functions (see c. 204, §1). The faculties necessary for ministry also pertain to all three dimensions of the Church's activity. Accordingly, faculties are authorizations or powers for performing acts of the *munus sanctificandi*, the sanctifying function of the Church; acts of the *munus docendi*, the teaching function of the Church; and acts of the *munus regendi*, the ruling function of the Church. The following are examples of some faculties, whether given by law or personal delegation, as classified according to these categories.

> **Sanctifying function**—faculties to confirm, hear confessions, assist at marriages, preside at blessings and other sacramentals, celebrate Mass twice on a weekday, preside at the liturgy of the hours.

> **Teaching function**—faculties to exercise the ministry of the word and to preach in a church or oratory.

> **Ruling function**—faculties to grant dispensations, commutations, permission, consent, mandates, approval; to delegate and subdelegate; to make contracts; to appoint and remove parish or diocesan officials; to make binding decisions within an area of competence.

This categorization is particularly useful with respect to faculties for lay ministers, because it assists the bishop and his advisors in conceptualizing the kinds of faculties that must be delegated for lay directors of parishes or other ministries. Unlike clerics, who are empowered by law at ordination for many ministerial acts of the sanctifying and teaching functions, the laity must receive faculties in virtue of an office or by delegation to perform these acts in the name of the Church. As for the ruling function, both clerics and lay persons must be empowered for specific acts by faculties of office or by delegated faculties. No faculty of the ruling function is granted at ordination.[7]

---

7. This is true even of bishops. Bishops receive the ontological *munus regendi* at their ordination, as do presbyters and deacons (c. 1008), but this function of ruling

This categorization of faculties also helps ministers and officials in determining whether a faculty they have may be delegated or sub-delegated. As we shall see in chapter 3, faculties of the ruling function that involve the exercise of the power of governance may freely be delegated and subdelegated according to the rules on executive power of governance (cc. 137–142), unless delegation or subdelegation is restricted by law or by the person delegating. Faculties of the sancti-fying and teaching functions may not be delegated, except when per-mitted by law. The notable exception is the faculty to assist at mar-riage, which is a faculty of the sanctifying function that may be delegated and subdelegated in accord with the rules on executive power.

4.2 Authorization or Power of Governance

Faculties, in addition to being divided according to the three functions of the Church, can also be classified according to whether they are authorizations or the power of governance. This categorization is fun-damental and will be recalled frequently in this work. Further infor-mation on these categories may be found above on pages 10–13.

Authorizations

An authorization is the legal empowerment, granted by means of an administrative act of the competent authority, which enables a per-son to perform lawfully an act of ministry or administration other than an act of the power of governance. An authorization is any non-jurisdictional faculty. Authorizations enable the minister to perform some act of ministry or administration lawfully, apart from an act of the power of governance. This empowerment may affect validity or

---

is not ordered to action without a canonical mission, in particular, by an office of some kind, such as the office of diocesan bishop, an auxiliary bishop appointed to the office of vicar general or episcopal vicar, a bishop appointed to offices in the Roman Curia, etc.

only liceity, depending on the requirements of the law. The law indicates an authorization is necessary by using various terms, as when it says the minister or other agent must have a permission, approval, consent, faculty, mandate, delegation, etc., before performing some non-jurisdictional act.

Some authorizations are required for the validity of the act; these include the faculty to confirm, hear confessions, assist at marriage, celebrate certain sacramentals (dedications and consecrations), etc. Other authorizations are needed for liceity only; they include the faculties to baptize, celebrate the Eucharist at a mixed marriage, binate or trinate, celebrate a penitential service, preside at the liturgy of the hours, preach, catechize, etc. Diocesan faculties that are authorizations pertain mainly to the sanctifying and teaching functions of the Church, although they may also be given for non-jurisdictional ruling functions, such as, for example, a faculty given to a deacon or lay director of a parish without a pastor to perform acts of financial administration on behalf of the parish.

Executive Power

Faculties for the exercise of the power of governance, also called "jurisdictional faculties," allow the minister, official, or delegated person to perform *(ponere)* juridic acts that could not validly be performed without this power. The power of governance is divided into legislative, executive, and judicial power (c. 135, §1). No diocesan faculty can be given for the exercise of legislative power, since only the supreme authority of the Church—the pope or the college of bishops—can validly delegate legislative power (c. 135, §2). Judicial power is exercised by judges and judicial colleges who may not delegate their judicial power, but may only permit others to assist them in acts preparatory to a decree or a sentence (c. 135, §3). Therefore, the only power of governance that may be delegated on a diocesan *pagella* is executive power.[8]

---

8. Nothing in the code bars the bishop from delegating his judicial power, but this would not be done by means of the standard diocesan *pagella*. In any case,

The exercise of executive power of governance is routine in church administration. All singular administrative acts are acts of executive power. Examples include the granting of dispensations, commutations, sanations, and other favors; the granting or denial of authorizations (permission, consent, mandate, etc.); appointment to office and transfer and removal from office; the delegation, subdelegation, and removal of faculties; granting incardination; giving a *mandatum* to teach a theological discipline in a university; issuing a precept; imposing a penalty after an administrative process; remitting a penalty; imposing a prohibition on a subsequent marriage following a declaration of invalidity;[9] etc. At the level of parish ministry, some common acts of the power of governance include dispensations, commutations, permissions, the delegation and subdelegation of faculties, and appointment to and removal from office of lay parish officials. The bishop is free to delegate his executive power, observing the rules of law.

Two important consequences follow from the distinction between authorizations and powers of governance. First, faculties involving the exercise of executive power of governance may be further delegated and subdelegated. Authorizations for a ministerial act may not be subdelegated, with few exceptions, the most notable being the faculty for assisting at marriage, which is an authorization that may be subdelegated. In the above examples in section 4.1, all the faculties in the sanctifying and teaching functions are authorizations, and all the faculties in the ruling function—with the exception of the faculty to make contracts[10]—involve the exercise of executive power of gover-

---

bishops do not normally delegate their judicial power. Instead, they appoint judges who function in virtue of their office.

9. This is the prohibition, or *vetitum*, of c. 1077, §1, which is an act of executive power. A *vetitum* may also be imposed judicially after a second affirmative decision of an appeal court (c. 1684, §1). Canon 1684, §1 also mentions the prohibition of the local ordinary.

10. Authorization is needed to make contracts in the name of the Church, but no power of governance is required. One simply must be capable of making a contract in the civil law (c. 1290).

nance. While authorizations may be given for acts of the sanctifying, teaching, or ruling function, the power of governance pertains only to acts of the ruling function.

The second important consequence of the distinction between executive power and authorizations concerns who may be delegated faculties that involve the exercise of executive power. In the canonical system today, clergy are normally preferred to lay persons in performing acts of the power of governance. (See cc. 129; 274, §1; 1421, §1.) This implies that if both a cleric and a lay person are equally available and equally competent to perform an act of power of governance, the bishop should choose the cleric before the lay person for offices or tasks involving the exercise of power of governance. However, when it is necessary for the common good and the spiritual benefit of the faithful (the *salus animarum*), the bishop has the authority to grant to lay persons, by particular law or personal delegation, some faculties involving executive power needed for their ministry or office. The bishop's power for the exercise of his pastoral function, which is rooted in the divine law since he is a successor of the apostles,[11] can be limited only by a law or decree of the pope (c. 381, §1). Since no such law or decree exists, nothing prevents the bishop from delegating executive power to lay persons for specific tasks when he judges this to be necessary or beneficial. This is one way lay persons can cooperate in the exercise of power of governance (c. 129, §2).[12]

Summary

This chapter has introduced fundamental canonical principles, concepts, and categories related to diocesan faculties. A faculty may be

---

11. See Vatican II, *Lumen gentium*, chapter 3, esp. nn. 24, 27; and *Christus Dominus* 2, 8.

12. For documentation and further information, see my study, "The Power of Governance and Its Exercise by Lay Persons: A Juridical Approach," *Studia Canonica* 35 (2001) 59–96.

defined as an ecclesiastical power or authorization necessary for performing lawfully an act in the name of the Church. The faculty is either a *power of governance* or an *authorization* to perform an act of some kind. It is a power or authorization of *ecclesiastical* or human origin, not of divine origin; a divine law power of order is not called a faculty in canon law. The *act* to be performed is an act of ministry or administration that cannot lawfully be done without the faculty. A faculty is necessary for performing an act *lawfully*—for validity and/or liceity, depending on the nature of the act. Without the faculty, the minister or church administrator cannot licitly perform the act, and the act in question in many cases will also be invalid. With the faculty, the act is performed lawfully, and the minister acts *in the name of the Church*, not solely in virtue of being baptized and in full communion with the Catholic Church.

There are three purposes of diocesan faculties and two sources of them. The purposes of diocesan faculties are to ensure that persons are competent to perform certain acts of the ministry or administration, to facilitate diocesan and parochial administration, and, rarely, to benefit ministers personally. The two sources of diocesan faculties are the law itself *(a iure)* or delegation from a person *(ab homine)* competent to grant the faculty. Moreover, faculties by law may be divided according to whether they are granted at ordination (power of order of ecclesiastical law), by office, or by law apart from an office. Diocesan faculties are habitual faculties, faculties that may be used repeatedly. The bishop or his delegate grants the faculties listed on a *pagella* to individual ministers and officials. He may grant them for a determinate period or indeterminately.

Faculties may be categorized as pertaining to the sanctifying, teaching, or ruling functions of the Church, as well as according to whether they are faculties for the exercise of executive power of governance or authorizations. Faculties for the exercise of the power of governance may be delegated and subdelegated in accord with the rules in the code; faculties that are authorizations may not be further delegated unless this is permitted by law or legal custom, or unless the competent authority expressly delegates the power to subdelegate the faculty.

In the next chapter, we shall explore the canonical rules governing the grant and revocation of diocesan faculties. We shall also see how the law supplies a missing faculty in certain situations when a minister or official performs an act without having the faculty by office or by personal delegation.

CHAPTER TWO

The Grant, Supply, and Revocation
of Faculties

In the first chapter, we examined fundamental matters concerning diocesan faculties—their purposes, sources, juridic nature, and the ways they may be categorized. This chapter treats the grant of faculties by the diocesan bishop and their revocation by him. It also explains the supply of faculties by the law (c. 144).

The chapter has four main sections. The first section explores the juridic nature of the act of granting, or delegating, faculties.[1] This is necessary to determine the canonical norms that must be observed by the bishop when he grants faculties or, as we will see in chapter 3, when ministers delegate or subdelegate their own faculties. Having clarified the juridic nature of faculties in chapter 1 and that of the act of granting them in the first section of this chapter, it will then be possible, in section 2 of this chapter, to give the canonical rules that govern the granting of faculties by the diocesan bishop.[2] Section 3 treats

---

1. The grant *(concessio)* of faculties and the delegation *(delegatio)* of faculties are juridically equivalent terms; they are the same juridic act observing the same rules. However, we shall use the term "grant" to refer to the act of the bishop in giving habitual faculties; "delegation" will likewise be used in this sense and also to refer to the act of the minister or official who further delegates a habitual faculty received.

2. This same foundation will make it possible, in chapter 3, to explain the pertinent canonical rules on the use, delegation, subdelegation, and cessation of diocesan faculties.

the supply of faculties by the law itself in situations of common error and positive and probable doubt (c. 144). Finally, we shall examine the act of revocation of faculties by the bishop and the rules applicable to it. The revocation of faculties has a juridic nature different from the act of granting faculties, necessitating the observance of canonical rules that are different in significant ways from the rules for granting them. The removal of faculties is a subject widely misunderstood, even by bishops and chancery officials. This fourth section explains how diocesan faculties may be lawfully removed, and how faculties are lost by removal from office or by certain canonical penalties.

The subject matter of this chapter primarily concerns diocesan officials as well as canonists and students of canon law.[3] Chapter 3 will deal with matters of direct concern to those who have faculties.

1. The Act of Granting Faculties

In chapter 1, we saw that diocesan faculties are granted by the personal delegation of the bishop or his delegate, and we examined the juridical nature of these faculties. We shall now explore the nature of the act of delegation *(delegatio ab homine)*. We shall see that the act of granting, or delegating, faculties is (1) a juridic act, (2) an act of the executive power of governance, and (3) a singular administrative act.

The act of delegation and the act of subdelegation have the same juridic nature. In this work, whenever rules are given for delegation, they also apply to subdelegation, unless it is clear from the context that the rule is intended only for one or the other. For that reason, subdelegation will be mentioned hereafter only when it is being distinguished from delegation. The reader should understand that, as a general principle, what is being said of delegation equally applies to subdelegation.

Before examining the nature of the act of granting faculties, it is necessary to clarify that the act of delegation, the faculty itself, and

---

3. The faculty supplied by law could also have been treated in the next chapter. It is included in this chapter due to its technical nature and to the fact that judgments on whether the law has or has not supplied the faculty in a particular case are typically made at the diocesan level by diocesan officials in consultation with canonists.

the act for which the faculty is given are each different juridic realities. The *faculty* is the power or authorization being delegated; it authorizes or gives power to a person to perform some act. The *act of delegation* is the means by which the faculty is granted. The *act for which the faculty is given* is some act of ministry or administration, be it an act of the sanctifying, teaching, or ruling function of the Church. These three distinct legal entities are sketched in the illustration on page 41.

The faculty itself may be either an authorization or the power of governance. The act of delegating a faculty, however, is always an act of the power of governance. For example, the diocesan bishop grants the faculty to a lay minister to preach in churches and oratories. The *delegation* of the faculty is the act of the bishop. The *faculty* itself authorizes the lay minister to preach lawfully in churches and oratories. The *act of preaching* is the act of the lay minister, an act of the teaching function of the Church. The act for which a faculty is given may pertain to the sanctifying, teaching, or ruling functions. The act of delegating the faculty, however, always pertains to the ruling function, because it is an act of executive power and a singular administrative act, as we shall see in this chapter.

Personal delegation *(delegatio ab homine)* is the act by which the competent authority grants a faculty to another person who lacks it. Canon law uses several terms for the act of granting power, such as to delegate *(delegare),* mandate *(mandare),* grant *(concedere),* provide *(instruere),* give *(dare),* or confer *(conferre, donare).* "Delegation" is used most especially in referring to the grant of power of governance, but it is also used in granting faculties for acts that do not entail the power of governance, such as, for example, delegation of the faculty to assist at marriages (c. 1111) or delegation of the faculty of blessing churches (c. 1207). It is not necessary in granting faculties that the precise word "delegation" or "grant" be used, as long as it is expressly stated in some way that the faculties in question are being granted.

We shall now examine more closely the nature of the act of delegating faculties. In the system of the 1983 code, the delegation of habitual faculties can be understood as: (1) a juridic act; (2) an act of the executive power of governance; and (3) a singular administrative act, subject to applicable rules for rescripts.

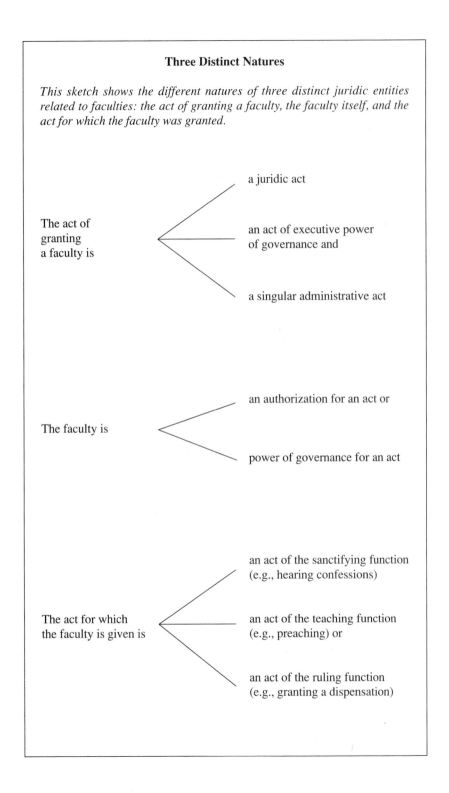

Three Distinct Natures

This sketch shows the different natures of three distinct juridic entities related to faculties: the act of granting a faculty, the faculty itself, and the act for which the faculty was granted.

The act of
granting
a faculty is

a juridic act

an act of executive power
of governance and

a singular administrative act

The faculty is

an authorization for an act or

power of governance for an act

The act for which
the faculty is given is

an act of the sanctifying function
(e.g., hearing confessions)

an act of the teaching function
(e.g., preaching) or

an act of the ruling function
(e.g., granting a dispensation)

1.1 A Juridic Act

The act of delegation is a juridic act, and the general rules on juridic acts—notably, canons 124–126—are applicable to the delegation of faculties. Juridic acts are acts of the will, performed by a capable and competent person, which have juridic effects specified in the law. All juridic acts have several common elements.

1. The act, for validity, must be performed by a person who is capable and competent in the law.

2. The person must have the intention to perform the act and do it with sufficient deliberation and freedom for the act to be valid.

3. For validity, certain formalities and requirements of law may have to be observed.

4. Specific effects recognized in law are brought about by the act.

Juridic acts are commonplace in the canonical system. Some examples of juridic acts are baptism, marriage, ordination, religious profession, transfer to another church *sui iuris*, vows and oaths, the promulgation of laws, singular decrees (e.g., assignment to an office, removal from office, canonical erection of a sacred place, erection of a parish, dedication of a church, establishment of an association of the faithful, establishment of a juridic person, suppression or division of a juridic person, etc.), granting a rescript (dispensation, privilege, commutation, sanation, other favors), judicial decrees and sentences, the imposition or declaration of penalties, alienation of ecclesiastical goods, contracts, wills and donations, and many more. Canons 124–128 are very important because they give the general rules governing the validity of *all* juridic acts, but here we are considering only the juridic act of delegating faculties.

For validity, the delegation of a faculty must: (1) be done by a capable and competent person, (2) include those things that essentially constitute the act itself, and (3) include the formalities and requirements imposed by the law for the validity of the act (c. 124, §1). Canon 124 is an invalidating law (c. 10), specifying what is necessary for juridic acts to be valid. We shall now look at each of these requirements.

The Capable Person

The person capable of granting diocesan faculties is the diocesan bishop. Many faculties may also be delegated by the other local ordinaries in the diocese, the vicar general and episcopal vicars. However, some powers are reserved in law to the diocesan bishop and are not given to local ordinaries in general. Therefore, if a *pagella* includes such faculties (as do all the lists of faculties in this book), the bishop must grant them himself, or he must expressly give a mandate to the vicar general, episcopal vicar, or some other official to do it. From a theological and pastoral perspective, it would be desirable for the bishop to grant the faculties in his own name. The issuance of faculties in the diocesan bishop's own name, signed in his own hand, tangibly conveys the role of the bishop as pastor of the local church and that of his clergy and lay ministers as his close collaborators in his sacred duty to sanctify, teach, and shepherd his people.

Constitutive Elements

The elements that essentially constitute a juridic act are those elements required by canon law (whether derived from divine or human law) that are essential to the act by its very nature. By the divine natural law, the *intention* on the part of the subject of the act is essential for all juridic acts. If the intention to perform the act and realize its effects is not present or is defective, the act is invalid. Since the essence of every juridic act is the will of a person to perform the act, the person delegating a faculty must freely intend to delegate it, or the delegation is invalid. For example, if the bishop intends to delegate faculties to the pastor, but mistakenly copies the name of the parish deacon and sends them to him, the deacon may not validly use them, even those that do not require the presbyteral order, because the bishop did not intend him to have them.

The other essential elements of the juridic act of delegation, as well as the various formalities and requirements of law, are found in the code in the titles on the common norms for singular administrative acts (cc. 35–47) and on the delegation of executive power of governance (cc. 133, 136–142). As we saw in the previous chapter, diocesan faculties are usually a mixture of those that are powers of governance and those that are authorizations. In either case, the delegation of habitual faculties is subject to the rules for delegated power of governance because the act of delegation is itself an act of executive power of governance.

1.2 An Act of Executive Power of Governance

The juridic act of granting a faculty is an act of power of governance. The power of governance is necessary in canon law to perform juridic acts that are legislative, executive, or judicial. When the bishop grants faculties, he is exercising his executive power, not his legislative or judicial powers (cf. cc. 135, §1; 381; 35). Therefore, applicable rules for the exercise of executive power must be observed (cc. 133, 136–144).

It is important to bear in mind the distinction made above between the *act of delegation* and the *faculty that is delegated*. While the *delegation* of a faculty is itself an act of the power of governance (executive power), the faculty so delegated might be, or might not be, the power of governance. For example, the *delegation* to a priest of the faculty to hear confessions is an act of executive power of governance, but the celebration of the sacrament of penance is not an act of power of governance; it is an act of the *munus sanctificandi*, the sanctifying function of the Church.

1.3 A Singular Administrative Act

The delegation of a faculty is a singular (or individual) administrative act (cc. 35–47). Even if the same faculties are given to many ministers at the same time, the granting of diocesan faculties is not a general act. It is neither a general legislative decree (cc. 29–30) nor a general act of executive power (cc. 31–34). Each person who is to receive diocesan faculties must be delegated. The diocesan bishop (or his delegate) must personally sign the document granting the faculties, and the document and list of faculties must be sent to each person who is intended to have them. The bishop should not delegate diocesan faculties by a general act. Were he to do so, many of the faculties he intended to give would not be given.

Faculties grant to ministers and officeholders additional authorizations and powers that they lack in the universal law. A general act of the bishop granting them such authorizations and powers would be invalid, because such a general diocesan policy (a general decree of cc. 29–33) would be contrary to higher law (c. 135, §2). Effectively, the bishop would be making his own particular law that contradicts the universal law. Since delegation *(delegatio ab homine)* is a singular administrative act, it cannot be done by a general act. In chapter 1 we saw that the bishop can create offices of particular law, and that faculties may be assigned by law to these offices. However, he cannot delegate the faculties of universal law by his own law, since the universal law requires that they be delegated individually.

For example, the bishop issues a policy stating that all priests have the power to dispense from the obligations of Sundays and holy days and days of penance. By means of this general policy, the bishop is intending to give this faculty to all priests, but what he is really doing is making a particular law, not delegating a faculty. The universal law gives this power only to the bishop himself (c. 87, §1) and to pastors and clerical superiors (c. 1245). Consequently, the bishop's policy is invalid, as it is contrary to higher law. To accomplish what he intends, the bishop must delegate his own dispensing power (c. 87) with respect to this matter. He can do this only by delegating each priest individually. Delegation *ab homine* is always a *singular* administrative act, not a general one.[4]

---

4. It would *not* be invalid to grant the same faculty to many persons at the same time by means of the same document. For example, the bishop grants to all pastors in the diocese the faculty to confirm baptized Catholics on Pentecost Sunday. This would still be a singular administrative act, even though granted to many

Certain permissions can be granted either by an individual faculty or by a general policy. For example, the diocesan bishop may permit holy communion to be given under both kinds whenever it seems appropriate to the pastor. He may do this if the faithful have been well instructed and there is no danger of profanation of the sacrament or the rite does not become cumbersome due to the large number of participants or some other reason (GIRM 283c). He can give this permission by a general act (a general decree or general executory decree), or he may permit it by means of a faculty on the diocesan *pagella*.

A general act would be entirely inappropriate for most permissions, for example, permission for a marriage to be celebrated in a suitable place outside a church or oratory (c. 1118, §2). For such acts, a judgment must be made that the permission is warranted by the circumstances of the case and that the conditions of the law are met. Often, it is very difficult to anticipate in a general act (a law) the many and varied circumstances that may arise. An individual judgment needs to be made in each case. Consequently, it is better that the bishop *delegate his power* to pastors or others by which they can make the judgment in individual cases that the conditions of the law are fulfilled and that the circumstances warrant the permission.

Individual delegation gives the bishop more control over the persons who should have the faculty. It also allows him to remove an individual's faculties when necessary. If a certain faculty, granted by individual delegation, is being abused by a single minister, it is easy to remove that faculty. If the permission was granted by general policy, the bishop could not withdraw it from an individual unless he first issued a penal precept followed by a penal process, if the abuse continued.

In some dioceses, general policies (cc. 29–34) affecting the ministry are given on the diocesan *pagella* together with faculties. These policies sometimes have the appearance of faculties but they are not. They merely serve as reminders of what the diocesan policy is. A typ-

---

individuals. However, this act would apply only to the priests who are pastors in the diocese at the time the faculty was granted, not to any others who would later be appointed pastor. The bishop has no power to say all pastors, present and future, have the faculty to confirm baptized Catholics; that would be tantamount to a particular law contrary to universal law (cc. 882–883).

ical example would be worded like this: "You may baptize infants whose parents do not live within the territory of the parish, provided they are registered in the parish." This is not really a faculty needed from the bishop, since all clerics are ordinary ministers of baptism. Rather, it is a general policy or custom of the diocese concerning who can be considered parishioners. Even if the policy had not been promulgated (cc. 8; 31, §2), the minister could have celebrated such baptisms in virtue of legitimate custom or after consulting the pastor of domicile or quasi-domicile (cf. c. 530, 1°).

When a general policy is given on the diocesan *pagella*, it should be clearly indicated in some way that it is a policy or custom *(ius particulare)* and not a faculty. The reason for this is not simply canonical tidiness and theoretical elegance; there are practical consequences. It is especially important when a minister's faculties are removed. Both the individual affected and the community at large need to know what faculties actually are being removed, but a general policy of the diocese is not abrogated when an individual's faculties are revoked!

A Decree or a Rescript?

We have seen that the act of delegating faculties is a singular administrative act, but which kind is it? Singular administrative acts are divided into singular decrees (cc. 48–58) and rescripts (cc. 59–75). (Precepts are treated under singular decrees.) Canonical commentators generally avoid saying whether the delegation of faculties is a decree, a rescript, or some *sui generis* act. They simply say that it is a singular administrative act.[5] There is good reason for this reluctance.

A singular decree is a decision for a particular case or a provision for a particular case (c. 48). The delegation of faculties may be under-

---

5. See, e.g., Francisco J. Urrutia, "Facoltà abituali (Facultates habituales)," in *Nuovo Dizionario di Diritto Canonico*, 2nd ed. rev., ed. Carlos Corral Salvador, Velasio DePaolis, and Gianfranco Ghirlanda (Milano: San Paolo, 1996) 480; James H. Provost, "Faculties," in *Clergy Procedural Handbook*, ed. Randolph R. Calvo and Nevin J. Klinger (Washington: CLSA, 1992) 99; and Barbara Anne Cusack, "Special Authorizations or Faculties," in *Pastoral Care in Parishes Without a Pastor: Applications of Canon 517, §2* (Washington: CLSA, 1995) 13.

stood as a provision for a particular case, that of the individual who is being delegated the faculties to facilitate the ministry or administration. A decree does not require a petition, nor does the grant of faculties. Therefore, the grant of faculties could be considered a decree that is a provision. However, nearly all the rules on singular decrees apply to decisions, not provisions. So, calling the grant of faculties a "decree" will not offer guidance to the bishop on the canonical rules that must be observed in issuing faculties, nor to the recipients on the rules to be observed in using their faculties.

A rescript is a written response to a petition. Sometimes faculties are granted in response to the petition of a major superior or an individual. Moreover, rescripts may be issued *motu proprio* (c. 63, §1), on the initiative of the competent authority; they may be requested for another person even without that person's assent and take force even before the person accepts them (c. 61). All of this, so far, corresponds to the act of granting faculties. Moreover, as we have seen in the Introduction to Part I, the grant and use of faculties are subject to applicable rules on rescripts.

The difficulty with considering the grant of faculties to be a rescript is that rescripts grant favors (c. 59, §1), but faculties are rarely favors *(gratiae)* in the strict sense.[6] Unlike favors, faculties granted by a superior authority may not be refused, and they must be used on behalf of those for whom they were granted. Faculties are intended primarily for the benefit of the faithful and for the common good of the Church. Still, faculties may be understood as favors in the broad sense; they are favor*able* to persons in that they give them a new power or ability to perform some act lawfully that previously they could not lawfully perform.[7]

While there are good reasons for calling the grant of faculties a rescript, there are equally good reasons for calling it a decree. Given this dilemma, the bishop could decide to call the act of granting faculties neither a rescript nor a decree. The document granting faculties could simply be called, "Grant of Faculties" or "Delegation of Facul-

---

6. Favors benefit the individual personally and may be freely used or not, e.g., a faculty allowing a cleric to dispense himself from praying an hour of the divine office when impeded.

7. See footnote 19, p. 13.

ties." Nevertheless, if the bishop were to issue faculties and refer to the grant as either a rescript or a decree, it would be valid and licit. His intention to delegate faculties would be clear. What is necessary, in either case, is to observe the correct rules for granting the faculties.

2. Rules for Granting Diocesan Faculties

We have identified the act of granting diocesan faculties as a juridic act of executive power of governance, namely, a singular administrative act, which is also subject to applicable norms on rescripts. With the nature of the act of delegating diocesan faculties clarified, we can now look at the pertinent canonical rules governing the delegation of faculties and explain their meaning. These rules affect the liceity, and frequently also the validity, of the grant of diocesan faculties. The applicable rules are chiefly found in the following sections of Book I of the Code of Canon Law: common norms on singular administrative acts (cc. 35–47); rescripts (cc. 59–75);[8] juridic acts (cc. 124–128); and executive power of governance (cc. 129–144). Other relevant rules will also be cited from other parts of the code.

The following rules apply to the faculties granted by the diocesan bishop or his delegate to those ministering in the diocese. In the next chapter we shall see rules that apply to ministers and administrators delegating or subdelegating their faculties for acts of executive power and assistance at marriage.

1. *Faculties may be granted in response to a petition or given* motu proprio.

Faculties may be given in response to a petition or may be given *motu proprio*—on the initiative of the bishop (cf. c. 63, §1). Faculties given to clergy who belong to religious institutes and societies of apostolic

---

8. Not applicable to diocesan faculties are cc. 64, 68–70, and 72, which deal with rescripts granted by the Apostolic See or rescripts requiring an executor. Canon 74 is not applicable, since true faculties do not grant dispensations or privileges. The applicability of cc. 63 and 65 is dubious. They cannot be used because the validity of acts cannot depend on laws of doubtful applicability (cf. c. 14).

life are generally granted in response to a request from the major superior of the institute or society (cf. c. 61). Faculties of extern priests who
are in the diocese temporarily are given at the request of the priests
themselves or their ordinaries. Faculties given to the clergy of the diocese and to lay ministers and officials are usually granted *motu proprio*
by the bishop without an explicit request from the cleric, minister, or
official. However, there is an implicit petition for diocesan faculties in
the desire of everyone who wants to minister in the diocese in a capacity for which faculties are given. Implicit in one's wish to be ordained
for a diocese or to minister in a certain pastoral role or office (pastor,
chaplain, parochial vicar, parish deacon, lay pastoral administrator, etc.)
is the request to have all the standard faculties of that order or office.

2. Faculties must be given in writing.

Faculties must be given in writing because they concern the external
forum (c. 37). A faculty given orally is valid but illicit, unless the law
requires for validity that a specific faculty be given in writing (see c.
1111, §2). From a practical perspective, it is not feasible to delegate
diocesan faculties orally, because each minister must be delegated
expressly and individually and both the diocese and the individual
ministers should have a record of the faculties granted and received.
For validity, the bishop or his delegate must sign the grant of faculties in his own hand. For liceity, the document should be countersigned by the chancellor or other notary (cc. 474, 483, §1), although
this is not strictly necessary if the bishop himself signs it personally.[9]
The date and the place are to be noted (c. 484, 2°). A copy of the document is to be kept in the diocesan archives (c. 486) or in the person-

---

9. Canon 474 requires that acts of the curia must, for validity, be signed by the
ordinary from whom they emanate and, for liceity, must also be signed by the chancellor or a notary. This canon is in the section on the diocesan curia. Some canonists
maintain that, since the diocesan bishop is not part of the curia but over it, c. 474
does not apply to him. Against this view is the interpretation of the "proper meaning
of the words" of the text (c. 17), which would hold that the "ordinary" includes the
bishop. It appears there may be a doubt of law (c. 14), in which case the grant of
faculties need not be countersigned by the chancellor or other notary if the bishop
himself signs it, but it must be countersigned if a delegate of the bishop signs it.

nel files if these are not in the archives. The original should be sent or delivered to the intended recipient. It should not be sent by e-mail attachment or fax, except as a preliminary indication that the faculties, already granted, are to be subsequently delivered.

3. *The document granting faculties must express the will of the bishop to grant the faculties.*

Every juridic act is in essence an act of the will, and therefore the act must express, in the way prescribed by law, the intention of the one performing the act (cf. c. 124). The act of granting faculties must express the intention that they are being granted. It is not sufficient merely to send out a list of faculties without any indication that they are actually now being granted. There must be some document—even in the form of a letter or an introduction to the *pagella*—which expresses the fact that the bishop or his delegate is now granting these faculties to the specified person.

4. *No one other than the bishop may grant the diocesan faculties without a special mandate from the bishop.*

A juridic act can be performed only by a capable and competent person (c. 124, §1). All local ordinaries, including the vicar general and episcopal vicar, may grant those faculties that they are competent in law to grant, including faculties to assist at marriage, hear confessions, binate and trinate, etc. However, in many instances, the law specifically names the diocesan bishop as the authority competent to grant some faculty, whether it be an authorization or a delegation of power (cf. c. 479). Since diocesan *pagellae* typically contain some faculties that can be granted only by the bishop, it is necessary that such lists of faculties be granted by the bishop himself, or by someone who has been expressly delegated by him. Even the vicar general and episcopal vicar must have a mandate in order to grant such faculties validly. Moreover, a chancellor or other official who is not a local ordinary may not validly grant any of the diocesan faculties without such a mandate. If the bishop grants a mandate to the vicar general, chancellor, or another delegate to sign the document granting faculties, a record of this mandate should be kept in the archives.

5. *Each person must be individually delegated.*

The delegation of faculties is a singular administrative act (cc. 35–47). Most faculties on a typical diocesan *pagella* cannot be granted by means of a general act (cc. 29–34). The bishop cannot validly issue a general decree or policy stating that ministers are to have such faculties. Since the delegation of faculties is a singular administrative act, each person must be individually granted the faculties. The recipient should be named in the grant of faculties or otherwise identified so there is no doubt for whom they are intended.

Since the issuance of faculties is a singular act, new diocesan policies may not be validly promulgated by their being listed on the *pagella*. A policy requires promulgation by means of a general decree (cc. 29–33) or publication as instructions (c. 34). Moreover, diocesan policies already in force should not as a rule be included on the *pagella* of faculties, since they are not faculties and cannot be delegated or revoked. If policies (whether laws, executive norms, or customs) are included for the sake of necessary information, they should be clearly demarcated and identified in such a way as to avoid confusing them with the faculties.

6. *Faculties must be in keeping with laws and customs.*

A faculty that is contrary to the law or against a legal custom may not be given (c. 38). Such a faculty would be invalid. For example, canon 905, §2 states that, if there is a shortage of priests, the local ordinary may permit priests to binate on weekdays for a just cause and to trinate on Sundays and holy days of obligation if pastoral necessity requires it. The bishop could not grant the faculty to priests to trinate on weekdays, nor could he permit them to binate without a just cause or trinate on Sundays and holy days when there is no pastoral necessity.[10]

This rule needs to be understood correctly, lest the whole purpose of granting faculties be vitiated. Faculties grant authorizations and

---

10. The bishop could, however, dispense in particular cases of necessity, for example, if the sole priest in a parish has on Saturday a funeral Mass, a wedding Mass, and the anticipated Mass of Sunday, and no one is available to assist him. He could also delegate his own power to dispense in such cases of necessity.

powers that persons lack in the law. However, granting them is not contrary to law, provided it is done lawfully. For example, the universal law says that pastors may dispense from the obligations of holy days and days of penance (c. 1245). As noted above, the bishop can delegate his own dispensing power to others besides pastors and clerical superiors to allow them to give the same dispensation. There is nothing contrary to the law in a bishop delegating the power that is his own to another person capable of exercising it.

7. The grant of faculties should indicate the extent of their use.

In the following chapter, we shall see the rule that faculties may be used throughout the diocese, unless they are given to parish ministers or chaplains in virtue of their pastoral office. Then they may only be used within their pastoral jurisdiction. Because there is no explicit canon on this in the law, the bishop should indicate, in his grant of the faculties, the extent of the use of each one. As a rule of thumb, faculties given to all priests may be used anywhere in the diocese. Faculties given to parish ministers in virtue of their office or function may be used only in the parish. Faculties given to chaplains and rectors of churches in virtue of their office may be used only within the scope of their pastoral assignment. The faculty delegated by the local ordinary for hearing confessions may be used for any penitent, anywhere in the world (c. 967, §2).

Faculties that are for the exercise of executive power can be used in the territory of the parish or diocese, or outside it, in keeping with the rules of canon 136. These rules may be summed up as follows:

a) Executive power may be used on behalf of residents of the territory whether they are in or outside the territory.

b) Ministers and others who have executive power may exercise it for themselves or for residents[11] of the territory when they (those who have the power) are in or outside the territory.

---

11. The term "resident" in this work refers to one who has domicile or quasi-domicile. See c. 102.

c) If the faculty is for an act of the power of governance that enables a favor to be granted, it may be used within the territory also for travelers *(peregrini)* who are in the territory temporarily. For example, the pastor, for a just reason, may dispense a visitor who is in the parish territory from the obligation of Friday abstinence (c. 1245).

The model faculties presented in Part II of this book indicate the appropriate extent of the use of the faculties: when the use of a faculty should be limited to the territorial parish or personal jurisdiction, when it may be exercised throughout the diocese, when it may be exercised outside the diocese for subjects of the diocese, and when, exceptionally, the law permits a faculty to be used for non-subjects outside the diocese, namely, the faculty for hearing confessions.

Some dioceses grant the same faculties to all priests for use throughout the diocese. From time to time, canonists hear of cases where a priest or deacon has assisted at a wedding in a chapel or oratory located within the boundaries of the parish, and the pastor only learns of it secondhand. No one knows whether the pre-marital formation was given or the canonical inquiry was conducted, and the marriage is not recorded anywhere. This is a violation of numerous universal and particular laws. Giving a diocesan-wide faculty for assisting at marriage to all priests and deacons enables, perhaps even encourages, the perpetration of such abuses, and it makes the work of tribunal personnel far more difficult when these marriages end in divorce and a declaration of invalidity of marriage is sought.

Faculties that are for particular parochial functions should not be delegated to all priests. While doing so is valid, it is not a good practice canonically. For the good order of the Church, the observance of all laws regarding the preparation for and celebration of sacraments and sacramentals, and the protection of parochial rights (c. 530), the use of certain faculties on the diocesan *pagella* should not be permitted outside the parish where the minister functions (especially assistance at marriages and the celebration of confirmation). If the need arises to function in another pastor's territory, special delegation can be granted.

Likewise, the use of certain other faculties that are for executive power, even though they may be validly and licitly used outside the diocese, should be restricted to the territory of the diocese, as their use may encroach on the good order of other dioceses and the rights of the bishops and pastors there. These restrictions, too, are noted on the model faculties given in Part II. If it is not appropriate that a certain faculty be used outside the parish, or outside the diocese, or outside the chaplain's jurisdiction, this fact may even be expressed as a condition on the grant of faculties, as seen in the following rule (no. 8).

8. *Conditions for the valid use of faculties must be expressly stated.*

If the bishop wants to attach any conditions for the valid use of a faculty, he must expressly state that it is for validity or, in a conditional clause, he must use the words "if," "unless," or "provided that" (c. 39). If the bishop wants to restrict the use of a faculty to the parish, he could say: "This faculty may be used validly only within the territory of the parish." This would provide juridic certainty on the extent of its valid use.

3. Faculty Supplied by Law

Given the complexity of the canonical norms on the grant of faculties, it is very likely that many administrative acts and many celebrations of certain sacraments would be invalid because the faculty for them was not given or the grant of the faculty was defective. Likewise, the numerous and detailed canons on the provision of office might be overlooked or misinterpreted (cc. 145–183), and pastors or other officials could be invalidly appointed, meaning that none of their faculties by office would be effective and any acts attempted would be invalid. Canon law provides a remedy for these real problems that likely occur daily around the world. In certain cases, when there is the possibility that many acts could be invalid, the Church, by means of *the law itself*, supplies the faculty that is missing.

The supply of the faculty is applicable to all acts of executive power and explicitly to three authorizations: the faculty for a presbyter to confirm, the faculty to hear confessions, and the faculty to assist at marriage. These are the only authorizations on a typical diocesan *pagella* that are necessary for validity, but even if there were other such habitual faculties, canon 144 provides a comprehensive remedy for ministerial acts, acts of administration, and acts of executive power performed without proper faculties.[12] However, the faculty is not supplied in all cases. The Church supplies the faculty only when the *common good* is at risk, that is, when there is the potential for harm to the common good due to repeated acts being invalid as a result of the lack of the necessary faculty by the same minister or administrator. The Church does not supply the faculty when only a private good is at stake, namely, when the validity of only one or a few acts is at stake.

Canon 144, §1 states: "In common error of fact or of law and in positive and probable doubt of law or of fact, the Church supplies *(Ecclesia supplet)* executive power of governance both for the external and the internal forum." The second paragraph of the canon applies this rule also to the faculties for confirmation, penance, and marriage. Some of the concepts in this canon are familiar: "executive power of governance," "external forum," and "internal forum." We need to examine now the meaning of the other concepts.

The faculty for assisting at marriage will be used throughout our explanation of these concepts. Canon 144 can be applied in the same way to the faculty for confirmation and all faculties for executive power as it is for marriage. The application is somewhat different in the case of the sacrament of penance, as will be seen.

3.1 Common Error

Common error is a mistaken judgment by the community. The community judges that its minister has the faculty but he does not. This is not

---

12. In virtue of c. 132, §1, c. 144 also applies to other authorizations necessary for validity, if they are habitual faculties. For example, the bishop grants all pastors the habitual faculty validly to make acts of extraordinary administration up to a maximum amount (cf. c. 1281, §1). This faculty is an authorization. If, then, a certain pastor were unknowingly appointed invalidly to office, the law would supply the necessary faculty and his acts of extraordinary administration would be canonically valid.

simply ignorance. There must be a situation when even persons who know the law judge, or would judge, that a priest or deacon should have the faculty to assist at marriages, when in truth he does not.

The community that makes the error is the one in which the minister functions. If the error regards a faculty of a pastor, parochial vicar, deacon or lay minister in a parish, or priest resident in a parish, the community is the parish. It is not the community that gathers for a specific wedding, which would include many non-parishioners.

Common error of fact (de facto) occurs when the community actually makes an error, thinking that the priest or deacon has the faculty but he does not have it. This would mean that the majority of parishioners see the minister presiding at a wedding and consciously judge that he has the faculty to assist. This does not happen in the real world!

Common error of law (de iure) occurs when the circumstances are such that the community *would judge* that the priest or deacon has the faculty, but it does not actually make this judgment. For the Church to supply the faculty in this situation of common error, there must have been some public fact that was the cause of the error or the potential error. Without this public fact, there is only ignorance, not error. The Church supplies the faculty when the priest or deacon exercises some function in the parish that would lead the people into believing he had the faculty *by office* or *by general delegation.* The activity of the priest or deacon in the parish is the public fact that is the basis for the common error. We shall look at three cases, one illustrating common error concerning the faculty by office, and two on common error concerning the faculty by general delegation.

Common Error Concerning the Faculty by Office

Pastors have the faculty to assist at marriage by law in virtue of their office, but if a pastor's appointment to office was invalidly made, then he is not the pastor and he does not have the faculties of a pastor by law. Still, the community would have good reason to consider him their pastor, as he has taken possession of the parish, was installed in office by the bishop, and has begun functioning as their pastor. Surely, the members of the parish have very good reason to be in error; they would be quite surprised if they learned he was never their pastor.

Appointment to office can be invalid for a number of reasons. For example, canon 153, §1 says that an office must be vacant before it can be filled. In other words, the outgoing pastor must be out of office before the new one is appointed. This sounds simple enough, but it must be read together with canon 191, §1 which says that, in a transfer to a new office, the first office is vacated only after the person takes possession of his new office (unless the law provides otherwise or the competent authority has prescribed otherwise). Let us consider the following scenario.

1. Fr. A., the pastor of St. George's, is being transferred to another pastorate.

2. Fr. B. is appointed new pastor of St. George's as of July 1, but the bishop neglects to make a provision with respect to the rule of canon 191, §1.

3. Fr. A. moves out of St. George's on June 30, but first goes on vacation and does not take possession of his new parish until August 1.

4. The office of pastor at St. George's is not vacant when Fr. B. takes charge, yet everyone (including the bishop) thinks he is the new pastor.

In this scenario, which often occurs, Fr. B. is not validly appointed, nor does his invalid appointment become sanated as of August 1. He remains invalidly appointed until a new decree of appointment is issued. Everyone—bishop, pastor, and parishioners alike—are in error because they think Fr. B. is their validly appointed pastor. In such a case of common error, in order to avoid many invalid acts, the Church supplies all the necessary executive powers plus the faculties for hearing confessions, confirming, and assisting at marriage (and any other delegated habitual faculties that are authorizations required for the validity of an act). Doubtless, the common good is at stake, so the Church supplies the faculty—*Ecclesia supplet facultatem.*

Common Error Concerning General Delegation

Case 1. Parochial vicars and parish deacons are typically granted general delegation for assisting at marriages in the parish as one of their diocesan faculties. However, in a certain diocese, the bishop leaves it to the pastor to determine whether the deacon may assist at marriage. Pastor X tells the parish deacon that he wants the deacon to preside at weddings in the parish on a regular basis. However, a general delegation for assisting at marriage cannot validly be given orally; it must be in writing (c. 1111, §2).[13] Consequently, all the marriages at which this deacon would assist would be invalid, but they are not invalid because the Church supplies the faculty in this case. The community, seeing the deacon assisting at marriage, would erroneously judge that he was given general delegation by the pastor (though they do not have to actually make this judgment). Due to the harm to the common good that would be caused by this deacon assisting at many weddings without the faculty, the Church supplies the faculty and all the marriages are presumed valid. *Ecclesia supplet facultatem.*

Case 2. A priest who is a university professor is in residence in a parish rectory and he regularly celebrates Mass and hears confessions in the parish, but he does not have the faculty to assist at marriage. One weekend the pastor is out of town and the resident priest is celebrating all the Masses. On Saturday afternoon, a bridal party appears unexpectedly at the church doors. It seems the secretary had mistakenly written the date of the marriage for the following week. The priest professor steps in and celebrates the marriage rite. The marriage is valid because the Church supplies the faculty. The public fact of his residency, together with his functioning publicly and regularly in a liturgical capacity in the parish, is the cause that would lead the community into the error of judging that he had general delegation, when

---

13. The Latin text of c. 1111, §2 is clearer on this point than any of the published English translations of the code, but the commentators note that the requirement is for validity. It is also evident from the acts of the commission that drafted this canon. See *Communicationes* 8 (1976) 41.

he does not. Moreover, there is the potential danger to the common good of invalid marriages happening on a repeated basis, even though this is unlikely. *Ecclesia supplet facultatem.*

Cases Involving a Lack of Special Delegation

Common error does not apply to cases of *special delegation* of a faculty. (The faculty for hearing confessions is a special case, treated below.) The Church does *not* supply the faculty if special delegation should have been given, but was not, to a visiting priest or deacon from outside the parish. No one who knows the law would judge that a visiting priest or deacon has general delegation for marriages in that parish (and the law always presumes knowledge of the law). The lack of delegation in this case applies to only one marriage; harm to the common good is not at stake.

If the Church supplied the faculty in such a case, there would be no need for the law requiring priests and deacons to have a faculty, because the Church would nearly always supply it when it was lacking. This would defeat the purposes of having faculties, among them, to promote good order within the Church through the observance of proper procedures and obligations, to protect parochial rights, and to ensure qualified ministers who are in the full communion of the Church and act in its name. If any minister could enter another parish or diocese anywhere in the world and begin functioning validly, there would be inevitable abuses and conflicts. The requirement of faculties for ministerial and administrative acts serves to prevent such problems.

Some dioceses give all priests and deacons the faculty to assist at marriage anywhere in the diocese. Where this is the case, the boundaries for the operation of common error are not the parish but the entire diocese. Only a priest or deacon coming from outside the diocese could invalidly assist at marriage due to a lack of a faculty. This may sound like a reason to recommend the practice of giving all priests and deacons the faculty to assist at marriage everywhere in the diocese, but there are other cogent reasons against it, above all, to prevent abuses and protect parochial rights.

The Faculty Not Supplied

Canon 144 is a legal remedy that works only in some kinds of cases but not in all. By no means is it an excuse for ministers to ignore canon law and assume *Ecclesia supplet*, that the Church always supplies a missing faculty. Some cases when the Church does *not* supply the faculty are:

- a minister who is excommunicated or suspended when the censure has been imposed or declared;

- a minister not in communion with the Catholic Church (e.g., a priest of the Society of St. Pius X);

- a minister whose faculty was revoked and a new one not given;

- a personal pastor who assists at a marriage in his parish when neither party is in his personal jurisdiction;

- a Latin Catholic pastor who assists at the marriage of a Catholic parishioner and a Protestant, but the Catholic is an Eastern Catholic;

- a cardinal or papal nuncio who assists at a marriage without delegation;

- a diocesan bishop who assists at marriage outside his diocese without delegation;

- a pastor who assists at the marriage of his parishioners in a parish oratory, but the oratory is outside his parish boundaries;

- when special delegation was not given expressly, whether explicitly or implicitly, to a specified person or persons;

- when the special delegation was not given for a specified marriage or marriages;

- when the subdelegation for a marriage was granted without the authorization of the one delegating.

Confirmation

Although the principles and application of canon 144 are identical for
the faculties for assisting at marriage and for presbyters to confirm,
one caution must be noted. It is possible for many individuals at the
same celebration to be invalidly confirmed if the presbyter lacks the
faculty, that is, if he should have had a special delegation but did not
have it. Unlike assistance at marriage, for which special delegation
generally involves only one couple at one wedding, special delegation
for confirmation could involve confirming scores of persons at one
celebration. The Church does not supply the faculty based on the
number of people invalidly confirmed at one celebration, but on
whether there is a good reason for the community to err in thinking
the presbyter had general delegation for confirmation or the faculty by
office. This is the basis for potential harm to the common good,
because the celebrations of confirmation could occur numerous times
on an ongoing basis, not just at one or several celebrations.

For example, the policy in a certain diocese is not to give presbyters
general delegation for confirmation; they must request special delegation
each time they want to confirm someone whom they cannot confirm in
virtue of their office (c. 883, 2°). At a parish celebration of confirmation,
the bishop forgets to come and he cannot be located. After waiting a half
hour, the pastor himself proceeds to celebrate the rite and confirms over
fifty children. They are all invalidly confirmed, because there is no legal
basis or public fact that would lead the community to conclude that the
pastor had been delegated.[14] The community was expecting the bishop,
so they rightly would presume that the pastor does not have special delegation for a confirmation at which the bishop was to preside. (If they
actually thought he had the faculty, it would be ignorance, not error.)

Supplied Faculty for Hearing Confessions

We have seen that the most common applications of canon 144 with
respect to the faculty for assisting at marriage (and diocesan faculties in

---

14. It is possible to induce common error, e.g., if the pastor announces before
the celebration that the bishop had delegated him, but this would be morally dubious.

general) are the following: (1) when a pastor was invalidly appointed, but the parish community believes him to be their pastor; (2) when the parochial vicar or parish deacon, who should normally have the faculty by general delegation, was not granted it or it was granted invalidly; (3) when the community errs concerning the status of the priest or deacon, thinking him to have general delegation because of some public fact that suggests this (like residence in the rectory and regularly celebrating the Eucharist in the church). The law does not supply the faculty when special delegation should have been given but was not, because the common good is not at stake.

While, in principle, the application of canon 144 is also the same for the faculty to hear confessions, there is a key difference. In practice, the mere fact that a priest is in the confessional or other place where penance is ordinarily celebrated, and the place is unlocked so that the possibility exists for the community to enter, is sufficient to form the foundation for common error. The community would judge that any priest in good standing who is hearing confessions there has the faculty, even if few or no people witness the celebration of the sacrament and make this judgment. The reason why the Church supplies the faculty is the potential of harm to the common good. If a priest without the faculty is hearing only one confession in an open church, the possibility exists that many people could enter and want to confess, with all of them being absolved invalidly. Although the rite is celebrated for only one person, there is the potential for many invalid celebrations. To avoid such potential harm to the common good, the law supplies the faculty, no matter how few confessions are actually heard.

If a priest is hearing confessions outside a place where penance is ordinarily celebrated, the Church would not supply the faculty because there would be no basis for the community to believe that such a priest should have the faculty. For example, if a passenger approaches a priest at the airport and asks to confess before boarding the plane but the priest does not have the faculty, the Church would not supply the faculty based on common error. The members of the community to make the error are not there even potentially and, even if they were, they would have no justification for concluding that the priest should have the faculty.

Again, the faculty is supplied only for a priest in good standing. If the priest no longer has his faculty due to an act of the external forum (the imposition or declaration of a censure, the revocation of the faculty, the loss of the clerical state), or if the priest is not in full communion with the Church, the faculty is not supplied. The law presumes knowledge of such external forum facts, even if they are not really known. Such a priest may validly celebrate the sacrament of penance only for someone in danger of death (c. 976).

3.2 Positive and Probable Doubt of Law and Fact

The law also supplies the faculty in cases of positive and probable doubt of law or doubt of fact. A doubt is *positive* when there is a good reason for thinking one has the faculty, but there is also a reason for thinking one does not. A negative doubt is based only on a slight reason for thinking one has the faculty. A negative doubt is tantamount to ignorance; it is not sufficient for the Church to supply the faculty. A doubt is *probable* if the reason is based on an objective fact or facts such that any reasonable person would conclude that the faculty could well exist, although there is no certainty. If both the reasons for and against thinking one has the faculty are equal, the doubt is still probable because the contrary reasons are not strong enough to overcome the reasons in favor. In other words, for the Church to supply the faculty in doubt, the reasons in favor of having the faculty must be as strong as, or stronger than, the reasons against having the faculty.

A doubt, like error, does not arise from ignorance. It presumes someone knows the law. *Positive and probable doubt of law* refers to a *dubium iuris*,[15] that is, when some canonical norm itself is unclear such that even experts in the law can interpret it differently. One opinion leads to a probable conclusion that one has the faculty, while another opinion leads to a conclusion that one does not have it.

---

15. The Latin word *ius* is used in the expression *dubium iuris*, not the word *lex*. The word *lex* only refers to laws promulgated by a legislative authority. The word *ius* includes any binding norms: legislation, customs, and normative acts of executive power.

For example, in a certain diocese, permanent deacons begin their ministry in a parish before completing their entire formation. They are granted the faculty to assist at marriage, but its valid use is contingent upon a diocesan policy. This policy holds that the deacons' faculty to assist at marriage may be used only in necessity until they have completed their required formation. This policy could easily lead to doubts in concrete cases involving a deacon who has not completed the required formation. What is a "necessity"? Does it demand the physical impossibility of the presence of the pastor, or does it also include moral impossibility (e.g., when the pastor is overworked and needs the deacon's assistance)? Does it mean that, when the pastor cannot be present for the wedding, he must try to find another priest, or a deacon with the required formation, to assist at the marriage? Does the lack of completing "the required formation" imply specifically the marriage segment of the diaconate formation program of the diocese, or could the deacon have obtained the necessary formation from another source, for example, through the pastor's own instruction?

There are good reasons for thinking the deacon can proceed to assist at marriage despite any of these doubts. Indeed, canon law requires the broad interpretation of favorable laws, like the diocesan policy (cf. c. 18), and of favorable administrative acts, like the grant of this faculty (cf. c. 36, §1). Broad interpretation of "necessity" and "required formation" leads to the probable (though not certain) conclusion that the deacon has the faculty. No reasons would lead to complete certainty regarding these doubts, so the *dubium iuris* would still exist. In all these doubtful cases, the pastor may permit the deacon to assist at the marriage without fearing that the deacon lacks the faculty. *Ecclesia supplet facultatem.*

A *positive and probable doubt of fact* occurs when, in a concrete case, there are reasons pro and con for the existence of some fact that is necessary for the valid use of the faculty. For example, the pastor is going out of town for the week and he asks a priest-friend to celebrate the Eucharist and reconciliation while he is gone. He also asks the priest if he would officiate at the wedding on Saturday afternoon, and the priest agrees. After the pastor has gone, the visiting priest discovers that the wedding on Saturday afternoon was canceled recently, but another wedding is scheduled for Saturday morning. The doubtful fact is whether the pastor forgot or did not know that the marriage originally scheduled in the afternoon had been cancelled and he had intended to delegate his friend for that marriage, or whether he made a mistake about the time of day for the wedding for which he intended to delegate the priest. The visiting priest has good reason to believe that the pastor made a simple mistake, and that he actually was granting him special delegation for the wedding on Saturday morning, as there is no other marriage taking place in the parish on Saturday afternoon. This doubt, under the circumstances, is positive and probable. The priest may proceed to assist at the marriage even though he has no explicit faculty for a marriage in the morning. *Ecclesia supplet facultatem.*

3.3 The Values Behind Canon 144

The canonical doctrine on the supplied faculty may appear to be so much casuistic "splitting of hairs," but it serves to protect important values:

- to uphold the actual will of the superior (bishop, religious superior, etc.) or other person delegating faculties, such that the person he invalidly delegated, neglected to delegate, or invalidly appointed to office still has the faculties as intended by the superior, since the essence of the act of delegation or provision of office is the intention of the one performing the act;

- to protect the common good, so that even in the case of someone who was not given the faculty, there will be no danger of many invalid acts on a regular basis, while at the same time not supplying the faculty merely for a private good, such as for a few marriages or a single celebration of confirmation, because that would defeat entirely the purpose of having faculties;

- to ensure that ministers are acting in the name of the Church, and thus the faculty is not supplied to those under censure, who have had their faculties removed, or who are not in the full communion of the Catholic Church;

– to reassure the community and its leaders and relieve consciences so that in doubtful cases ministers and administrators may proceed to act for the common good of the Church and the spiritual welfare of the faithful.

4. Revoking Diocesan Faculties

In this section, we gather the canonical rules that must be observed in revoking faculties. The first, and principal, topic to be treated is the revocation of an individual minister's diocesan faculties, namely, those faculties granted by personal delegation. We shall see that the act of revocation is a singular administrative decree, which requires that specific canonical rules be observed for this act. The more important of these rules will be explained and illustrated. We then shall briefly consider the revocation of diocesan faculties when the bishop is replacing them with a new *pagella* and the removal of faculties of office, which is accomplished by removal from office. We shall conclude with some remarks on the suspension or privation of faculties as a penalty for the commission of a canonical crime.

4.1 Revoking an Individual's Faculties

The person capable of revoking faculties is the one who granted them or his successor in office (cf. c. 142, §1). The diocesan bishop may directly revoke faculties given by him or his predecessor, or by any other official of the diocese subject to him. He may revoke one, several, or all delegated faculties.

Like the grant of faculties, the revocation of faculties is a juridic act, a singular administrative act, and an act of executive power of governance. Unlike the granting of faculties, which observes pertinent rules for rescripts, the revocation of faculties is a singular administrative decree. Therefore, in addition to the canons on juridic acts, singular administrative acts, and the exercise of executive power of governance, the canons on singular decrees (cc. 48–58) must also be observed whenever one or more faculties are revoked.

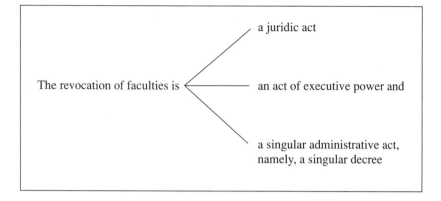

Singular Decree

A singular decree is defined in canon 48 as "an administrative act, issued by a competent executive authority by which, for a particular case, a decision is given or some provision is made; by its nature it does not presuppose that anyone requested it." The revocation of faculties is a decision made by the bishop. Unlike rescripts, which grant something favorable to a person and are given to the willing, singular decrees may have negative consequences and can be imposed on subjects against their will.

The form of a singular decree varies. Decrees that are provisions often simply take the form of a letter from the bishop or other authority. Even when a decree is a decision, it does not have to state explicitly that it is a decree, although this is preferable when faculties are being removed so that the subject knows exactly what is at stake canonically.

The decree must always express some provision or decision or give some command. A decree cannot be a mere request, a recommendation, or an invitation to do something. Revocation would not occur by a statement like this: "After due consideration of all the factors, it would be better, Fr. X, if henceforth you did not exercise the faculties of the diocese." As worded, the bishop would be merely giving his own recommendation about the exercise of the priest's faculties; the priest could consider this recommendation and then proceed to do what he wanted. He would still have his faculties and would be free to exercise them. Rather, the bishop must give a direct and clear command, such as: "I hereby revoke all the faculties delegated by me, my predecessors, or any other official or minister of this diocese at any time." The rest of the letter may be gentler in tone, if this is warranted, but there would be no mistake about the intent and interpretation of such a clear decision.

Necessary Information and Proofs

Among the general norms on singular decrees, the most important, procedurally, are canons 50 and 51. According to canon 50, the authority who wishes to issue a decree must gather the necessary information and proofs and, insofar as possible, should hear the person whose rights could be harmed by the decree. The purpose of this canon is to prevent arbitrary actions on the part of ecclesiastical authority, which might offend against justice, charity, and the rights of persons, including their right to a good reputation (c. 220). The necessary information and proofs are those that form the basis for the bishop's decision to revoke one or more faculties. For example, if the bishop is contemplating the revocation of a deacon's faculty to preach, the necessary information and proofs would consist of whatever led him to this determination—complaints of parishioners, the report of the pastor, review of formation records, etc. Those who could be harmed by the decree are most certainly the deacon himself and possibly the pastor, if the pastor needs the deacon's services for preaching. Thus, the bishop should hear the deacon's reply before he issues a decree revoking his faculty. He should also hear what the pastor thinks about the revocation of the faculty.

After hearing the deacon and the pastor and considering the other evidence, the bishop is in a good position to make an informed judgment. If the bishop thinks the deacon has given reasonable assurances that he will put more effort into preparation and seek additional formation, the bishop might then decide not to issue the decree of revocation and wait for further developments. Or he might decide instead to issue a precept (c. 49), enjoining the deacon to a specific course of action, such as taking further homiletic instructions, with a threat to remove his faculty if there is no significant improvement within a certain period of time. Or he may decide that the gravity of the situation warrants an immediate revocation of the faculty.

In Writing

Canon 51 says the decree is to be issued in writing and, if it is a decision, the reasons for the decision are to be given, at least in summary fashion. A decision in writing is necessary for its enforcement (c. 54, §2). If nothing is given in writing, the recipient of the decree can claim that he still has his faculties, and proof to the contrary is lacking. Moreover, an oral decree deprives the subject of the means for recourse (cc. 1732–1739) and therefore would be unjust as well as unlawful. An unjust and unlawful decree does not have to be observed.[16]

According to canon 55, the decree of revocation can be delivered orally only if "a very grave reason" prevents the bishop from delivering a written decree. Sometimes a person may refuse to accept a decree and it is returned to the bishop unopened. Such defiance would constitute a very grave reason for using the oral procedure. This procedure requires that the decree be read to the person in the presence of a notary or two witnesses. All present are then to sign a document. The document should include the text of the decree, a statement that it was read in the presence of the subject and the undersigned, and the date and place. If the subject refuses to sign, this fact should be noted on the document. Thus, even the oral process results in a written document that is proof of the issuance of the decree.

Reasons Expressed

The motivation for the decree must be given in its introductory part. This consists of the reason or reasons why the bishop is revoking one

---

16. Revoking faculties orally would also be an empty gesture, because the law would supply executive power and the faculties for confirmation, hearing confessions, and assisting at marriage due to common error. An oral decree given privately to a subject is not an external forum act about which the community would be presumed in law to have knowledge, so there would be common error about the existence of this faculty and the law would supply it.

or more faculties. Instead of giving some general reasons (like "the common good of the diocese"), it is preferable to express the reason or reasons that truly motivated the decree. It should not be some secondary reason that was not decisive or a reason that may sound like a personal opinion. For example, if the principal reason for removing the deacon's faculty to preach is the feedback the bishop has received from parishioners about his bad preaching, the bishop should mention this. He should not say something so generic that the deacon could attack it on recourse, such as, "As it appears that you lack preaching skills," or "Given that you do not have sufficient formation to preach..." The deacon could prove, on recourse, that he has had the same formation as other deacons and he could furnish his own testimonials from his supporters and friends who affirm his preaching. The bishop may be motivated by compassion to "cushion the blow" in not citing the real evidence for his decision, but this approach often seems unfair to the recipient of the decree and may result in a time-consuming recourse that would not have been taken if the facts had been disclosed from the beginning.

Accusations of Sexual Misconduct

In some dioceses, the bishop removes a cleric's faculties immediately upon an accusation of sexual misconduct, even if no penal process has been initiated.[17] In such a case, the bishop or his delegate still must hear the cleric first, issue the decree of revocation of faculties in writing, and give the motivating reason. The reason for the revocation of faculties should be carefully considered so it would hold up if recourse were to be taken against the decree.

---

17. In truth, the bishop often tells the accused that he must cease all ministerial activities. However, the bishop has no power to do this unless he commences a penal process.

In 2002, the USCCB enacted particular law on this matter. The policy states that, in applying the norms, "the processes provided for in canon law must be observed, and the various provisions of canon law must be considered." See Essential Norms for Diocesan/Eparchial Policies Dealing with Allegations of Sexual Abuse of Minors by Priests or Deacons, 13 November 2002, *Origins* 32 (2002) 415–418.

Although such a decree may well result in the cleric's ceasing to minister altogether, legally, it only bars him from those acts that require diocesan faculties delegated *ab homine* and the faculty to preach, which is a faculty of the law subject to the bishop's control. Other faculties by law and powers of order would not be affected. The penal process must already be under way to prevent the cleric from ministering altogether (c. 1722). In the meantime, the cleric can only be advised to refrain voluntarily from exercising the ministry for his own good.[18] Removal from office and penalties are treated below in Sections 4.3 and 4.4.

Faculty for Hearing Confessions

Canon law provides some special rules for the revocation of the faculty to hear confessions (c. 974). The faculty for hearing confessions habitually cannot be revoked except for a *grave cause*. If the local ordinary who revokes the faculty is the ordinary of the place of the priest's incardination or domicile who granted the faculty, then the faculty is lost everywhere in the world. If some other local ordinary revokes the faculty, the priest loses it only in that territory. A local ordinary who revokes a priest's faculty to hear confessions must inform that priest's ordinary of incardination or, if he is a religious, the competent superior. All the other rules must also be observed: the necessary information and proofs must be collected; the priest must be heard before the decree is issued; the decree must be in writing; and the motivating reason(s) must be expressed.

4.2 Replacing the Pagella

In granting a new *pagella* of faculties, the diocesan bishop should mention in the grant that he is replacing the old *pagella* with the new

---

18. It would not be sufficient simply to rely on a diocesan protocol barring public ministry without attending to the universal law. Any provision of a policy of particular law that is contrary to universal law is invalid (c. 135, §2), unless the Holy See has specifically approved it.

one (cf. c. 67, §2). Otherwise, the old faculties continue in force, even those that do not appear on the new *pagella*. A simple statement suffices, such as: "This list of faculties replaces any previous list of diocesan faculties granted by me, my predecessors, or by any other diocesan official." This is the statement used in the model documents for granting faculties found in Appendix II. If the bishop mentions in the document granting the faculties that the old *pagella* is replaced by the new one, then the ministers and officials will lose their old faculties immediately upon receiving their new ones (cf. c. 47). If the new faculties are not to take effect immediately, the bishop should mention explicitly that the old faculties are revoked on the same date that the new ones take effect.

4.3 Faculties of Office and Removal from Office

The bishop may not revoke faculties granted by the law unless this power is expressly given in the universal law. In general, the diocesan bishop has no authority to revoke faculties he has not given. Therefore, he cannot revoke faculties that belong to clerics in virtue of their ordination. Nor can he revoke faculties attached by law to an office.[19] Two exceptions to this rule are expressly stated in the universal law. (1) Canon 764 allows the competent ordinary to restrict or remove the cleric's faculty for preaching, which is given by the universal law at ordination to the diaconate.[20] (2) Canon 975 allows the competent authority to revoke the faculty for hearing confessions of those who have it by office. Those who have the faculty by office, below the pope, are all local ordinaries (including vicars general and episcopal vicars), the canon penitentiary, pastors, and those who take the place

---

19. Canon 143, §1 says that ordinary power (power by office) ceases by the loss of the office to which it is attached. Since it is a general principle of law, it applies to offices of particular law as well as universal law.

20. Canon 764 says the faculty may be restricted or taken away by the competent ordinary, and that particular law may require express permission to use it. Thus, the faculty is granted by the universal law to all clerics, but particular law can restrict its use and the competent authority may restrict its use or remove it.

of pastors (c. 968, §1).[21] The local ordinary must have a grave reason to remove the faculty and must observe all the norms of law, as explained above.

To remove any other faculties granted by office, the bishop should remove the person from office. Faculties granted by the law itself in virtue of an office are those that are necessary for fulfilling the obligations of that office. If there is a reason for removing any such faculty, it has to be serious enough to warrant removal from office, because that is what it takes to remove such faculties (with the exception of the faculty for hearing confessions, as noted above). To remove someone from office, the applicable canons must be observed (cc. 35–58, 143, 192–195, 1740–1747). Suspension of faculties involves a penal process.

4.4 Penal Processes

The use of faculties, both delegated and granted by law, may be suspended or prohibited by a penalty. They may also be removed by penalty (privation), unless they are granted at ordination. The punishment for many canonical crimes results in the privation of faculties or a prohibition against their exercise. Privation applies to delegated faculties *(ab homine)* and faculties by office, but not to powers of order and faculties granted at ordination (c. 1338, §1). The prohibition of the use of faculties applies to all categories of faculties. Given the complexity of penal law and procedures, the bishop and his canonists must consult more detailed commentaries before embarking on a penal process.[22] The treatment here will be limited to

---

21. Bishops and cardinals have the faculty by law (c. 967, §1). On the faculty by law of superiors of clerical religious institutes and societies of apostolic life, see c. 968, §2.

22. For a useful summary and practical application of penal law, see Gregory Ingels, "Processes Which Govern the Application of Penalties," in *Clergy Procedural Handbook*, ed. Randolph R. Calvo and Nevin J. Klinger (Washington: CLSA, 1992) 206–237.

For lists of canonical delicts and their corresponding penalties, many of which affect the use of faculties, see Thomas J. Green, "Sanctions in the Church," in *Code*

a description of the kinds of penalties in canon law that affect the use of faculties.

There are two categories of penalties in canon law—censures and expiatory penalties. The three censures—excommunication, interdict, and suspension—each involve the loss of faculties to one extent or another. The penalty of excommunication prohibits the exercise of all faculties; the penalty of interdict prohibits exercising some faculties; the penalty of suspension prohibits the use of some or all faculties.

Excommunication. A person who is excommunicated is prohibited from: (1) having any ministerial participation in the Eucharist or any other liturgical ceremonies; (2) celebrating the sacraments and sacramentals and receiving the sacraments; (3) exercising ecclesiastical offices, ministries, or functions and performing acts of governance (c. 1331, §1).[23] In short, the excommunicated person cannot exercise any faculty, whether of order, office, or personal delegation. The sole exception is for priests, who always retain the faculty by law to hear the confession and remit the censures of a person in danger of death (c. 976).

Interdict. A person who has been penalized with an interdict is prohibited from: (1) having any ministerial participation in the Eucharist or any other liturgical ceremonies; and (2) celebrating the sacraments and sacramentals and receiving the sacraments. The penalty of interdict affects only faculties for liturgical acts; it does not affect faculties for exercising executive power (see c. 1332).

Suspension. The penalty of suspension affects only clerics. A suspension prohibits: (1) either all or some acts of the power of orders (including faculties by law at ordination); (2) either all or some acts of the power of governance; (3) the exercise of all or some of the rights or functions of office. The extent of the suspension is determined either in the law, by precept, or by the sentence or decree imposing the penalty (c. 1334, §1).

Expiatory penalties. Five expiatory penalties in canon law are listed in canon 1336. Three of the five affect the exercise of faculties:

---

of Canon Law: A Text and Commentary, ed. James A. Coriden, Thomas J. Green, and Donald E. Heintschel (New York/Mahwah, N.J.: Paulist Press, 1985) 932–940.

23. Canon 1331, §2 gives further effects of an excommunication that is imposed or declared.

(1) privation of a power, office, function, right, privilege, faculty, favor, title, or insignia; (2) a prohibition against licitly exercising any of these, or a prohibition against licitly exercising them in a certain place or outside a certain place; (3) dismissal from the clerical state. The penalty in the first and second categories may be limited to one or more specific faculties, depending on the nature of the crime. The third penalty—dismissal from the clerical state—results in the loss of all faculties granted by the bishop in virtue of one's clerical status, the loss of all faculties granted by law in virtue of a clerical office, and the prohibition of the exercise of all powers and faculties of orders.

Summary

The act of granting a faculty is a juridic act, an act of executive power of governance, and a singular administrative act, and all the canons of the code on these acts must be observed in the grant of diocesan faculties. The grant of faculties, moreover, is subject to the applicable canons on rescripts. On the basis of these numerous canons, eight key rules must be observed for the valid and/or licit grant of diocesan faculties by the bishop or his delegate. Faculties can be granted by law as well as by personal delegation, and one of the ways they are granted by law, or supplied, is in cases of common error of fact or of law and in positive and probable doubt of law or of fact. The law supplies the necessary faculty in these situations to avert danger of harm to the common good due to the possibility of a minister performing an invalid act repeatedly.

Like the grant of faculties, the revocation of faculties is also a juridic act, an act of executive power of governance, and a singular administrative act. Unlike the grant of faculties, which observes applicable rules on rescripts, the revocation of faculties is a singular administrative decree that makes a decision. It follows that the canons on all these matters must be observed in revoking faculties. Before issuing the decree of revocation, the bishop must gather the necessary facts and information and listen to those whose rights may be harmed. He must issue the decree in writing and give the reason(s) for revocation. If the bishop is presenting a new *pagella*, he must revoke the old one, which may be done simply by stating that the new list of faculties replaces the former one. The bishop can revoke only those faculties granted by him, his predecessor, or one of his subjects. He cannot revoke faculties granted by law, unless the law gives him this power. He can, however, remove an official from office, observing all the applicable canons. Moreover, if a minister or official has committed a canonical delict, the suspension or privation of faculties is frequently the result of canonical penalties, both censures and expiatory penalties.

The matters of this chapter are principally the concern of canonists and diocesan officials who are involved in the grant and revocation of faculties and the determination of whether the law supplies a faculty when a person has acted without the faculty. The next chapter treats the use, delegation, and cessation of faculties, matters that pertain to all those who have any faculties by law or delegation.

CHAPTER THREE

The Use, Delegation, and Cessation of Faculties

The previous chapter was directed primarily to the diocesan bishop, officials of the diocesan curia, and canonists, since it dealt with rules for the granting and revoking of faculties and the determination of when the law supplies a missing faculty. The present chapter is directed not only to them but also to the ministers and administrators given the faculties. This chapter has three sections treating the use, the delegation and subdelegation, and the cessation of diocesan faculties. As we have seen, habitual faculties are governed by applicable canonical norms on executive power of governance, singular administrative acts, and rescripts. The rules discussed in this chapter are principally based on these norms.

1. Rules for the Use of Faculties

The following rules mainly apply to diocesan faculties granted by the bishop or his delegate, but several rules equally apply to faculties granted by law in virtue of an office. Rule six is on faculties granted at ordination and rule seven is on faculties granted by the law in virtue of an office.

1. Diocesan faculties ordinarily take effect on the date of issue.

If the bishop specifies no date for when the faculties take effect, they go into force immediately on the date they are issued, even before they are received (cf. c. 62). For example, a religious priest arrives in the parish from another diocese, but he has not yet received his faculties. He calls the vicar general's office and is told they are in the mail. He can immediately begin using his faculties, that is, those faculties that he knows he will be receiving.

Faculties granted to an officeholder in virtue of his office do not take effect until the person is in office. This is in keeping with the intention of the bishop in granting the faculties, and the intention is the essence of every juridic act. For example, if the bishop delegates special faculties to pastors beyond the general faculties given to all priests, those additional faculties do not become effective until the priest takes canonical possession of the parish, the act by which he takes office (c. 527). The bishop intends the faculties to be used only by pastors; therefore, they cannot be used until the priest is a pastor, even if they are dated and received before he takes office.

2. Faculties can be used only by the intended person.

If a minor mistake is made regarding the recipient of the faculties, they are valid and may be used, but a substantial error renders them invalid (see c. 66). Minor mistakes include the spelling of the minister's or official's name, the wrong address, the confusion of one name with another (provided the intended person received the proper faculties), or a similar kind of error. Such faculties are still valid and may be used. Substantial errors would include mistakes about the person, office, or status of the recipient of the faculties. If they are issued to the wrong person entirely, then that person may not use them; examples of such instances would include faculties for the pastor being mistakenly granted to the parochial vicar or deacon, or faculties for a priest being granted to a religious brother.

3. *Diocesan faculties do not require acceptance before use.*

We shall see in section 2 of this chapter that, when a priest or deacon delegates a faculty, the one being delegated must accept it. However, faculties given by a superior to a subject do not require acceptance (cf. c. 61).[1] Faculties granted by law also do not require acceptance and cannot be refused. In truth, the bishop does not impose faculties on unwilling ministers; they want the faculties because the faculties facilitate their ministry. Implicit in one's petition for holy orders or in one's request to minister in a certain pastoral role or office is the request to have all the standard faculties of the diocese for that order or office.

4. *Diocesan faculties are to be used for the benefit of the faithful.*

Diocesan faculties are, for the most part, not intended for the minister's personal benefit (cf. c. 71). They are given for the benefit of the faithful. Therefore, their use is obligatory whenever they promote the common good or favor the spiritual welfare of the faithful—the *salus animarum*, which is the supreme law of the Church (c. 1752). We see a forceful demonstration of this general rule in canon 885, §2 regarding the faculty to confirm: "A presbyter who has this faculty [to confirm] must use it for those in whose favor the faculty was granted." The presbyter *must use* the faculty; it is not his option to use it or not. Most faculties are not favors that the minister can use or not; they are intended for the benefit of the faithful.

In some dioceses, the bishop grants presbyters the faculty to confirm all baptized Catholics who are older than the normal age for confirmation in the diocese. The presbyter who has this faculty cannot refuse a person who requests the sacrament, unless he has a reason based in the law (cc. 889, §2; 843, §1). For example, the presbyter cannot refuse because he thinks that only bishops should confirm; the law says otherwise (cc. 883–884).

---

1. See Francisco López-Illana, "La suplencia de la facultad de asistir al matrimonio," *Ius Canonicum* 37 (1997) 116–122.

5. *Diocesan faculties may be used anywhere in the diocese, unless the bishop restricts their use or unless the faculties were granted in virtue of an office.*

Since the bishop has jurisdiction over the entire diocese, he can grant faculties for use throughout the diocese. Faculties granted to priests in general nearly always may be used anywhere in the diocese. However, additional faculties given to priests in virtue of their parochial office (pastors, parochial vicars) and faculties given to deacons and lay ministers in virtue of a parochial office may be exercised only in the parish boundaries. Likewise, faculties granted to ministers in personal parishes, chaplains, and rectors of churches in virtue of their pastoral office may be only used within the limits of their pastoral charge.[2]

6. *Faculties granted at ordination can be used anywhere in the world, unless the universal law permits a restriction on their use.*

Faculties granted by ecclesiastical law at ordination—traditionally called powers of order of ecclesiastical law—are given to the cleric absolutely. They can be used anywhere in the world with at least the presumed permission of the competent authority of that place—local ordinary, pastor, religious superior, chaplain, rector, etc. (cf. cc. 561; 764; 903). For example, a deacon visiting a parish in another diocese can be permitted by the pastor to preach, assist at Mass, give holy communion, baptize infants, preside at blessings, etc. Faculties from the local bishop are not needed, since the deacon already has these faculties in virtue of his ordination.

The universal law may place, or allow the bishop to place, additional restrictions on the use of such faculties. For example, the faculty to preach, granted to clergy at diaconate ordination, may be used anywhere in the world with at least the presumed consent of the rector

2. There is no explicit rule on this in the code. However, it is the custom of the Church, and various canons support it by showing that the pastoral jurisdiction of pastoral ministers is their own parish, chaplaincy, or church. See cc. 107, 518, 519, 526, 530, 545, 564, 566, 887, 1108–1111.

of the church, "unless the faculty is restricted or removed by the competent ordinary or express permission is required by particular law" (c. 764). Preaching to religious in their own churches or oratories requires permission of the competent religious superior (c. 765).

Visiting clergy. The diocesan bishop is the moderator of the apostolate and public worship in the diocese. He could require visiting clergy, if they intend to stay at least three months, to obtain permission of the local ordinary to exercise the public ministry. He could not make a policy binding clergy who intend to stay less than three months. Since they are not his subjects, they are not bound to his particular laws. Even if this is considered a matter of public order (c. 13, §2, 2°), such a law or policy would be impossible to enforce, given the mobility of people who enter dioceses for vacations, conferences, and other matters. Diocesan law could require *pastors* to notify the local ordinary and/or obtain his permission before permitting a visiting priest or deacon to function publicly. However, it would be an unnecessary burden on pastors and an undue restriction on the rights of visiting clergy if such a policy were required for clergy who are only staying less than a month (the period of time for a pastor or parochial vicar's annual vacation specified in cc. 533, §2; 550, §3).

7. Faculties granted by law in virtue of an office may be used only within the jurisdiction of that office, excepting the provisions in canon 136.

In rule five above, we saw that faculties *delegated* by the bishop to persons in virtue of their office may be used only within the person's own jurisdiction, for example, within the territory of the parish. This rule is the same, except that it applies to faculties granted *by law* in virtue of an office. These also may be used only within the jurisdiction of the officeholder (pastor, parish deacon, chancellor, chaplain, etc.). Exceptions to this rule are seen below in rules eight and nine.

8. Faculties for acts of executive power of governance may be used outside the diocese for one's subjects and oneself in accord with canon 136.

The rules of canon 136, with application to diocesan faculties, are as follows: (1) Faculties for acts of executive power may be used on behalf of one's subjects. (2) Executive power may be used whether the subjects at the time are in the diocese or outside it, and whether the person using the faculty at the time is in the diocese or outside it. (3) An act of executive power for one's own benefit may be used in or outside the diocese.

This rule applies to faculties for an act of executive power, whether the source of the faculty was delegation from a person or by law in virtue of an office. The identity of the subjects depends on the extent of the faculty. If the faculty may be used anywhere in the diocese, then the subjects of the exercise of such a power are all those who are residents of the diocese, whether by domicile or quasi-domicile. If the faculty was given in virtue of an office, such as, for example, faculties for a pastor or parochial vicar, the subjects are the parishioners of that parish.

9. *Faculties that are authorizations may not be used outside the diocese unless permitted by universal law.*

Canon 136, as seen in rule eight above, applies only to faculties that are for acts of executive power of governance, not to authorizations.[3] This is so for two reasons. (1) It is not the custom of the Church for such faculties to be used outside the diocese. (2) The code expressly states that the use of certain key faculties that are authorizations is limited to one's own jurisdiction (e.g., cc. 887, 1111). (3) The use of ministerial faculties outside one's diocese would infringe on the rightful authority of the bishop and pastor of that place. The bishop of one's own diocese has no power to authorize ministerial acts in another bishop's diocese. Therefore, to perform an act outside one's diocese that requires an authorization (assistance at marriage, celebrating confirmation, etc.), the competent authority of that diocese must grant the

---

3. Canon 136 itself allows for an exception to its own rule whenever "it is clear from the nature of the matter or by prescript of law" *(ius). Ius* includes both custom and written law.

faculty or the permission to use the faculty, unless universal law permits the act. The universal law allows the faculty to hear confessions to be used anywhere on behalf of subjects or non-subjects, in accord with canon 967, §2. This rule applies to the faculty granted by the local ordinary or by law in virtue of an office.

10. *Faculties may be used within one's own jurisdiction for the benefit of travelers and transients, unless restricted by law.*

Faculties may be used for the benefit of travelers *(peregrini),* whether they are from outside the parish or even outside the diocese, provided the minister is using the faculty within his or her own jurisdiction, for example, within the territory of the parish. Diocesan faculties may also be used for the benefit of transients *(vagi);* they are subjects of the ordinary and the pastor of the place where they are staying (c. 107, §2). Rule ten applies both to faculties delegated by a person and to those granted by law in virtue of an office.

Occasionally, the use of faculties that are *authorizations* is restricted by law when the beneficiary of the faculty is a traveler (one who does not reside in the territory). The restriction is the requirement of permission for the licit use of the faculty or a provision allowing the local ordinary to block the use of the faculty. A presbyter who has the faculty to confirm may licitly confirm persons from outside his territory, unless their own ordinary prohibits this. For the valid use of the faculty, he must be in his own territory (c. 887). The faculty to assist at marriage can be used validly within one's territory on behalf of subjects and non-subjects, provided at least one party is in the Latin church *sui iuris* (cc. 1109, 1111). For liceity, the permission of the local ordinary or the pastor of one party is necessary for travelers, unless either party has resided in the parish at least a month (c. 1115). With transients, permission of the local ordinary is necessary (c. 1071, §1, 1°). Note that, in either case, the restriction on the use of the faculty affects liceity only, not validity. For validity, the minister can use the faculty only in his own territory.

With respect to faculties that are for *acts of executive power*, canon 136 says in part that this power can be used for travelers who are in the territory if it is a question of granting a favor. The word "favor" should be understood to include both favors in the strict sense (dispensations, commutations, remission of censures, etc.) and related acts that favor the welfare of individual persons or the common good (permissions, subdelegations, authorizations, etc.). This principle of broad interpretation is discussed in rule twelve below. Moreover, it is the custom of many, perhaps most, dioceses in North America to regard as one's parochial subjects not only those who live in the territory of the parish but also others registered in the parish and/or active in it.

11. *A faculty may still be used, even if a new law is contrary to it.*

No law, universal or particular, can revoke a delegated faculty unless it does so expressly (cf. c. 73). The code acknowledges that its canons do not affect acquired rights (c. 4), and this includes rights acquired by the delegation of faculties. This is one example of the general principle of law stated in canon 9: "Laws concern the future, not the past, unless they expressly provide for the past." In recent years, some lay ministers have experienced doubts about the use of one faculty or another in light of documents of the Holy See which, they fear, restrict the pastoral charge given them by the bishop. Knowledge of this rule will eliminate such doubts. A faculty legitimately granted by the diocesan bishop is not lost by a new law, unless the law expressly revokes faculties contrary to it.

In the previous chapter, we saw the rule that a faculty cannot be granted if it is contrary to a law or a legal custom. This rule is different, in that the contrary law took effect *after* the faculty was granted. Once the faculty has been granted, a new contrary law does not affect it, unless the law expressly states this.

12. *Diocesan faculties are subject to broad interpretation.*

In keeping with canons 138 and 36, §1, faculties of office and faculties granted by general delegation are subject to broad interpretation.[4]

---

4. Broad interpretation of favorable matters is always required. Rule 15 of the *Regulae Iuris in Sexto* states: "It is fitting that odious things be restricted and

Broad interpretation means that the law should be understood as encompassing all cases that can be included in the proper meaning of the wording of the faculty, without going beyond what the faculty says. For example, the bishop grants the faculty to priests to trinate on Sundays and holy days, when there is a pastoral necessity. "Pastoral necessity" is to be interpreted broadly. A strict interpretation of pastoral necessity would hold that the priest may not celebrate a third Mass unless the people could not satisfy their obligation at any other Mass. Broad interpretation of pastoral necessity would include the spiritual welfare of the faithful, such as celebrating an additional Mass for a wedding, for a special gathering of the faithful, etc., even though the priest has already celebrated two Sunday Masses.

13. One who has a faculty is understood also to have everything necessary to exercise the faculty.

This rule, also found in canon 138, serves to remove doubts about what ministers or officials may do in using their faculties. They may do anything and everything that is necessary to accomplish the purpose for which the faculty was given. Although canon 138 treats the exercise of executive power, it also is applicable to habitual faculties that are authorizations (cf. c. 132, §1). For example, the bishop gives gen-

---

favorable ones extended" (translation in Albert Gauthier, *Roman Law and Its Contribution to Canon Law* [Ottawa: Faculty of Canon Law, Saint Paul University, 1996] 108).

Canon 36, §1 speaks of broad interpretation of administrative acts in a case of doubt, with exceptions given when strict interpretation is required. If there is no doubt, it is to be understood according to the proper meaning of the words and the common manner of speaking. However, even if the wording is clear and no doubt exists, a favorable administrative act should still be interpreted broadly, because broad interpretation does not extend the interpretation beyond the proper meaning of the words. In a case of true doubt, the meaning of the words is open either to a strict or a broad interpretation, thus the rule that the broad interpretation is the correct one. Strict interpretation is given only to the exceptions mentioned in the canon: on matters of litigation, threatening or inflicting penalties, restricting the rights of a person, harming acquired rights, or an act contrary to a law that benefits private persons.

eral delegation to a lay minister in a parish without a resident priest to assist at marriages in the absence of the priest who supervises the pastoral care (c. 517, §2). With the grant of this faculty, it should be presumed, unless otherwise established, that the lay minister also has the authority to instruct the couple, undertake the premarital investigation, conduct the wedding rehearsal, register the marriage, etc.

14. *If a faculty grants the power to dispense, the rules on dispensations must be observed in the use of that faculty.*

This rule, which is based on the final canon on rescripts (c. 75), serves as a reminder that the code has a title containing special rules for dispensations (cc. 85–93), which anyone who has the power to dispense must observe. For example, the diocesan bishop grants to parochial vicars and chaplains the faculty to dispense from the obligations of feast days and days of penance. This is a faculty that pastors and clerical superiors have by law (c. 1245). In using this power, the priests in question must observe the canonical rules on dispensations, in particular canon 90, which requires that there be a just and reasonable cause for the dispensation. Without a just and reasonable cause, the dispensation would be invalid.

15. *A faculty for the internal forum, inadvertently placed after the lapse of the time limit for which it was granted, is valid (c. 142, §2).*

Diocesan faculties are often granted for a time limit to extern priests who are staying temporarily in the diocese. This rule pertains only to faculties used in the internal forum. With respect to diocesan faculties, this applies to the sacrament of penance. The canon is treating the exercise of delegated power of governance. Thus, it includes the remission of a censure during the sacrament of penance, since many diocesan *pagellae* contain a faculty for the remission of one or more *latae sententiae* (automatic) penalties, most notably remission of the possible excommunication for the crime of abortion and for the crimes of apostasy, heresy, and schism. The rule of canon 142, §2 also applies to the faculty for hearing confessions itself, which is an

authorization.[5] For example, a priest of a religious institute on sabbatical in the diocese, who has no domicile (cc. 103, 106), is given faculties for six months. He remains in the diocese past six months and
hears confessions, not adverting to the fact that his faculties have
expired. The absolutions are valid. Although the faculty has expired, it
is prorogued by the law itself.

16. *Faculties do not cease when the see is vacant or when a new
bishop takes office.*

This rule follows from canon 46, which says that an administrative act
does not cease when the authority of the one who performed the act
ceases, unless the law expressly provides otherwise. Above we saw
that the delegation of faculties is an administrative act. Thus, diocesan
faculties remain in force and can continue to be used even when the
bishop who issued them is not in office.

2. Rules for the Delegation and Subdelegation of Faculties

The previous chapter enumerated the rules the bishop must observe in
granting faculties. The following rules are compiled for ministers and
administrators who have faculties by office or by delegation from the
bishop and who wish to delegate or subdelegate a faculty to another.
These rules apply to all faculties given for acts of the executive power
of governance and for the authorization of a priest or deacon to assist
at marriage. No other diocesan faculty that is an authorization may be
delegated, unless the bishop grants the power to delegate it.

In illustrating these rules, we shall use the example of the faculty
to assist at marriage, since it is routinely delegated in the pastoral

---

5. This is clear not only from the rule of c. 132, §1, but is based also on c. 6,
§2, which requires that canons of the code referring to the prior law must be
assessed in accord with canonical tradition. In the 1917 code, the faculty for hearing
confessions was considered a power of jurisdiction. Since c. 142, §2 is based on a
rule of the previous code (1917 c. 207, §2), it must be interpreted in keeping with
canonical tradition; therefore, it is applicable to the faculty for hearing confessions,
as well as for acts of executive power in the internal forum.

ministry. The faculty to assist at marriage is necessary for the valid observance of the canonical form of marriage. The canonical form requires the parties to manifest their consent to marry in the presence of two witnesses and a priest or deacon who has the faculty to assist; the priest or deacon must ask for and receive the consent of the parties in the name of the Church (c. 1108).

Although we shall be using the example of the faculty to assist at marriage, which is an authorization, the reader should not lose sight of the fact that these rules apply to all faculties for acts of executive power. Any ministers or administrators may freely subdelegate any of their diocesan faculties given for such acts, unless the bishop prohibited this when the faculty was granted.

We shall first look at some general rules on delegation and subdelegation applied to diocesan faculties. Then, we shall look at diocesan faculties that may not be delegated.

2.1 General Rules

Before taking up rules of delegation, we must stress again that the rules of this section *do not apply to most authorizations*. Thus, one could not delegate one's own faculty to hear confessions, to preach, to binate, etc. That could be done only if the bishop granted the *power* to delegate.

1. *Faculties attached to office (ordinary power) may be delegated for single cases or for all cases.*

This rule is based on canon 137, §1: "Ordinary executive power may be delegated both for an individual case (*ad actum*) and for all cases (*ad universitatem casuum*), unless something else is expressly stated in law." Delegation for an individual case or determined cases is commonly called "special delegation." Delegation for all cases is commonly called "general delegation."

The pastor has the faculty by law to assist at marriages celebrated in the parish (c. 1109). This is akin to an ordinary "power" of office, although it is not a power of governance. The pastor can freely delegate another priest or deacon the faculty to assist at marriages in the parish. This may be for a single case or several single cases, which is special delegation. Or he may give the faculty for any and all marriages in the parish, which is a general delegation. For validity, general delegation must be given in writing (c. 1111, §2).

General delegation to assist at marriage is routinely given to parochial vicars and parish deacons on the diocesan *pagella* of faculties. In most dioceses, the faculty is limited to the territory of the parish of assignment. In some places, the faculty is good throughout the diocese, in which case, general delegation is also given to pastors for use outside their own parish.

This rule applies only to faculties granted *by law* in virtue of office. The pastor and other officials may *not* grant a general delegation for faculties delegated to them by the bishop in virtue of their office. Such faculties can be delegated only in individual cases, as seen in the next rule.

2. Diocesan faculties can be subdelegated in individual cases.

This rule is based on part of canon 137, §3, which says that executive power delegated for all cases by any authority other than the Apostolic See may be subdelegated only for individual cases. Parochial vicars and deacons who have general delegation to assist at marriages may subdelegate the faculty only for a specified marriage or marriages. They cannot validly give a general delegation. Likewise, pastors and other officials who have executive powers delegated by the bishop in virtue of their office may subdelegate them only in individual instances; a general delegation would be invalid.

This rule may appear pastorally inflexible, but a solution for situations of need is available. The bishop can delegate to pastors, chancery officials, and others *his own power to grant general delegation.* For example, the grant of faculties could contain an introductory faculty like this:

> When you are on vacation or otherwise legitimately absent from the parish for no more than one month, you may grant to the priest who replaces you all the faculties on the diocesan

pagellae for priests and pastors. The delegation must be in writing, dated, and signed by you, and a copy must be retained in the parish archives. It should be worded as follows: "I, [name of pastor], hereby grant to you, [name of visiting priest], all the faculties of the diocese for priests and pastors as indicated on these *pagellae*, which faculties are valid until [give the date of your return, which may not be more than a month]." A copy of the *pagellae* for priests and pastors should be attached to the document of delegation.

The pastor would not be delegating his own delegated powers, which would be invalid under rule two. Rather, the bishop would be mandating him to grant the standard faculties of the diocese, just as if he would mandate the vicar general or chancellor to do this. Such a mandate would also include, of course, the power to delegate the faculties that are authorizations, not just executive powers and the faculty to assist at marriage.

Special delegation, unlike general delegation, is given only for a specific case or cases. Special delegation for marriage must be given for a specific marriage or marriages (c. 1111, §2). The marriage is specified by giving the names of the parties, or the hour and place of marriage, etc. A valid special delegation would be the pastor saying: "I delegate [name] to assist at the next six marriages scheduled in the parish." These are specific marriages that have already been scheduled; no other marriages are included, not even an unscheduled marriage before the sixth one is celebrated. An invalid delegation would be the pastor saying: "I delegate you for any marriage within the next month." This is not delegation for specific marriages; it is a general delegation to assist at marriages, which can be given validly only in writing.

3. *One who has a faculty by special delegation cannot subdelegate it except by the express grant of the person who originally delegated it.*

This rule is based on a part of canon 137, §3, which says that power delegated for a specified act or acts may not be subdelegated except by the express grant of the one delegating. For example, Pastor A will be away on a Saturday when a wedding is scheduled in the parish. He calls a neighboring priest, Pastor B, and delegates him the faculty for that marriage; this is a special delegation for an individual case. Pastor B needs delegation for this wedding, because his faculty by office is valid only in his own parish territory. Pastor A also tells Pastor B that, if he is impeded, he can subdelegate the faculty to another cleric. At the last minute, Pastor B falls ill, so he subdelegates his faculty to the deacon of his parish. If Pastor A had not stated that the delegated pastor could subdelegate the faculty, he could not have done so. He would have had to reach the local ordinary to get delegation for the deacon.

4. *One who has been subdelegated a faculty cannot again subdelegate it unless the person who originally subdelegated it expressly granted this power.*

This rule, based on canon 137, §4, is virtually the same as rule three, but now it applies to a person who has been subdelegated a faculty and wishes to subdelegate it to another. That can only be done if the person who first subdelegated the power expressly stated that it could be further subdelegated. For example, the pastor is away and the parish deacon is in charge of the pastoral care of the parish in his absence. The deacon is unable to preside at a scheduled wedding, so he subdelegates a neighboring pastor and tells him that he can further subdelegate the faculty to another priest or deacon. If the deacon had not expressly granted this power to the pastor, the pastor could not have subdelegated the faculty to anyone else.

5. *For the delegation or subdelegation of a faculty to be valid, it must be expressly given to a specified person.*

This rule is stated explicitly in canon 1111, §2 regarding the faculty to assist at marriage, but it applies to the delegation of any faculty. Delegation is a singular administrative act, so it must be directed to an intended person, as are all singular administrative acts. Being a juridic act, delegation must be express, that is, there must be a positive act of the will of the delegator manifested in some way, either explicitly or implicitly, which indicates that the faculty is being delegated.

Both general and special delegation for marriage must be given to a specified person or persons (and general delegation must be in writing). The person may be explicitly mentioned by name or by office, or delegation can be manifested implicitly. Some examples of implicit delegation are: (1) the pastor, knowing the identity of the priest who will assist at the marriage, prepares everything for the wedding, although he never meets the visiting priest; (2) the pastor hands the keys of the church to the visiting priest and tells him what he should do to prepare for the wedding, but never explicitly delegates him; (3) a party asks the pastor if her uncle, a deacon, can perform the marriage, and the pastor responds yes. In all cases, the one delegating must know the identity of the one delegated (by name, or office, or relationship to the party, etc.), and the delegation must be at least implicitly given for a specific marriage by means of a positive act of the will on the part of the one delegating.

Delegation is not express if: (1) it is presumed, that is, delegation is not granted in any way, but it is erroneously believed to have been given; (2) it is interpretative, that is, there are some conditions present that would lead one to think it was granted, but it was not; (3) it is tacit, that is, the pastor intended to delegate but he gave no external manifestation of that intention; (4) the wedding is merely tolerated but the delegation was not given.

The priest or deacon is not sufficiently designated when the pastor notifies the superior of a monastery that he delegates as the priest to assist at the marriage whatever priest the superior will select to send to the parish.[6] This is not a valid delegation, because no one specifically is granted the faculty, not even implicitly. However, several ministers may be delegated for the same wedding. For example, the pastor may say to the superior: "I delegate all the priests of your monastery the faculty to assist at this marriage, and you may send whomever you wish."[7] He could also say to the superior: "I delegate

---

6. Code Commission, reply, 20 May 1923, CLD 1:540–541.

7. Although the pastor is delegating all the priests in the monastery, this is still a singular administrative act. It applies only to the priests assigned to that monastery at that moment, not to other members of the institute who may be assigned after the delegation was given but before the wedding takes place.

you to assist at the marriage, and you may subdelegate another priest of your community."

Although special delegation may be validly granted orally, giving the faculty explicitly and in writing is always best. In this way, a copy of the delegation may be placed in the marriage file for proof of valid observance of canonical form. Explicit delegation would be: "I delegate you, N., to assist at the marriage of N. and N. on [date], at St. Mary's Church in [city or town]." The problem with oral delegation and implicit delegation is that often no public record exists of the delegation, and thus no certain proof in later years, when memories fail, that the faculty was ever given. Moreover, delegation of a faculty is a singular administrative act which, for liceity, must be given in writing (c. 37).

6. *The one delegated must accept the delegation to use the faculty validly, unless the one delegating is the superior of the one delegated.*

This rule is not in the code but is rooted in natural law and canonical tradition.[8] No one who lacks legal authority can exercise power over others by mandating them to perform some act that they do not want to do. That is contrary to the freedom and dignity of the human person. Moreover, from a practical point of view, the delegator has no assurance that the act is going to be performed unless the one being delegated accepts the mandate.

Acceptance of the delegation may be implicit, as when one knows he or she has been delegated and proceeds to use the faculty as specified, even without explicitly accepting it. However, if the faculty is positively refused, the person could not perform the act, even in necessity; a new delegation would be necessary. For example, the pastor sends a note to the deacon at the neighboring parish, delegating him to assist at a wedding when the pastor will be away. The deacon telephones, says he is too busy, and declines. The pastor gets another priest to celebrate the wedding, but this priest forgets and cannot be found on the day of the wedding. The parish secretary, in desperation,

---

8. See c. 6, §2; López-Illana, "La suplencia de la facultad de asistir al matrimonio," 116–122; D'Ostilio, "Tipologia ed esecuzione degli atti amministrativi," 255.

calls the deacon who had originally been approached for the wedding; he steps in at the last moment to officiate at the wedding. The deacon invalidly assists at the marriage because he did not accept the faculty and a new one was not given. To make this marriage valid from the moment of consent, the pastor should request a radical sanation from the diocesan bishop (cc. 1163, §1; 1165, §2).

As seen above, the requirement of acceptance of a faculty does not apply to faculties granted by law or faculties delegated by a superior to a subject. Diocesan faculties granted by the bishop or his delegate do not require acceptance to be valid. We saw in the previous chapter that a priest, newly arrived in the diocese, who begins his ministry although his faculties have not arrived, validly functions if he learns that his faculties were already issued, even if he has not yet received them or even asked for them. That is because diocesan faculties delegated by the bishop come from a superior to a subject, and they are given for the benefit of the faithful and the common good of the Church. This is not true when a pastor delegates his faculty to another priest or deacon. The pastor is not the canonical superior of the cleric; the ordinary is.

2.2 Faculties That May Not Be Delegated

1. *Most faculties that are authorizations may not be delegated.*

This general rule is not explicitly found in the law but is the practice of the Church. Faculties for preaching, confirmation, hearing confessions, presiding at Sunday celebrations in the absence of a priest, giving blessings, etc., may not be delegated, except by the competent authority who, most often, is the diocesan bishop himself or his delegate, and sometimes also the other local ordinaries (the vicar general and episcopal vicar). The faculty to assist at marriage may be delegated and subdelegated to other priests and deacons, but not to a lay minister. Only the diocesan bishop or his delegate validly grants the faculty to a lay minister to assist at marriage.

It should be recalled that the diocesan bishop can delegate his own power to grant an authorization. That is different from ministers attempting to delegate an authorization on their own. For example, the diocesan bishop grants the faculty to priests to hear confessions. They may not delegate this faculty unless the bishop also gives them a second faculty to delegate it for a particular reason, for example, to a visiting priest who will be helping in the parish for a brief period.

2. Faculties granted by law at ordination may not be delegated except when permitted by the competent authority in accord with universal law.

This rule, too, is based on the practice of the Church and is not expressed as such in canon law. Since the supreme legislator determines which powers and faculties are to be given by the ecclesiastical law at the ordination of deacons, presbyters, and bishops (the powers of order of ecclesiastical law), such faculties may be delegated only when permitted by universal law. A deacon, for example, cannot delegate his faculty to preach to someone else. A priest cannot delegate to a lay person his faculty to baptize, unless the bishop has given him this power (c. 861, §2). Sometimes, the law permits the diocesan bishop to delegate to presbyters a faculty that is usually reserved to bishops, for example, to celebrate certain sacramentals (see, e.g., c. 1169, §1). Powers of order of the divine law (e.g., the power to confect the Eucharist) cannot be delegated by anyone, since they are obtained from God by means of the sacrament of holy orders itself, not from the Church.

3. Rules for the Cessation of Faculties

In chapter 2, we considered one way that faculties cease—by revocation. Now we shall look at rules for all the ways that a faculty ceases.

1. A faculty ceases if expressly revoked by a law.

Above we saw that a faculty may continue to be used, even if a law contrary to it is promulgated, unless the law expressly revokes the faculty (cf. c. 73). Here we see the same rule with applicability to the cessation of faculties. A faculty ceases by a law when the law expressly revokes the faculty. An example of express revocation is found in the 1997 Instruction on Certain Questions Concerning the Cooperation of the Lay Faithful in the Ministry of Priests. At the end of the document is this clause: "Particular laws and customs and likewise faculties granted *ad experimentum* by the Apostolic See or by any authority subject to it, if they are contrary to these norms, are revoked." This clause revokes not all contrary faculties but only faculties granted *ad experimentum* that are contrary to the norms in the instruction.

2. Temporary faculties cease by the expiration of the time for which they were granted.

This rule, as well as rules three, four, and five below, are based on canon 142, §1.[9] Temporary faculties may be granted to visiting priests *(peregrini)*—those who intend to stay in the diocese for less than three months. Likewise, temporary faculties are given to priests who intend to establish only a quasi-domicile in the diocese for some reason, such as higher studies, a sabbatical, short-term pastoral assistance, etc. This rule also applies to faculties granted to an officeholder who has a fixed term of office, although in this case the faculties are not lost until the officeholder is notified in writing of the loss of office (c. 186).

3. The cessation of the purpose for the delegation automatically causes a faculty to cease.

In chapter 1, we saw several general purposes of diocesan faculties, but the overarching purpose, the *causa finalis*, is to empower the per-

---

9. According to c. 142, §1, delegated power ceases "by fulfilment of the mandate; by the expiration of the time or completion of the number of cases for which it was granted; by the cessation of the purpose *(causa finalis)* for the delegation; by the revocation of the one delegating directly communicated to the delegate; and by the resignation of the delegate made known to and accepted by the one delegating; it does not cease, however, when the authority of the one delegating expires unless this appears in attached clauses." Several of these means of cessation are pertinent to diocesan faculties, not only faculties involving the exercise of executive power but also authorizations.

son for ministry in the diocese. If this purpose ceases, the faculties cease by the law itself. For example, the bishop grants the priestly faculties of the diocese to a religious priest, but after three years the superior of the religious institute transfers him outside the diocese. His faculties are lost the very moment he leaves the territory of the diocese with the intention of taking up residence elsewhere.

This rule is also applicable to diocesan faculties given in virtue of an office. The purpose of such faculties is to facilitate the performance of one's duties of office. Special faculties may be given to various officeholders, such as, for example, the chancellor, the director of the diocesan office of worship, the pastor, the deacon or lay minister who cares for a parish without a priest, and others. Once the person ceases to hold the office, the faculties given for that office likewise cease, because the purpose for which they were given has ceased.

The rule equally applies to the special delegation of a faculty. For example, the pastor delegates a visiting deacon the faculty to assist at the marriage of his niece, but the couple quarrels and the wedding is canceled. The faculty ceases because its purpose has ceased.

In this rule, the loss of the faculty occurs by the operation of the law itself. However, not everyone is familiar with this rule, so it is preferable that the bishop, in granting faculties, should state expressly how they may be lost. This is done in the models for granting faculties presented in Part II of this book.

4. *Faculties cease upon their renunciation by the one delegated and the acceptance of the renunciation by the one delegating.*

Renunciation of diocesan faculties applies mainly to those who retire or resign from office. After the bishop accepts their retirement or resignation, all faculties granted in virtue of their office cease along with the office itself. For example, a pastor retires at age seventy-five. When he is notified in writing that his resignation has been accepted by the bishop (c. 186), he not only loses the office and faculties attached to the office by law, but also all delegated faculties given to him in virtue of his office. Priests who retire do not lose the general faculties of the diocese given to all priests, but only those faculties that were given in virtue of an office they held (pastor, parochial vicar, etc.).

Above we saw the rule that faculties granted by a superior to a subject do not require acceptance by the subject. The present rule is based on the same principle. The renunciation by a subject of a faculty granted by a superior has no validity unless the renunciation is accepted by the superior. For example, a deacon, frustrated by the pastor's criticism of his style of presiding at weddings, writes to the bishop and renounces his faculty to assist at marriage. The renunciation has no effect unless accepted by the bishop.

5. The diocesan bishop may directly revoke faculties for a grave reason.

The bishop may revoke one, several, or all faculties that he himself, his predecessor, or a subject of either had granted. The revocation must be directly communicated to the person, in writing, giving the reason(s) for the revocation at least summarily (cc. 37, 47, 51). The bishop may not revoke powers of order. The bishop cannot revoke faculties granted by the law at ordination unless the universal law permits it (as with respect to the faculty to preach in c. 764). Nor can he revoke faculties granted by the universal law either in virtue of an office or without an office. In general, the only faculties the bishop can revoke are those that he or his predecessor, or someone subject to either, has granted. He could suspend the use of other faculties, but that would involve a penal process, whether administrative or judicial. The revocation of faculties is treated more extensively in chapter 2.

Summary

This chapter has identified and explained the canonical rules governing the use, delegation, and cessation of faculties: sixteen rules on the use of faculties, eight on their delegation and subdelegation, and five on their cessation. All ministers and officials who have faculties are subject to these rules. They are based on canons of the code treating executive power of governance, general norms on administrative acts, rescripts, and individual canons in various places in the code treating particular faculties.

This concludes Part I of this book, which was devoted to canonical theory and rules on faculties, especially diocesan faculties granted by the bishop. Part II presents lists of model faculties for priests, deacons, lay ministers, and officials of the diocesan curia, and offers brief commentaries on them.

PART II
MODEL FACULTIES AND COMMENTARIES

Introduction to Part II

Part I established a theory on diocesan faculties that made possible the identification of the canonical rules to be observed in their grant and revocation, use and supply, and delegation and subdelegation. In Part II we turn our attention to a practical task: providing lists of model faculties for various ministries and offices in the parish and the diocese and offering brief commentaries on them.

Overview of Part II

Part II is divided into five chapters listing faculties for all priests; priests who are pastors, parochial vicars, chaplains, and rectors of churches; deacons; lay ministers; and officials of the diocesan curia. Appendix II contains sample documents for granting the faculties, which include provisions for their use, extent, delegation, and cessation.

Many faculties in the lists of Part II are routine and should be found on the respective *pagellae* in every diocese. Other faculties are offered as options from which the bishop may choose. The sources of the faculties are the Code of Canon Law, the liturgical books, the Directory for the Application of the Principles and Norms on Ecumenism, and other important documents from the Holy See. Regarding the liturgical books, citations are given to the typical editions *(editiones typicae)* and to the ICEL versions approved for the U.S.A. and Canada when the numbering in them differs from the typical edition. Citations of sources are abbreviated and appear in parentheses following the faculty.

Following the first presentation of each faculty, brief commentaries are given, unless the meaning and purpose of the faculty are evident. The technical commentary (TC) is intended for diocesan officials and for canonists. Each technical commentary begins by indicating whether the faculty in question is an act of executive power (EP) or an authorization (Au) for a non-jurisdictional act. (If there is no technical commentary, this notation is made in the pastoral commentary; these notations are not given on faculties by law.) Additional information about the faculty may follow, such as its purpose, applicability, and other useful information. These technical commentaries are *not* to be included on the *pagella*.

The pastoral commentary (PC) is intended for inclusion on the *pagella* under the corresponding faculty, without the abbreviation "PC." These commentaries help the minister to understand the meaning and application of the faculty.

The commentaries are omitted when the meaning of the faculty is self-evident or has already been explained in a previous chapter. Cross references in later chapters allow those compiling a *pagella* easily to find the commentaries on the faculties of that chapter. When the same faculty is intended for several categories of ministers, the faculties themselves are restated in their entirety in different chapters so that the reader does not have to keep turning back to previous chapters to discover which faculties are intended.

The numbering of the faculties simplifies cross-referencing in this book, but every diocese likely will have its own numbering system. Each faculty is preceded by two numbers separated by a period, as in faculty 3.2, which means the second faculty in section 3. (A few faculties are preceded by only one number.)

Before each faculty is a succinct heading that identifies the nature of the faculty. These headings, or variations of them, may be included on the *pagella* for ease of comprehension and quick reference. Following each faculty is an abbreviation for the source of the faculty in parentheses, such as (c. 905, §2). This should be included on the *pagella*, so the ministers or officials can easily find the sources and consult more detailed commentaries on them, if they wish. A list of abbreviations will be necessary for documents cited frequently.

Special lists of optional, additional faculties are given for priests in general, for pastors and chaplains with the full care of souls, and for deacons and lay ministers who share in the pastoral care of a parish without a resident pastor (c. 517, §2). Some or all of these may be granted when special circumstances of the diocese call for it. The special circumstances arise, in particular, from a shortage of priests in the diocese.

Most of the faculties are those to be granted personally *(delegatio ab homine)*, but some chapters also contain select faculties granted by universal law both to officeholders and to priests and deacons who do not have an office. These may be included on the *pagella* for the information of the ministers, as they may not be aware of all the faculties they have in virtue of their ordination or office. Although not juridically necessary, diocesan *pagellae* typically list certain faculties granted by law, especially if these faculties were traditionally included on the *pagella*. For example, under the law of the 1917 code, the faculty to preach had to be granted to priests by the local ordinary (1917 c. 1337). In the 1983 code, the faculty is granted by law to all clergy upon ordination to the diaconate (c. 764), unless the competent ordinary has restricted or taken away the faculty, or unless particular law requires express permission to preach. If faculties by law are to be included on the *pagella*, they should be separated from the other faculties in their own section, or they should be clearly identified as faculties by law.

To speak of "model faculties" does not mean every faculty on the lists is right for every diocese. No single list of faculties is suitable for every diocese, because needs and circumstances differ greatly depending on the size of the diocese, the extent of the shortage of priests, the kind of formation program offered to deacons and lay ministers, the number of persons working in the diocesan curia and their canonical competence, etc. Bishops' own management styles differ as well; some desire a more centralized administrative approach while others prefer to delegate routine faculties to others. The wording of these model faculties can, of course, be altered according to the circumstances of the diocese. The bishop himself has the right to decide which faculties are to be included and how they are to be worded, provided they do not conflict with the law. A process for making this determination is suggested below.

The faculties presented in subsequent chapters are intentionally not a complete list of all potential faculties. They consist of faculties that would be *reasonable* for the bishop to delegate, depending on the needs of the diocese.

Process for a New **Pagella**

Reading the lists of faculties in this book will likely reveal inadequacies or incompleteness, to a greater or lesser extent, in one's own diocesan *pagellae* for priests and other ministers, especially if the Code of Canon Law was the only source used. Consequently, the responsible officials and canonists of the diocese or province will want to revise the *pagella* for priests and to create or revise *pagellae* for other ministers and officials. To begin this task, diocesan officials and canonists should first conceive a process for determining which faculties should be given and how the ministers and officials are best to be informed about the meaning and application of the faculties they will receive. The outline of a process could take shape as follows.

1. A commission is formed consisting of the bishop (if he wishes to participate at this stage), his vicars, a representative from both the presbyteral council and the diocesan pastoral council, and possibly others (especially canonists); they each read this book and review the current diocesan *pagella(e)*.

2. After individual study of this book, the members of the commission have an initial brief meeting to decide whether revising the *pagella* for priests would be desirable; whether additional faculties should be given to pastors, parochial vicars, and chaplains; and whether *pagellae* for deacons, lay ministers, and chancery officials should be revised or created. Once the goals have been determined, one or more members of the commission are chosen to draw up a first

draft of the desired *pagellae*, choosing desired faculties from the models of this book. The first draft is distributed to commission members.

3. After studying the first draft of the various *pagellae*, the same commission meets again to discuss the texts and determine which faculties should be omitted or revised, or which additional ones not in the draft should be included. If there is disagreement, the matter is referred to the bishop. After the meeting, a redactor prepares a second draft of the *pagellae*, incorporating the changes agreed upon and pointing out areas of disagreement. The second draft texts are then submitted to the bishop and members of the commission.

4. The bishop approves the texts with any additional changes he wants. Before the faculties are issued, workshops or meetings are held separately for the distinct groups of ministers to explain their forthcoming faculties, answer their questions, and solicit their opinions. *Empowerment for Ministry* may be distributed or recommended to them to augment their canonical formation, particularly regarding the purpose and nature of faculties and their use, delegation, subdelegation, and cessation.

5. If necessary, the commission in no. 1 meets and discusses any remaining issues arising from the workshops or meetings, and final texts of the *pagellae* are prepared. The bishop issues the faculties in keeping with the rules in chapter 2 of this book, pages 49–55.

Formation of Ministers

It is necessary that local churches provide all those training for ministries in the Church with a solid education in canon law. This includes seminarians, candidates for the permanent diaconate, and lay persons preparing for full-time ministries such as administrator of a parish without a resident priest, chancellor, finance officer, etc. The diocesan *pagella* itself can serve as the text for several lectures to candidates for ministry before their ordination or appointment. Using the diocesan *pagella* as an educational tool allows students to apply their knowledge of canon law to the functions and ministries they will be undertaking. Certain faculties suggested in subsequent chapters (e.g., granting permission for a mixed marriage) require knowledge of canon law so that they can be used correctly. Without this formation, such faculties should not be given.

CHAPTER FOUR

Priests

The faculties in this chapter are intended for all priests in good standing, including retired priests, who have domicile or quasi-domicile in the diocese. Additional faculties for priests who are pastors, parochial vicars, chaplains, or rectors of churches are given in the next chapter. A sample document for granting faculties to priests is found in Appendix II, page 240.

1. Eucharist

Frequency of Celebration

1.1 For a good reason, you may celebrate Mass twice in one day and, if pastoral need requires it, three times on Sundays and holy days of obligation (c. 905, §2).

> **TC/Au.** The local ordinary may grant this faculty when there is a shortage of priests.

> **PC.** A just cause for binating would be not only pastoral necessity but also lesser causes: the desire of the priest to concelebrate at a special celebration, an urgent request of someone to celebrate a Mass for a special intention, such as imminent surgery; the desire to celebrate for a special group of the faithful, etc. To trinate on Sun-

days and holy days requires pastoral necessity, namely, when three Masses must be celebrated for the needs of the faithful.

The word "celebrate" here means both preside and concelebrate. With respect to the law of bination and trination, the anticipated Mass of Sunday counts as a Mass of Saturday, not Sunday, since the canonical day runs from midnight to midnight (c. 202, §1). The same is true for the vigil of holy days.

Masses with Children

1.2 You may use the adaptations described in nn. 38–54 of the Directory for Masses with Children at a Mass celebrated with adults in which children also participate, if the Mass is intended primarily for the benefit of children or for families with children.

> **TC/Au.** The Directory for Masses with Children, no. 19 says the bishop can permit the adaptations for children's Masses to be used at Masses for adults in which children also participate.

> **PC.** [The adaptations of the Directory for Children's Masses may be given here.]

Communion Under Both Kinds

1.3 At a Mass at which you preside, communion may be administered under both kinds, unless the pastor or other priest in charge of the community determines that it is not appropriate under the circumstances (GIRM 283c).

> **PC/Au.** The General Instruction of the Roman Missal, no. 283c says that, with this faculty from the bishop, communion under both kinds may be given if the faithful have been well instructed and there is no danger of profanation of the sacrament or the rite does not become more cumbersome due to the large number of participants or another reason. This latter concern can be addressed by a sufficient number of ministers of the chalice.

Infirm Priests

1.4 If you are unable to celebrate Mass standing, you may celebrate Mass while seated (c. 930, §1).

> **PC/Au.** When celebrating Mass publicly, you should inform the people before Mass that you have this faculty.

Mass in the Home of a Sick Person

1.5 You may celebrate Mass in the home of a sick person who would have difficulty coming to church, observing the law that you may not celebrate more than two Masses on a weekday or three on a Sunday or holy day of obligation (PCS 77; cf. cc. 905, §2; 932).

> **TC/Au.** *Pastoral Care of the Sick*, no. 77 says that the ordinary determines the conditions and requirements for a Mass in the homes of the sick. This faculty establishes some simple conditions and requirements.

Viaticum During Mass

1.6 You may celebrate Viaticum during Mass in accord with canon 911, §2 (OUI 94; PCS 164).

> **TC/Au.** Celebrating Viaticum during Mass may be done in the judgment of the ordinary (PCS 164). Bringing Viaticum to the sick apart from Mass is a faculty by law, which may be used in accord with the requirements of canon 911.

> **PC.** You have this same faculty *by law*, 5.3 below, of celebrating the rite of Viaticum for the dying *apart from Mass*. When celebrating Mass, you should allow the dying person the opportunity of receiving holy communion under both species. You may give communion under the species of wine alone to a person who cannot consume the consecrated host (c. 925; PCS 181).

2. Reconciliation

Hearing Confessions Anywhere

2.1 You may hear the confessions of any of the faithful anywhere in the world, unless in another diocese the local ordinary revokes the faculty for that territory (cc. 969, §1; 974, §2).

> **PC/Au.** Requesting the faculty when you are traveling in another diocese is unnecessary. You may presume the bishop there permits you to use it, unless you are informed otherwise. If you lose the faculty to hear confessions, you also lose the diocesan faculties of confessors (2.2–2.6).

Remission of Censures

2.2 You may remit in the internal forum the *latae sententiae* penalty of excommunication for abortion, apostasy, heresy, and schism, provided the penalty has not been declared. You may use this faculty for anyone when hearing confessions in the diocese, but when outside the diocese you may use it only for those who are residents of this diocese by domicile or quasi-domicile (cc. 1355, §2; 1398; 1364).

> **TC/EP.** Only the more commonly committed crimes are included. The bishop could grant a more extensive faculty, if he wished, to include the remission of additional *latae sententiae* penalties not reserved to the Apostolic See.

> **PC.** Whenever someone commits the crime of abortion or abandons the Catholic faith and adheres to another religion or to atheism or agnosticism, a possibility exists that the penalty of automatic excommunication may have been incurred (cc. 1321–1325, 1398, 1364). This faculty allows you, as confessor, to remit the penalty when you absolve the sin. For a penitent returning to the Catholic faith, you should admonish him or her to begin practicing the faith in some public way, such as by registering in a parish, so that there is some external forum evidence of the person's reconciliation with the Church. Under no circumstances, however, may any confessor him-

self use knowledge of sin, gained only from the sacrament, in the external forum (c. 984).

Dispensation from Irregularities

2.3 You may dispense in the internal forum from an irregularity to the exercise of an order already received, provided it is not reserved to the Apostolic See and provided the case is not publicly known. You may use this faculty when hearing confessions in the diocese, but when outside the diocese you may use it only for clergy who are residents of this diocese by domicile or quasi-domicile (c. 1047, §4).

> **TC/EP.** This faculty is principally based on canon 1047, §4 and related canons (cf. cc. 1040–1049). It is intended to unburden the conscience of a cleric who incurred an irregularity not reserved to the Apostolic See, to allow him to exercise his order licitly. The faculty is valid only for occult cases and has no effects in the external forum, so a new dispensation from the ordinary would be necessary if the irregularity became public.

> **PC.** An irregularity is a perpetual impediment to ordination or to the exercise of an order already received. This faculty pertains only to *the exercise of an order already received* with respect to the following irregularities: (1) a cleric who was ordained unlawfully while he was affected by an irregularity to receiving orders; (2) one who gravely and maliciously mutilated himself or another, or who attempted suicide; (3) one who performed an act of order reserved to those in the order of the episcopate or presbyterate, while he himself did not have that order or was barred from its exercise by some declared or inflicted penalty.

> The faculty pertains only to cases in which the irregularity is not publicly known. You must tell the dispensed cleric that, if the case afterwards becomes public, he must seek a dispensation from the ordinary. Note that two irregularities to the exercise of an order are reserved to the Apostolic See even if they are not publicly known: intentional homicide and positively cooperating in the crime of abortion. See canons 1040–1049.

Dispensation and Commutation of Vows and Oaths

2.4 In keeping with canons 1196 and 1203, you may dispense from private vows and promissory oaths, provided the vow or oath does not affect anyone else in the external forum. Likewise, you may commute the obligation of a private vow or oath to a lesser good. You may use this faculty when hearing confession within the diocese, but outside the diocese only for residents of this diocese by domicile or quasi-domicile.

> **TC/EP.** This extends to confessors, for the internal forum, a faculty that local ordinaries and pastors have in the external forum (cc. 1196, 1°; 1203). It is a delegation of executive power (c. 137, §1).

> **PC.** This faculty cannot be used if the dispensation will negatively affect others in the external forum, especially if their acquired rights could be harmed or if they refuse to remit the obligation of a private vow or oath. Pastors have this faculty by law in the external forum (cc. 1196, 1203).

Dispensation and Commutation of Obligations

2.5 In individual cases and for a just cause, you may dispense from the obligation to attend Mass and/or abstain from work on Sundays and holy days of obligation, or you may commute the obligation to another pious work. Under the same conditions, you may dispense from or commute the obligations of fast and abstinence on a day of penance. You may use this faculty when hearing confessions in the diocese, but outside the diocese only for penitents who are residents of this diocese by domicile or quasi-domicile (c. 87, §1).

> **TC/EP.** This faculty extends to confessors, for use in the internal forum, a faculty that pastors have in the external forum. It is a delegation of executive power (c. 137, §1).

> **PC.** Pastors have this faculty by law and may use it also in the external forum (c. 1245).

Freedom to Choose Your Own Confessor

2.6 You may grant another priest the faculty to hear your own confession. This faculty may be used in the diocese; outside the diocese, it may be used only if the priest receiving the faculty has a domicile or quasi-domicile in our diocese.

> **TC/EP.** This faculty would not generally be necessary, but some priests may find it helpful. It is the delegation of the *power* to grant the faculty to another priest to hear that priest's own confession (c. 137, §1). It is given as a favor to the priest to simplify his choice of a confessor. Its delegation and use follow the rules for executive power of governance.[1] One of these rules is that executive power may be used for one's own subjects anywhere and for externs when they are in one's own territory (cf. c. 136).

> **PC.** This faculty enables you to choose any priest as your confessor, even if that priest lacked the faculty, such as, for example, a retired religious who has not requested the faculties of the diocese. You may use this faculty in the territory of the diocese even if the priest receiving the faculty is not resident in the diocese. The faculty can be used outside the diocese only if the priest to whom you grant the faculty has a domicile or quasi-domicile in our diocese (cf. c. 136).

3. Ecumenism

Reader at Mass

3.1. On exceptional occasions and for a just cause, if you are presiding at the Eucharist, you may permit a member of a non-Catholic church or ecclesial community to be a reader at the eucharistic celebration (DAPNE 133).

---

1. See Code Commission, response, October 16, 1919, AAS 11 (1919) 477; CLD 1:410–411; William H. Woestman, *Sacraments: Initiation, Penance, Anointing of the Sick* (Ottawa: Faculty of Canon Law, St. Paul University, 1996) 253.

PC/EP. A typical just cause would be verified at weddings, funerals, and like celebrations when the baptized non-Catholic has some kind of relationship to the Catholic family members and they want to involve this person more actively in the celebration. It could also be done in Catholic schools at Masses that are attended by baptized non-Catholics, and in similar situations. Before using the faculty, you should have assurances that the designated person is capable of reading intelligibly in public.

Sacramental Sharing in Cases of Grave Need

3.2 Observing the conditions of canon 844, §4, you may administer the sacraments of penance, Eucharist, and anointing of the sick to validly baptized non-Catholics who are in danger of death or who live in areas or institutions where they do not have regular access to a minister of their own. [Additional cases can be listed here as determined by the conference of bishops and/or the diocesan bishop.]

> **TC/Au.** A delegated faculty is not needed for administering these sacraments to Eastern Christians and members of like churches, as that faculty is given in the law (c. 844, §3). This faculty is granted on the basis of canon 844, §4 for "other Christians," namely, Anglicans (Episcopalians) and Protestants. The faculty for the case of danger of death is a faculty by law (c. 844, §4). The other case (persons who live in areas or institutions where they do not have regular access to a minister of their own) is based on examples given in documents of the Holy See, but these cases still need to be authorized by the diocesan bishop or conference of bishops. Thus, if there is no diocesan policy, this faculty can provide for situations of grave need as envisioned in canon 844, §4. (See also DAPNE 131–131; Secretariat for Promoting Christian Unity, instruction *In quibus rerum circumstantiis*, 1 June 1972.)

> **PC.** You have the faculty *by law* to administer the sacraments of penance, Eucharist, and anointing of the sick to members of the *Eastern churches* that do not have full communion with the Catholic Church, if these persons ask on their own for the sacrament and

are properly disposed. The same applies to members of other churches which, in the judgment of the Apostolic See, are in a condition equal to the Eastern churches in reference to the sacraments. See canon 844, §3.

This faculty applies, therefore, to other validly baptized Christians who cannot approach a minister of their own community, who ask for the sacrament on their own, and who manifest Catholic faith in the sacrament. In case of doubt regarding the proper disposition, you should admonish the person to make an act of perfect contrition before receiving holy communion or the anointing of the sick. In case of doubt as to whether the person has the necessary faith in the sacrament, you should ask for an explicit manifestation of faith in these or similar words, as recommended by the Holy See: "Do you accept the faith in the sacrament of (penance, the Eucharist, or anointing of the sick) as Christ instituted it and as the Catholic Church has handed it down?" (See Secretariat for Promoting Christian Unity, instruction *In quibus rerum circumstantiis*, no. 5, 1 June 1972.)

The faculty may be used: (1) anywhere in the world on behalf of someone in danger of death; (2) within the territory of the conference of bishops for cases established by the conference; (3) within the diocese for cases established by the diocesan bishop.

Mixed Marriage in Non-Catholic Church

3.3 You may attend or participate in the celebration of a mixed marriage outside a Catholic church or oratory when a dispensation from canonical form has been given. If invited to do so by the non-Catholic minister, you may offer prayers, read from the scriptures, give a brief exhortation, and/or bless the couple. However, you may not ask for and receive the consent of the parties (DAPNE 157).

PC/Au. The minister who asks for and receives the consent of the parties must be the minister of the host church. With a dispensation from canonical form, that minister is the non-Catholic.

Participation of Non-Catholic Minister

3.4 Upon the request of the couple, and if you have the faculty to assist at marriage, even by special delegation, you may invite the minister of the party of the other church or ecclesial community to participate in the celebration of the marriage by reading from scripture, giving a brief exhortation, and/or blessing the couple (DAPNE 158).

> **PC/Au.** If you do not have the faculty to assist at marriages in the parish, you must obtain it from the local ordinary or pastor or, in the absence of the pastor, from the priest or deacon who has general delegation in the parish. Permission for a mixed marriage must also be granted in accord with canons 1124–1125.

Ecumenical Meetings

3.5 You may take part in meetings with other Christians aimed at improving ecumenical relations and resolving pastoral problems in common. This faculty may be used within the territory of the diocese (DAPNE 91b).

> **TC/Au.** Pertinent directives of the Directory for the Application of the Principles and Norms on Ecumenism or guidelines of the diocesan ecumenical commission could be summarized in the pastoral commentary, if desired.

4. Select Faculties Granted by Law

The following faculties are for your information. You already have these faculties as a validly ordained priest in good standing.

Preaching

4.1 With at least the presumed consent of the rector of a church or the competent religious superior, you may preach everywhere, unless the competent ordinary has restricted or removed this faculty (c. 764).

PC/Au. The rector of the church, in this context, refers to the one in charge: the pastor, chaplain, cathedral or shrine rector, religious superior, or other priest in charge. Canon 765 states that preaching to religious in their churches or oratory requires the permission of the competent religious superior, including lay superiors. A priest invited to celebrate the Eucharist or another liturgical act may presume the permission to preach, as the homily is part of the liturgy itself (cf. c. 767, §1). Apart from the liturgy, the rector's or superior's permission to preach must be express, for example, the preaching of a retreat.

Designation of Eucharistic Minister

4.2 You have the faculty to appoint a qualified person to distribute communion for single occasions when you are the presiding celebrant and there are too many communicants and insufficient ordinary and extraordinary ministers of communion, or when it is necessary to bring Viaticum to a dying person and no ordinary or extraordinary minister is available (GIRM 162; c. 911, §2). This faculty may be used everywhere with at least the presumed consent of the pastor.

PC/EP. The priest commissions the minister by blessing him or her and saying: "Today you are to distribute the body and blood of Christ to your brothers and sisters. May the Lord + bless you, N." Response: "Amen." When this ministry will be exercised during Mass, the commissioning occurs after the breaking of the bread.

Remission of Censures

4.3 Confessors have the faculty to remit in the internal sacramental forum an undeclared *latae sententiae* censure of excommunication or interdict if it is burdensome for the penitent to remain in the state of grave sin during the time necessary for the competent superior to make provision (c. 1357, §1). This faculty may be used anywhere in the world.

TC/EP. Confessors may be given the delegated faculty, as above in 2.2, to remit outright, without the obligation of recourse to higher authority, the censure of excommunication for the crimes of abortion, apostasy, heresy, and schism (or additional censures not reserved to the Apostolic See, if desired).

PC. This faculty pertains to the remission of all *latae sententiae* penalties that have not been declared, including those reserved to the Apostolic See. The use of this faculty is subject to the rule of canon 1357, §2: "In granting the remission, the confessor is to impose on the penitent, under the penalty of reincidence, the obligation of making recourse within a month to the competent superior or to a priest endowed with the faculty and the obligation of obeying his mandates; in the meantime he is to impose a suitable penance and, insofar as it is demanded, reparation of any scandal and damage; however, recourse can also be made through the confessor, without mention of the name."

Dispensation from Marriage Impediments by Confessor

4.4 Whenever an impediment is discovered after everything has already been prepared for the wedding, and the marriage cannot be delayed without probable danger of grave harm until a dispensation is obtained from the competent authority, **confessors** may dispense in occult cases from all impediments except prior bond, impotence, consanguinity in the direct line and the second degree of the collateral line, sacred orders, and a public perpetual vow of chastity in a religious institute of pontifical right (c. 1080, §1). This faculty may be used anywhere in the world.

PC/EP. Some impediments are of their nature public, such as, for example, lawful consanguinity or affinity, bond of marriage, holy orders, a public perpetual vow of chastity in a religious institute, disparity of worship, adoption. Sometimes one of these may be occult in fact. Other impediments are of their nature occult, for example, illegitimate consanguinity or affinity, or crime. Yet they may be in fact public, since it may happen that they are capable of proof owing to the particular circumstances of the case. Some impediments may be public in one place or at one time but occult elsewhere or later. Therefore, several times the code speaks of occult *cases*.

Dispensations granted in the sacrament of penance are not written down or recorded anywhere. If the impediment later becomes public, a dispensation in the external forum will be necessary.

Anointing of the Sick

4.5 You may administer the anointing of the sick to anyone validly baptized who is seriously ill, observing canon 844, §§ 3–4 if the person is not Catholic. When celebrating the rite, you have the faculty by law to bless the oil in a case of necessity, but only within the sacrament (OUI 17; PCS 21; cc. 999, 2°; 847, §1). This faculty may be used anywhere in the world with at least the presumed consent of the pastor (c. 1003).

> **PC/Au.** A case of necessity is demonstrated when two circumstances exist: (1) someone gravely ill requests the sacrament, and (2) you do not have time to get the oil of the sick blessed by the bishop. In that case, you may bless olive oil or any plant oil during the rite itself (PCS 123). On anointing a baptized non-Catholic, see faculty 3.2 above.

5. Faculties by Law in Danger of Death

Baptism

5.1 You may baptize anyone not yet validly baptized, including a fetus, provided the person is alive (cc. 864, 871). Those who had the use of reason at any time during their life may not be baptized without having manifested this intention; they must also have some knowledge of the principal truths of the faith and must promise to observe the commandments of the Christian religion (c. 865, §2). This faculty may be used anywhere in the world.

PC/Au. The Rite of Christian Initiation for the Dying, from *Pastoral Care of the Sick*, is to be used, if the ritual is available. The one to be baptized demonstrates "some knowledge of the principal truths of the faith" and the "promise to observe the commandments of the Christian religion" by an affirmative answer to the four questions you are to ask at the beginning of the rite (PCS 282). After asking the questions, if death is imminent, it suffices to observe what is necessary for validity: water baptism and the Trinitarian formula (cc. 850, 853; PCS 277). If the sacred chrism is available, the person—whether adult or infant—should be confirmed immediately afterward. Viaticum should be given as below in faculty 5.3. The baptism and confirmation are registered in accord with canons 877–878 and 895–896.

Confirmation

5.2 You have the faculty to confirm anyone validly baptized, including an infant or non-Catholic, who is in danger of death (cc. 883, 3°; 891; RC 7c). This faculty may be used anywhere in the world.

PC/Au. A validly baptized non-Catholic should not be confirmed unless he/she intends to become a Catholic. If the baptized non-Catholic lacks the use of reason, he/she may be confirmed if the parent or guardian wants the infant to become a Catholic. The confirmation is recorded in the diocesan archives or the parish of the person's domicile. If the person was baptized a Catholic, the confirmation is also recorded in the parish of baptism (c. 895). See also the commentary on faculty 5.1.

Viaticum

5.3 You may bring Viaticum to a person who is dying, with at least the presumed permission of the pastor, chaplain, or superior, who must be notified afterwards (c. 911, §2). You may also give Viaticum to a baptized non-Catholic who is in danger of death, in accord with the law (c. 844, §§ 3–4). This faculty may be used anywhere in the world.

PC/Au. The dying person must request the sacrament and be properly disposed. You should celebrate the sacrament of reconciliation first, if possible. If the baptized person is not a Catholic, the conditions of canon 844, §§ 3 and 4 must be observed. See faculty 3.2 above. Viaticum may be administered under both kinds or even under the form of wine alone if the dying person cannot consume bread (cc. 866, 925; PCS 181, 276). See the delegated faculty, 1.6 above, on celebrating Viaticum during Mass.

Penance

5.4 Even if you lack the faculty to hear confessions by office or delegation, you may validly and licitly absolve any penitent in danger of death from any censures and sins, even if an approved priest is present (c. 976). You may also absolve any baptized non-Catholic, observing canon 844, §§ 3–4. This faculty may be used anywhere in the world (RCIA 280; PCS 276).

> **TC.** The faculty for absolving sins is an authorization; that for remitting censures is the grant of executive power.

> **PC.** The absolution from censures applies only to Catholics, since only they are subject to the penal laws of the Church. If the censure being remitted was imposed or declared in the external forum, or if its remission is reserved to the Apostolic See, you must inform the penitent that, after recovering, he or she must request the permanent remission of the penalty from the competent authority (c. 1357, §3). This should be done within a month, and normally you or another confessor should apply for the remission on the penitent's behalf without mentioning the penitent's name.

General Absolution

5.5 Even if you lack the faculty to hear confessions by office or delegation, you may grant a general absolution without previous individual confession when the danger of death is imminent and there is insufficient time to hear the confessions of the individual penitents (c. 961, §1, 1°). This faculty may be used anywhere in the world.

> **PC/Au.** If there is time, you should exhort the penitents to make an act of contrition and inform them that they must intend to confess any serious sins in individual confession within a suitable period of time. The absolution is valid only for those who are contrite and intend to confess their grave sins in individual confession later, if they survive (c. 962).

Dispensation from Marriage Impediments

5.6 When a party to a marriage is in danger of death, **confessors** may dispense from occult impediments to marriage for the internal forum, within or outside the act of sacramental confession. If you lack the faculty to hear confessions by office or delegation, you may grant this dispensation only within the act of sacramental confession (c. 1079, §3). This faculty may be used anywhere in the world.

> **PC/EP.** The faculty of canon 1079, §3 is granted only to confessors, namely, to those who have the faculty to hear confessions. A priest who lacks the faculty is given it by law in order to hear the confession of someone in danger of death. Therefore, a priest lacking the faculty to hear confessions can grant this dispensation only within the act of sacramental confession, because outside of this act he is not a confessor.
>
> The confessor may dispense impediments that are occult in nature or that are public by nature but occult in fact (cf. c. 1074). The dispensation is not recorded and is not made known to anyone by the confessor. If the impediment should later become public, a further dispensation for the external forum should be sought and duly recorded, if possible (cf. cc. 1081–1082). Note that, in this internal forum situation, the law does not speak of the danger of death being urgent. This indicates that the danger of death for an internal forum dispensation may be more remote than for a dispensation in the external forum.

Marriage Dispensations

5.7 Even if you lack the faculty to assist at marriage, when one or both parties is in danger of death and when the local ordinary cannot be reached, you may dispense the parties to marriage both from the form to be observed in the celebration of marriage and from each and every impediment of ecclesiastical law, whether public or occult, except the impediment arising from the sacred order of the presbyterate (c. 1079, §2).

> **PC/EP.** The local ordinary is not considered accessible if he can be reached only by telegraph or telephone (c. 1079, §4), e-mail or fax.
>
> If you lack the faculty, the marriage is celebrated according to the extraordinary form (c. 1116, §2). In that case, no dispensation from form is necessary unless another witness is unavailable.
>
> If you have the faculty to assist, you should dispense from the form if: (1) the marriage is being celebrated outside the territory of the parish; (2) two witnesses are unavailable.
>
> If there is time, you should exhort the parties to make an act of perfect contrition or hear their confessions, if they are baptized and want to confess.
>
> All impediments may be dispensed except prior bond, impotence, consanguinity in the direct line and second degree of the collateral line, and the sacred order of the presbyterate. You should dispense as follows: "I dispense you from the canonical form and/or from the impediment of _____."
>
> The parties must be present together and must express their consent to marry each other, even by signs if one party cannot speak (c. 1104). If you lack the marriage ritual and are unsure of the formula for asking for and receiving the consent of the parties in the name of the Church, you may use equivalent words of your own (c. 1108, §2).

If the dispensation is for a public impediment, you are to notify the local pastor and local ordinary immediately afterward so that the dispensation may be properly recorded (cc. 1081–1082).

If it is a mixed marriage between a Catholic and baptized non-Catholic, no permission is necessary in danger of death (c. 1068).

CHAPTER FIVE

Pastors, Parochial Vicars, Chaplains, and Rectors of Churches

In addition to the faculties of chapter 4 that are to be granted to all priests, there are special faculties for priests with various pastoral offices. The offices are those of pastor and parochial vicar of both territorial and personal parishes, chaplains with the full pastoral care of a community and other chaplains, and rectors of churches. Priest supervisors of parishes without a pastor are subsumed in the category of pastors, since they have all the faculties of pastors (c. 517, §2).

The presumption of this chapter is that the faculties of chapter 4 are also given to all the priests of the diocese or the military ordinariate on a separate *pagella*. None of the faculties of chapter 4 is repeated in this chapter, which contains additional faculties for priests in the specified pastoral offices.

Pastors and Chaplains with Full Pastoral Care

The faculties of sections 1–9 of this chapter are intended, in the first place, for pastors and for priest chaplains who have the full pastoral care of the faithful in their charge, such as military chaplains and chaplains assigned to migrants or similar groups who do not have their own parish. (Such chaplains may celebrate infant baptism, adult initiation, marriages, funerals, etc.) Some or all of the faculties in sections 1–9 are also appropriately granted to the priest supervisor of a parish without a pastor, as discussed below. The faculties by law of pastors, given in section 10, are also faculties by law of military chaplains, unless the nature of a matter or particular statutes determine otherwise.[1] It would be pastorally beneficial in many situations for other chaplains who have the full pastoral care of some community also to have the faculties of section 10. Such chaplains do not have these faculties by law, so a grant *ab homine* would be necessary.

The technical and pastoral commentaries of this chapter refer only to the office of pastor. The pastoral commentaries, to be included on the actual *pagellae* for other offices, can be easily modified simply by changing the word "pastor" to the other office in question.

Other Chaplains

Only some of the faculties of this chapter should be given to chaplains who do not have the full pastoral care of a community (chaplains of health care institutions, houses of lay religious, educational institutions, etc.). The faculties appropriate for such chaplains are indicated by the abbreviation "Chpl" in parentheses following the heading for the individual faculty. Other faculties may be added, depending on the pastoral charge of the chaplain (c. 566).

Parochial Vicars

Some faculties given to pastors may be given to parochial vicars (also called assistant pastors, associate pastors, or curates). These are shown after the heading for the faculty by the abbreviation "PV" in parentheses. Section 11 contains three additional faculties that may be granted to parochial vicars and chaplains who are to assist at marriage. The faculties given to parochial vicars should be on their own *pagella*, distinct from that given to pastors. This can easily be done by compiling a list of desired faculties marked with a "PV" and adding

---

1. John Paul II, apostolic constitution *Spirituali militum curae*, April 21, 1986, AAS 78 (1986) 481–486, no. VII; CCLA, pp. 1161, 1163. The military ordinary is normally a bishop who has all the rights and obligations of a diocesan bishop. He can grant all the faculties of this book that are appropriate for the chaplains of his jurisdiction. See ibid., no. II, §1, p. 1159.

desired faculties from section 11. Moreover, many faculties of section 10 are faculties by law of parochial vicars.

Rectors of Churches

A rector of a church is the priest in charge of a church that is not a parish, a capitular church, or a church connected to a house of a religious community or a society of apostolic life (c. 556). In North America, the most common example of churches that have rectors in this sense are shrine churches. Rectors of cathedrals established as parishes are canonically pastors, not the rectors of churches treated in canons 556–563. Faculties that should, as a rule, be given to rectors of churches are indicated by the abbreviation "R." Additional faculties of pastors can be given, depending on local needs and customs.

Priest Supervisors for Parishes Without a Pastor

When a parish lacks a pastor due to a shortage of priests, the bishop may appoint a deacon or a lay minister as administrator or a community of persons who participate in the exercise of the pastoral care of the parish (c. 517, §2).[2] In this case, the bishop must also appoint a priest to oversee the pastoral care, and this priest is endowed with *(instructus)* the powers and faculties of the pastor. Actually, it is unnecessary to speak of both powers and faculties, because the notion of "faculties" includes powers.

The powers and faculties of the priest supervisor mentioned in canon 517, §2 are properly understood as his ordinary faculties, not his delegated faculties. Since "priest supervisor" is an office, albeit without any precise title in the universal law, the faculties of this office are faculties by law, not by delegation. The priest receives these

---

2. The titles "pastoral administrator" and "priest supervisor" are used in this book. The former title indicates that the minister is not just taking care of financial administration but also shares in the pastoral care of the parish. The title "priest supervisor" indicates that this priest oversees the pastoral care of the parish. Since the universal law itself has no titles for this office, an appropriate title may be established in particular law, whether by the conference of bishops or by each bishop for his diocese.

ordinary faculties by the law itself when the bishop confers the office
(c. 145, §2). In his decree appointing the priest supervisor, the bishop
should acknowledge that the supervisor is endowed with all the faculties of a pastor for this parish. This can be done in a simple statement:
"By means of this office of priest supervisor, you have all the powers
and faculties of a pastor in universal and particular law, which you
can freely exercise in [St. Mary's Parish]."

Besides the faculties of office, the bishop should grant to the
priest supervisor some or all of the diocesan *delegated* faculties of
pastors, namely, the faculties given to other pastors from sections 1–9
below. Even if he is a resident pastor in another parish and has these
faculties for that parish, he must be given another grant of faculties
for the parish where he is supervisor, since the delegated faculties he
has as pastor of his own parish are, for the most part, only valid there.

If the bishop wants the pastoral administrator to participate in the
pastoral care of the parish as envisioned by canon 517, §2, he cannot
appoint the priest the actual pastor of the parish because, by constitu-
tive law, the provision of this canon applies only to a parish that has
no pastor.[3] If the priest were appointed the pastor, he would be bound
to all the canonical obligations of a pastor for that parish, which he
could not fulfill. Priest supervisors typically have one or more other
apostolates elsewhere and do not have the time properly to fulfill all
the obligations of a pastor in that parish. Thus, canon 517, §2 shows
pastoral wisdom in saying that the priest is endowed with the powers
and faculties of a pastor, not that he is the pastor.

The Document Granting Faculties

Four separate sample grants of faculties for these several offices are
provided in Appendix II, nn. 2–5. The documents differ according to
office, extent of pastoral jurisdiction, and power to delegate. Pastors,
both personal and territorial, as well as rectors of churches, military
chaplains, and like chaplains, have the faculty to delegate all their

---

3. See John A. Renken's commentary on this canon in *New Commentary on
the Code of Canon Law*, ed. John P. Beal, James A. Coriden, and Thomas J. Green
(New York/Mahwah, N.J.: Paulist Press, 2000) 684–688.

diocesan faculties to the priest who replaces them for up to a month for their vacation, and for shorter periods of travel, retreat, etc. If the pastor has one or more parochial vicars, he also has the faculty to grant the diocesan faculties for priests and parochial vicars to another priest who replaces the parochial vicar for up to one month. This faculty will be useful in dioceses that allow pastors to find their own temporary replacements without the intervention of a diocesan official.

All four sample grants of faculties (Appendix II, nn. 2–5) state that the priest can subdelegate any of his faculties in individual cases, unless otherwise noted. Saying this with respect to faculties for the exercise of executive power is unnecessary, since the universal law already permits it (c. 137, §3). However, authorizations generally cannot be subdelegated, unless this is permitted in the law or the one granting the authorization also grants the power to subdelegate.

Non-Territorial Offices

The paradigm for the faculties below in sections 1–9 is the territorial pastor. The wording in some faculties needs to be modified for other offices. The pastoral jurisdiction of chaplains and of pastors and parochial vicars of personal parishes is personal rather than territorial, so the extent of the use of the faculties must always be considered in rewording the faculties. For example, instead of saying, "This faculty may be used for parishioners in or outside of the parish territory," the faculty could read: "This faculty may be used for your subjects wherever they are." Also, the faculties and commentaries that refer to parishes and parishioners should be reworded when the faculty is being granted to chaplains.

1. The Catechumenate and Baptism

Deputation of Catechists

1.1 You may depute catechists, truly worthy and properly prepared, to celebrate the minor exorcisms of the catechumenate and the blessings of the catechumens when a priest or deacon cannot be present (OICA 44, 48, 109, 119; RCIA 12, 16, 91, 97).

TC/EP. This faculty pertains to the diocesan bishop in the general law. The word "catechist" here applies both to RCIA catechists and catechists in missionary territories.

PC. The minor exorcisms and blessings are found in OICA 109–124, 374; RCIA USA and Canada 90–97.

Abbreviated Catechumenate in Exceptional Circumstances

1.2 You may permit the abbreviated rite for the initiation of an adult in the exceptional circumstances envisioned in the law: sickness, old age, change of residence, long absence for travel, or a depth of Christian conversion and a degree of religious maturity in the catechumen. In all other cases, the permission of the diocesan bishop is necessary to use the abbreviated rite (c. 851, 1°; OICA 240, 274; RCIA USA 331–332, Canada 307–308).

TC/EP. The simple, or abbreviated, rite involves a shorter catechumenal process than is normally required. Without this faculty, permission from the diocesan bishop is required in each case to use this abbreviated catechumenate. Although the bishop could delegate the power to pastors or others to use the abbreviated rite in other exceptional circumstances besides those listed in the law, this would not be advisable. Some parishes have not organized a catechumenal program, despite the requirements of the law. A diocesan faculty that broadly allowed pastors to permit the abbreviated catechumenate could be abused to avoid the standard catechumenate.

PC. The abbreviated rite is found in OICA 240–247 [RCIA USA 340–369, Canada 316–345].

Dispensation from Scrutinies

1.3 For a serious reason, you may dispense a catechumen from participating in one scrutiny or, in extraordinary circumstances, from two. The extraordinary circumstances for granting the dispensation from two scrutinies are those mentioned in faculty 1.2 (OICA 52, 66, §3; RCIA 20, 34, §3).

TC/EP. The universal law permits the diocesan bishop to dispense from one scrutiny for a serious reason, or from two scrutinies in extraordinary circumstances.

PC. The three scrutinies take place normally on the third, fourth, and fifth Sundays of Lent. The scrutinies are special presidential prayers of the celebrant that intercede for the catechumens. A serious reason for dispensing from participation in a scrutiny might be the catechumen's inability to come to the Mass on a particular day when the scrutiny is to take place. The scrutinies are found in OICA 152–180; RCIA USA 141–177, Canada 125–164.

Rite of Election

1.4 You may celebrate the Rite of Election or Enrollment of Names when a catechumen or godparent is unable to participate in the rite celebrated by the bishop on the first Sunday of Lent, provided it is celebrated on the Sunday before or after the first Sunday of Lent or, if that is impossible, at a weekday Mass during the week before or after the first Sunday of Lent.

TC/Au. The bishop or his delegate celebrates the Rite of Election or Enrollment of Names on the first Sunday of Lent. This faculty authorizes pastors to celebrate the rite. (See OICA 44, 138–139; RCIA USA 12, 125–126, Canada 12, 112–113.)

PC. There are two conditions for the use of the faculty. The first is that the catechumen or godparent is unable to come to the diocesan celebration on the first Sunday of Lent. The second condition is mentioned in the law itself: When the rite cannot be celebrated on the first Sunday of Lent due to urgent pastoral reasons, it must be celebrated the week before or after the first Sunday of Lent.

Baptism of Adults (PV)

1.5 You may baptize those seven years of age and older who have the use of reason, without referring them to the bishop, and confirm them in the same rite (cf. c. 863). This faculty may not be validly subdelegated.

TC/Au. Canon 863 states: "The baptism of adults, at least of those who have completed their fourteenth year, is to be deferred to the diocesan bishop so that he himself administers it if he has judged it expedient." Although the canon mentions only baptism, confirmation is a necessary part of the rite of initiation of adults, that is, of those seven years of age and older with the use of reason (c. 852, §1). The pastor and parochial vicar have the faculty to confirm by law when baptizing those who are no longer infants (c. 883, 2°).

Baptism in a Private Home (PV)

1.6 Besides the case of danger of death, you may confer baptism in a private house for a grave condition that makes it difficult for the one to be baptized to leave the house (c. 860, §1).

TC/Au. Canon 860, §1 states: "Apart from a case of necessity, baptism is not to be conferred in private houses, unless the local ordinary has permitted it for a grave cause." (See also RBC 12.) In this faculty, the local ordinary identifies a grave cause in which baptism may be celebrated in a private house. This faculty also has a didactic value, because it educates ministers that they are not supposed to baptize outside the church except in a case of necessity. In danger of death, anyone with the right intention may baptize anywhere.

PC. Ordinarily, baptism is to be celebrated in the parish church (c. 857). In an emergency, it may be celebrated anywhere. This faculty is not needed in danger of death but is intended for use with a person who has a serious disability or illness that makes it difficult to come to the church.

Participation of Christian Minister (PV)

1.7 For pastoral reasons, in particular circumstances, you may invite a minister of another church or ecclesial community to take part in the celebration of baptism by reading a lesson, offering a prayer, or the like. The actual baptism is to be celebrated by the Catholic minister alone (DAPNE 97).

PC/Au. This faculty would be used typically at the baptism of an infant of parents in a mixed marriage, when the non-Catholic party is active in his or her own denomination, or if the non-Catholic minister is a friend or relative of the couple. The Directory for the Application of the Principles and Norms on Ecumenism, no. 97, states: "According to Catholic liturgical and theological tradition, baptism is celebrated by just one celebrant. For pastoral reasons, in particular circumstances, the local ordinary may sometimes permit a minister of another church or ecclesial community to take part in the celebration by reading a lesson, offering a prayer, etc. Reciprocity is possible only if a baptism celebrated in another community does not conflict with Catholic principles or discipline." You should not participate in the baptism of another church or ecclesial community if either parent of the one being baptized is Catholic (cf. cc. 1125, 1366), or the baptism of that community is invalid.

2. Reception into Full Communion

Conditional Baptism (PV)

2.1 If, after a serious investigation, a doubt remains about the validity of a candidate's non-Catholic baptism, and after explaining to the candidate the Church's teaching on valid baptism, you may conditionally baptize. Conditional baptism may be done only in a private ceremony, omitting non-essential rites if desired, but always retaining the renunciation of sin, the profession of faith, the water baptism, and anointing with sacred chrism. Afterwards, at a public celebration such as the Sunday Eucharist, you confirm the person, observing the Rite of Reception of Baptized Christians into the Full Communion of the Catholic Church. (See c. 869 and DAPNE 99.)

> **TC/Au.** The rite of reception states in part: "The local ordinary shall determine, in individual cases, what rites are to be included or excluded in conditional baptism." (See OA 7; RCIA USA 480, Canada 393.)

> **PC.** The Rite of Reception into the Full Communion of the Catholic Church, appended to the Rite of Christian Initiation of Adults, is

used in receiving Anglicans and Protestants into the Church. It is used for those seven and older who have the use of reason. Confirmation and first communion are an integral part of the rite, which may not be delayed, even with children who are below the normal age of confirmation in the diocese but who are at least seven. For children under seven, it suffices that either parent declares his or her intention that the child be received into the Church, and that this be noted in the baptismal register, along with pertinent entries concerning the child's baptism.

For those baptized in a separated Eastern Church, this rite is not observed; they need only make a profession of faith.

For those who might have been invalidly baptized, but who think they were validly baptized, the ceremonies should be minimal. For those who believe their baptism was not valid, or who themselves ask for a fuller liturgical celebration, additional ceremonies, even all the ceremonies of baptism, may be used. Those whose baptism is not doubtful should not be required to fulfill the complete catechumenate, nor should they participate in the Rite of Election, unless they do not consider themselves Christian. A private celebration of baptism is not publicized in any way; having a godparent or witness present is sufficient, but the presence of guests should not be encouraged.

Gesture of Welcome (PV)

2.2 Following the confirmation of the newly received Christian into full communion, you may substitute a handshake or the kiss of peace as a sign of friendship and acceptance in place of taking into your own hands the hands of the person newly received (OA 18; RCIA USA 495, Canada 408).

> **TC/Au.** The *Ordo admissionis*, no. 18 states: "After the confirmation the celebrant greets the newly received person, taking his hands as a sign of friendship and acceptance. With the permission of the ordinary, another suitable gesture may be substituted depending on local and other circumstances." (See RCIA USA 495, Canada 408.) This permission could also be given by means of a general policy.

3. Confirmation

Older Confirmandi (PV)

3.1 You may confirm baptized Catholics who are over the age when children are normally confirmed in the diocese. Confirmation in such cases should take place at Mass, usually on a Sunday, so that the person may complete Christian initiation by participating fully in the Eucharist (c. 884, §1; RC 8, 13).

> **TC/Au.** In a case of need, the bishop may delegate the faculty to confirm to presbyters. The need may arise on the part of the bishop, for example, if he does not have time to confirm many isolated cases that arise outside the normal times for confirmation in a parish. Or the need may be on the part of the *confirmandi*, when they physically are unable to get to an episcopal confirmation without serious inconvenience, or when they morally cannot go there, as in the case, for example, of an adult who feels embarrassment at being confirmed with children or adolescents. By delegating his faculty, the bishop is determining that the need exists on both his part and that of the older candidates—that he has more pressing responsibilities than to be confirming in isolated cases, and that the candidate whose confirmation has already been put off too long has a need for the sacrament.

Delay of Confirmation until After Marriage (PV)

3.2 When the preparation of baptized adults for confirmation coincides with preparation for marriage and it is foreseen that the conditions for a fruitful reception of confirmation cannot be satisfied, or if confirmation cannot be conferred without grave inconvenience, you may defer confirmation until after the marriage (c. 1065, §1; RC 12). If the party wants to be confirmed before marriage and you are opposed, you must refer the case to the local ordinary.

> **TC/Au.** The Rite of Confirmation, no. 12, says that the local ordinary will judge whether deferring confirmation until after the marriage is better. Although the local ordinary's intervention is not

mentioned in canon 1065, §1, the two texts must be harmonized (c. 21), since this liturgical law was not emended following promulgation of the code, as were many other liturgical laws. The final sentence, referring the case to the local ordinary if the pastor refuses to confirm, is necessary to protect the right of the baptized Catholic to the sacrament and to uphold the law that favors confirmation before marriage.

PC. Confirming before marriage is preferable, since the assumption that the party will return for confirmation after the wedding is often unrealistic. Because confirmation, theologically, is a continuation of sacramental initiation begun at baptism, it is not necessary to precede confirmation with a lengthy catechetical program. Therefore, the pastor or parochial vicar ordinarily can confirm an engaged party after a minimal catechesis about the meaning and importance of baptism and confirmation and the obligations of the Christian life that flow from sacramental initiation. In rare cases, when there is not sufficient time even for this, or if the party maintains that confirmation before marriage would be a grave inconvenience (c. 1065, §1), it may be delayed until after the wedding.

4. Eucharist

Extraordinary Ministers (R, Chpl)

4.1 You may appoint suitably instructed lay persons for a term of one to three years to serve as extraordinary ministers of holy communion, both at Mass or outside Mass, whenever it is necessary for the pastoral benefit of the faithful and sufficient ordinary ministers [or instituted acolytes] are lacking or unavailable. You may also commission them for their ministry after the homily at a Sunday Eucharist in accord with the Rite of Commissioning Special Ministers of Holy Communion (EDM art. 8, §1; HCWE 17; c. 230, §3).

TC. The 1997 Instruction, *Ecclesiae de mysterio*, article 8, §1, says that the diocesan bishop appoints extraordinary ministers of holy communion. Given the regular use of extraordinary ministers in many places due to the lack of clerics and the large number of communicants, the bishop may find it fitting to delegate this faculty to pastors. Since most dioceses do not have instituted acolytes, other than a few seminarians, this is bracketed, to be included or not according to the circumstances of the diocese. The appointment of the ministers is an exercise of executive power; the second part of the faculty is an authorization to allow the pastor to commission the ministers.

PC. At the pastor's discretion, the minister may be reappointed to successive terms.

Lay Minister of Exposition (R, Chpl)

4.2 In the absence of a priest, deacon, [instituted acolyte,] or extraordinary minister of communion, you may appoint another person to expose publicly the Eucharist for the adoration of the faithful, and afterward to repose it. You may also determine the suitable vesture for this minister to wear, whether an alb, choir robe, religious habit, or worthy secular attire (HCWE 91–92; c. 943).

PC/EP. Only a priest or deacon may give the benediction.

Holy Thursday (R)

4.3 You may permit a second Mass of the Lord's Supper on Holy Thursday if any of the following conditions is applicable: (1) there are too many faithful to accommodate at one Mass on Holy Thursday; (2) you have the care of more than one parish, and coming together at a single church is not possible; (3) Mass is celebrated in more than one language, and having a multi-cultural celebration is not feasible. The Mass may not begin before evening without the express permission of the bishop in a case of genuine necessity. This faculty may not be subdelegated.

TC/EP. The *Roman Missal*, in the rubrics for Holy Thursday, says the local ordinary may permit a second Mass for pastoral reasons. In this faculty, pastoral reasons are specified. The Masses must be celebrated in the evening. To celebrate an earlier Mass, the universal law requires a case of genuine necessity, and it may be done exclusively for those faithful who are unable to come in the evening. It would be best if only a very few parishes in the diocese were designated for a Mass of the Lord's Supper earlier in the day for the benefit of those who cannot go in the evening.

5. Reconciliation

Delegation of Diocesan Faculties (R, Chpl)

For the celebration of the sacrament of penance in an individual case, you may grant the faculty to hear confessions and all the diocesan faculties of confessors to a priest in good standing (c. 969, §1).

TC/EP. This faculty is unnecessary if the document granting the faculties includes the power to subdelegate faculties in individual cases. However, since canon 969, §1 says that the local ordinary *alone* may grant the faculty to hear confessions of any of the faithful, it may be prudent to include this faculty by which the local ordinary explicitly delegates the power to grant the faculty to hear confessions in individual cases.

All priests have the power by the divine law to absolve from sins in the sacrament of penance, but the faculty is needed, by ecclesiastical law, as authorization to use this power. Since the concession of this faculty is an exercise of executive power of governance, it can be delegated and subdelegated.[4]

PC. You may subdelegate the faculty to hear confessions and the diocesan faculties of confessors to a priest in good standing who will be celebrating the individual or communal rite of penance in

---

4. See Code Commission, response, October 16, 1919, AAS 11 (1919) 477; CLD 1:410–411; William H. Woestman, *Sacraments: Initiation, Penance, Anointing of the Sick* (Ottawa: Faculty of Canon Law, St. Paul University, 1996) 253.

the parish. If the priest already has the faculty to hear confessions from his own diocesan domicile, you need only subdelegate the diocesan faculties of confessors. You should subdelegate the faculty in writing or orally, using these or similar words: "I grant you, Fr. N., the faculty to hear confessions and the faculties of this diocese for confessors on the occasion(s) of [specify the individual instance(s)]. You should give him a copy of the Faculties for Priests, faculties 2.2–2.5. [See chapter 4, faculties 2.2–2.5].

6. Anointing of the Sick

Communal Celebration (Chpl)

You may decide when it is fitting to celebrate the anointing of the sick for several of the sick together in a sacred place or other suitable place, provided there is previous instruction on the eligibility requirements for the sacrament, in particular, that the recipients must be seriously ill or notably weakened due to old age. You may also designate other priests to anoint at these times (c. 1002; PCS 108).

TC/EP. Pastoral Care of the Sick, no. 108 (OUI 83), leaves it to the diocesan bishop[5] to judge whether there may be communal celebrations of the anointing of the sick when many sick people will be anointed at the same celebration. It also says the diocesan bishop is to designate the priests who may take part in such a celebration. Canon 1002 says that communal celebrations of the anointing of the sick for many of the sick together may be held in accord with the regulations of the diocesan bishop. If the diocesan bishop has not issued any particular laws or guidelines on this subject, having a faculty concerning it in the diocesan *pagella* would be useful.

PC. These celebrations should take place in a church, chapel, or other appropriate place where the sick and others can easily gather. On occasion, a communal anointing may also take place in hospitals

---

5. The text says "ordinary," but this was changed in 1983 to "diocesan bishop." See ELB, p. 23, no. 108.

and other institutions. The practice of indiscriminately anointing numbers of people on these occasions simply because they are ill or have reached an advanced age is prohibited. Only those whose health is seriously impaired by sickness or old age are proper subjects for the sacrament. (See PCS 108, 8–15; OUI 83–84, 8–15.)

7. Marriage

Faculties 7.1 to 7.4 are appropriately given not only to pastors and chaplains with the full pastoral care of a community but also to parochial vicars and any other priests who are granted the faculty to assist at marriage.

Permission for Mixed Marriage (PV)

7.1 After the conditions of canon 1125 have been fulfilled, you may, for a just and reasonable cause, permit a mixed marriage between a Latin Catholic and a baptized non-Catholic to be celebrated in the parish, provided there is no doubt about the validity of the baptism of the Catholic party (c. 1124).

> **TC/EP.** The policy of the conference of bishops could be included here, if desired.

> **PC.** The conditions of canon 1125 are: (1) The Catholic party declares that he or she is prepared to remove dangers of falling away from the faith and makes a sincere promise to do all in his or her power to have all the children baptized and brought up in the Catholic Church. (2) The other party is to be informed at a suitable time of the Catholic party's promises so that the non-Catholic party is truly aware of the promise and obligation of the Catholic party. (3) Both parties are to be instructed on the ends and essential properties of marriage that are not to be excluded by either party.

> "In order to judge the existence or otherwise of a 'just and reasonable cause' with regard to granting permission for this mixed marriage, the priest will take account, among other things, of an explicit

refusal on the part of the non-Catholic party to allow the children to be baptized and raised Catholic" (DAPNE 150).

Mixed Marriage to an Eastern Christian at Eucharist (PV)

7.2 At a marriage between a Catholic and an Eastern non-Catholic (c. 844, §3), you may use the Rite of Marriage Within Mass, and the non-Catholic party may receive holy communion if he or she asks for it and is properly disposed (OCM 36).

> **PC/Au.** You may also give communion to the Eastern Christian wedding guests, but you may not publicly invite them to holy communion, as their own discipline may prevent it and canon law requires that they ask on their own for it.

Mixed Marriages at Eucharist Involving Other Christians (PV)

7.3 Because of problems concerning eucharistic sharing that may arise from the presence of non-Catholic witnesses and guests, a mixed marriage between a Catholic and an Anglican or Protestant ordinarily should not take place during the eucharistic liturgy. For a just cause, however, you may permit the celebration of the Eucharist, provided the non-Catholic party comes from a eucharistic tradition and truly agrees to it, after informing both parties that the non-Catholic guests may not be invited to holy communion (OCM 36). If the non-Catholic party wishes to receive communion, permission should be requested from the diocesan bishop [or diocesan ecumenical officer] (cf. DAPNE 159).

> **TC/EP.** The local ordinary may permit the celebration of marriage at the Eucharist in a mixed marriage (OCM 36), but the decision as to whether to admit the non-Catholic party to holy communion is to be based on existent law, chiefly canon 844, §§ 3–4 (DAPNE 159). The director of the diocesan ecumenical office or another official of the diocesan curia could be delegated the faculty by the bishop to grant this permission.

PC. The words, "provided the non-Catholic party truly agrees to it," are important for ecumenical sensitivity, because frequently the Catholic party, or his or her family, requests the Eucharist without considering the wishes of the non-Catholic party and his or her family and guests. A "just cause" for celebrating the Eucharist would be better shown if the non-Catholic party comes from a eucharistic tradition and personally desires a wedding Mass.

Special Cases (PV)

7.4 You may permit: (1) the marriage of transients *(vagi)*, provided the diocesan marriage preparation program is observed, to the extent possible, and baptismal certificates or sworn affidavits show they are free to marry; (2) the marriage of a person who is bound by natural obligations toward another party or children arising from a previous union, provided these obligations are being fulfilled; and (3) the marriage of a Catholic with another Catholic who has notoriously rejected the faith, provided the norms of canon 1125 have been observed (c. 1071, §1, nn. 1, 3, 4; §2).

> **TC/EP.** Canon 1071 requires permission of the local ordinary for marriage in seven special cases. Three of them are treated in this faculty. It is recommended that the faculty to permit the other four not be delegated. These are for: (1) a marriage that cannot be recognized or celebrated according to the norm of the civil law; (2) a marriage of a person who is under censure; (3) a marriage of a minor child when the parents are unaware or reasonably opposed; (4) a marriage to be entered through a proxy.

> **PC.** [The conditions of canon 1125 could be given here.]

8. Other Acts of Divine Worship

Blessings (R, Chpl)

8.1 You may permit competent lay ministers and catechists to celebrate blessings from the *Book of Blessings* that are not reserved to a priest or deacon, provided sufficient clergy [or instituted acolytes and readers] are unavailable (DB/BB 18d).

> **TC/EP.** The *Book of Blessings*, no. 18d, says the local ordinary may grant this faculty to lay persons after ascertaining their proper pastoral formation and prudence in the apostolate. If instituted acolytes or readers are few, reference to them could be omitted.

> **PC.** The term "competent" refers to someone who is exercising a parish apostolate, such as religious education or visits to the sick, and who has been instructed on the celebration of the appropriate blessings. Those who preside at meetings of parish organizations may also give blessings.

Funerals of Unbaptized Children

8.2 You may permit church funeral rites for children who died before baptism, provided their parents had intended to have them baptized (c. 1183, §2).

> **PC/EP.** It suffices that one parent had intended to have the child baptized.

Funeral of Baptized Non-Catholic

8.3 You may permit the celebration of the Church's funeral rites for a validly baptized member of another church or ecclesial community, provided this would not be contrary to the wishes of the deceased person and provided the minister of the deceased person is unavailable (c. 1183, §3; DAPNE 120).

> **PC/EP.** The name of a non-Catholic may not be mentioned during the Eucharistic Prayer (DAPNE 121). It some cases it may be more suitable to celebrate the funeral liturgy outside Mass, especially if few Catholics will be present.

> The minister may be "morally" unavailable as well as physically unavailable, for example, if there is a church of the deceased per-

son's denomination, but he or she was unknown to the minister there. It sometimes happens that the spouse or next of kin of the deceased is Catholic, but he or she does not have a place for the funeral rites of the deceased person.

Funerals with Cremated Remains Present (PV, Chpl)

8.4 You may celebrate the funeral liturgy in the presence of the cremated remains of a deceased person, taking into account the concrete circumstances in each individual case, and always observing the following conditions: (1) There is no anti-Christian motive for choosing cremation (c. 1176, §3). (2) The cremated remains will be handled with respect and buried or entombed in a place reserved for this purpose. (3) There is no other canonical prohibition of a funeral liturgy, namely, for notorious apostates, heretics, and schismatics and other manifest sinners for whom ecclesiastical funerals cannot be granted without public scandal to the faithful (c. 1184). Doubtful cases are to be referred to the bishop [or delegate, named here].

> **TC/Au.** The diocesan bishop may permit the funeral liturgy to be celebrated in the presence of the cremated remains in the U.S.A., Canada, and other countries that have the indult from the Holy See. The advisability of granting this faculty to a chaplain depends on whether he may celebrate funerals and whether cremation is practiced in that community.

> **PC.** [For additional norms, see NCCB, *Order of Christian Funerals*, Appendix: Cremation, no. 426; CCCB, *Order of Christian Funerals*, Supplement for Cremation (1997), nn. 639–640.]

9. Exceptional Faculties

The faculties in this section would normally be granted by a diocesan official, not by pastors. Most of them would not be needed by pastors in a typical diocese, but some or all might be needed in dioceses, both large and small, depending on the organization of the diocesan curia and the extent of the shortage of priests. They are offered here as further options for the bishop and his advisors to consider.

Sunday Celebrations Without a Priest (Chpl)

9.1 In individual instances when you will be legitimately absent and no priest is available to celebrate Mass on a Sunday or holy day of obligation, you may appoint a deacon or, if there is no deacon, a lay minister who has had the necessary formation to preside at the liturgy of the word, morning prayer, or evening prayer at which holy communion is distributed in accord with the approved rite. This may be done only for the benefit of the faithful who are unable to go to another church for the Eucharist; it may not be done more than once a day in any one place or when Mass is celebrated there that day (DSCAP 24; EDM art. 7).

> **TC/EP.** The 2 June 1988 Directory for Sunday Celebrations in the Absence of a Priest, no. 24, says it belongs to the diocesan bishop, after hearing the presbyteral council, to decide whether Sunday assemblies without the celebration of the Eucharist should be held on a regular basis in his diocese. It also belongs to the bishop to set out both general and particular norms for such celebrations. In the absence of particular laws on this matter, the above faculty would be appropriate where it is needed. The restrictions on this faculty (not for those who can go elsewhere for Eucharist, once a day, etc.) come from the 1988 directory.

> The faculty is intended only for parishes with a pastor who, in individual instances, may be unable to find a priest to replace him during a legitimate absence. For parishes without a resident pastor where the need for Sunday celebrations is ongoing, a special mandate of the bishop is necessary. (See EDM art. 7, §1.)

> **PC.** No faculty is needed for a communion service on a weekday. The universal law permits such a service for a just cause, such as the absence of a priest to celebrate the Eucharist (HCWE 14; c. 918).

Dispensation from Disparity of Worship (PV)

9.2 You may dispense from the impediment of disparity of worship, provided the conditions of canon 1125 are fulfilled (c. 1086), and provided one or more of the following reasons is present: (1) fear of a marriage outside the Church if the dispensation were not granted; (2) fear of odium to the Catholic Church if the marriage were prohibited; (3) danger of spiritual or emotional harm to the Catholic party if the marriage were not permitted. [Additional reasons may be given.] The dispensation is valid only if granted in writing, noting as well the just and reasonable cause for it. A copy of the dispensation must be forwarded to the diocesan archives after the marriage has been celebrated; another copy is to be retained in the parish archives. This faculty may not be subdelegated. It may be used only for marriages being celebrated in the parish, or for the marriage of a parishioner being celebrated outside the parish with a dispensation from canonical form.

> **TC/EP.** The dispensation from disparity of worship is routine in areas that have a relatively high percentage of non-baptized persons and consequently many non-sacramental marriages. Listing some additional just and reasonable causes for which the dispensation could be granted may be desirable. Providing dispensation forms for each parish would also be helpful so that the dispensations can be granted in a uniform manner.

> The law requires that dispensations be given in writing (cc. 37; 59, §1). The condition added here that this is for validity is a matter of good order. If there is nothing in writing, it is difficult to prove in later years that it was truly given. The delegation of a faculty may contain a condition for validity (c. 39).

> **PC.** [If the diocese provides no dispensation form, this should be added]: The dispensation must be given in writing. You should use parish stationery and write: "I dispense (name of Catholic party) from the impediment of disparity of worship so that she might marry (name of unbaptized or doubtfully baptized party) at (name of church) on (date). The reason(s) for the dispensation is/are..."

You must sign and date the dispensation. One copy is sent to the local ordinary, retaining a copy for the marriage file.

Dispensations in Urgent Cases (PV)

9.3 You may dispense from any of the following impediments if the impediment is discovered shortly before the marriage and there is no time to reach the local ordinary: disparity of cult, consanguinity in the fourth degree, affinity, public propriety, and legal relationship (cc. 1086; 1091, §2; 1092–1094).

> **TC/EP.** The bishop may delegate his power to dispense other marriage impediments of ecclesiastical law, but this is not recommended, given the gravity of those impediments.

Mixed Marriage Outside Church or Oratory (PV)

9.4 If you are the pastor of the Catholic party, you may permit a mixed marriage to be celebrated according to the canonical form: (1) in the church of the non-Catholic party, with the consent of the non-Catholic minister; (2) in a nondenominational chapel; (3) in the place where the reception will be held, provided the place is suitable and free from noise and other distractions. The Rite of Marriage Outside Mass must be used, and the priest or deacon who assists must obtain the faculty to assist from the local ordinary or the pastor of the territory in which the marriage is celebrated. The marriage must take place in the territory of the diocese. This faculty may not be subdelegated (c. 1118, §2).

> **TC/EP.** The faculty is an application of the rule, found in canon 1118, §2, that marriage outside a Catholic church or oratory may be permitted by the local ordinary, provided the place is suitable. With this faculty, the pastor may grant this permission in a mixed marriage to be celebrated in any of the three places indicated.

10. Select Faculties of Pastors Granted by Law

This section contains selected faculties that pastors, parochial vicars, and military chaplains (unless otherwise regulated by statutes) have in virtue of the universal law. Listing faculties by law on the *pagella* is unnecessary, but it is helpful for the information of the ministers and it facilitates the delegation of faculties by the pastor to his replacement when he is away. He can simply delegate all his faculties on his *pagella*, including the faculties he has by law that are listed.

If the diocese has any priest chaplains in hospitals, prisons, or on voyages at sea, the faculty of canon 566, §2 may be included on their *pagella*. Such chaplains have the faculty, even apart from the danger of death, of absolving from *latae sententiae* censures that are not reserved or declared.

The following faculties by law should be listed in a separate section, as below, but if they are interspersed with the other faculties, it should be clearly stated on the *pagella* that they are faculties by law. The faculties parochial vicars have by law are indicated by the abbreviation "PV" in parentheses following the faculty heading.

Any faculty in this section for the exercise of executive power is ordinary power and can be delegated by the pastor, parochial vicar, or chaplain to another priest or deacon either by way of general delegation or special delegation (c. 137, §1). The pastor's faculty to assist at marriage may also be delegated for all cases or for individual cases (c. 1111).

Confirmation (PV)

10.1 When you baptize anyone seven years of age or older with the use of reason or receive the same into full communion with the Catholic Church, you have the faculty to confirm during those rites. This faculty may not be validly subdelegated (c. 883, 2°).

> **TC/Au.** This faculty is also given in the Rite of Confirmation and the Rite of Christian Initiation of Adults. (See RC 7 a, b; OICA 46, RCIA 14); OICA 227, RCIA USA 232, Canada 226; OICA 267,

RCIA USA 363, Canada 339; OICA 344, RCIA USA 305, Canada 281; OICA 362, RCIA USA 323, Canada 299; OA 8, RCIA USA 481, Canada 394.)

Faculty to Hear Confessions

10.2 Within the territory of the parish, you have the faculty to hear confessions (c. 968, §1). This faculty may not be validly subdelegated.

> **PC/Au.** The delegated faculty, given on the diocesan *pagella* for priests, may be used anywhere in the world.

Faculty to Assist at Marriage

10.3 Within the territory of the parish, you have the faculty to assist at a marriage involving at least one Catholic of the Latin church *sui iuris* (c. 1109).

> **PC/Au.** By law, you may delegate this faculty to another priest. General delegation, for validity, must be granted in writing (c. 1111). Special delegation, for liceity, also should be granted in writing (c. 37), so there is proof that the marriage was validly celebrated.

Marriage of a Catechumen (PV)

10.4 You may celebrate the marriage of a catechumen, even to a non-Catholic, according to the appropriate rite of marriage involving a non-baptized person, which may never take place at Mass (OCM 152).

> **TC/Au.** This faculty is included because many priests are not aware that a catechumen has the right to have a church wedding, even if not marrying a Catholic. Strictly speaking, it is not necessary that a

priest have the faculty to assist at the marriage of a catechumen and a non-Catholic, since the canonical form is not required for such a marriage. In cases involving a catechumen and a Catholic, this faculty can be used only by a priest who has the faculty to assist at marriage.

PC/Au. A catechumen is someone who has been accepted into the order of catechumens until baptism. The catechumen has the right to a church wedding, whether to a Catholic or a non-Catholic (OCM 152). The rite for non-sacramental marriages is to be observed, always celebrated outside Mass. If the marriage is between a catechumen and a Catholic, a dispensation from the impediment of disparity of worship is necessary.

Dispensation from Impediments (PV)

10.5 Whenever an impediment is discovered after everything has already been prepared for the wedding, and the marriage cannot be delayed without probable danger of grave harm until a dispensation is obtained from the competent authority, you may dispense in occult cases from all impediments except prior bond, impotence, consanguinity in the direct line and the second degree of the collateral line, sacred orders, and a public perpetual vow of chastity in a religious institute of pontifical right (c. 1080, §1). You may dispense either Catholic party, even if they live outside the parish territory, provided the marriage takes place in the parish, and you may dispense a parishioner even if the marriage is lawfully celebrated outside the parish territory.

PC/EP. The difference between this faculty and that given for confessors is that this faculty is used in the external forum, whereas that of a confessor is used in the internal forum. An external forum dispensation is reported to the local ordinary and recorded; a dispensation granted during a sacramental confession is not (c. 1081).

The dispensation should be granted in writing: "In virtue of the faculty of canon 1080, §1, I dispense N. from the impediment of _____ so that he/she may be free to marry N. on [date] at this church, [name of parish]. The reason for this dispensation is to avoid the probable danger of grave harm if the marriage is delayed while waiting for the dispensation from the competent authority." You should write the dispensation on parish stationery, sign and date it. A copy is to be sent to the local ordinary and another copy retained for the marriage file.

Some impediments are of their nature public, such as, for example, lawful consanguinity or affinity, bond of marriage, holy orders, a public perpetual vow of chastity in a religious institute, disparity of worship, adoption. Sometimes one of these may be occult in fact. Other impediments are of their nature occult, such as, for example, illegitimate consanguinity or affinity, or crime. Yet they may be in fact public, since it may happen that they are capable of proof owing to the particular circumstances of the case. Some impediments may be public in one place or at one time but occult elsewhere or later. Accordingly, the code sometimes speaks of occult *cases* (cc. 1047, §3; 1048; 1080, §1).

Funeral of a Catechumen (PV)

10.6 You may celebrate funeral rites for a deceased catechumen, omitting language referring to Christian baptism (c. 1183, §1). You have the discretion of celebrating the funeral liturgy outside Mass, especially if the immediate family is not Catholic (OE 45).

> **TC/Au.** This faculty is from the rite of funerals. (See OE 45; OCF USA 178, Canada 349.)

Feast Days and Days of Penance

10.7 In individual cases and for a just cause, you may dispense parishioners anywhere they are, and others who are in the parish territory, from the obligations to attend Mass and abstain from work on Sundays and holy days of obligation, or you may commute the obligation to another pious work. Under the same conditions, you may dispense from or commute the obligations of fast and abstinence on a day of penance (c. 1245).

> **TC/EP.** For chaplains and personal pastors, as suggested in the introduction to this chapter, the faculty should be worded: "In individual cases and for a just cause, you may dispense your subjects wherever they are staying from the obligations to attend Mass...."
>
> **PC.** A commutation is the substitution of one obligation for another that can be more easily done.

Vows and Oaths

10.8 In the external or internal forum, you may dispense from private vows, provided the dispensation does not injure the acquired rights of others. You may dispense from promissory oaths, unless dispensation from an oath would tend to harm one or other persons who refuse to remit its obligation. You may commute the obligation of a private vow or oath to a lesser good. This faculty may be used on behalf of parishioners wherever they are staying and within the boundaries of the parish on behalf of visitors (cc. 1196, 1°; 1203).

> **PC/EP.** This faculty does not apply to public vows, such as the vows taken by members of religious institutes.

11. Additional Faculties for Parochial Vicars and Chaplains

The following additional three faculties, especially the first, are recommended for delegation by the diocesan bishop to parochial vicars. Since they are faculties of pastors by law, they did not appear on the lists in nn. 1–9 above. All three faculties may also be given to chaplains who have the full pastoral care of a community (migrants, ethnic groups, etc.), but military chaplains generally already have these faculties in virtue of the law. Faculties 11.2 and 11.3 may also be given to other chaplains for the benefit of their subjects (in health care institutions, schools, convents, etc.).

Faculty to Assist at Marriage

11.1 Within the territory of the parish, you may assist at marriages involving at least one party who is a Catholic of the Latin church (cc. 1108, 1111).

> **TC/Au.** The pastor may also grant the faculty which, if it is a general delegation, must be in writing for validity (c. 1111). This faculty should be listed together with the other marriage faculties to be granted to parochial vicars (the above faculties 7.1 to 7.4 and 9.2 to 9.4).

> **PC.** You may also celebrate the appropriate marriage rite for a catechumen, even to another non-Catholic (OCM 152). As with any non-sacramental marriage, it cannot take place at Mass, and the appropriate rite of marriage must be used.

Feast Days and Days of Penance (Chpl)

11.2 In individual cases and for a just cause, you may dispense parishioners anywhere they are, and others who are in the parish territory, from the obligations to attend Mass and abstain from work on Sundays and holy days of obligation, or you may commute the obligation to another pious work. Under the same conditions, you may dispense from or commute the obligations of fast and abstinence on a day of penance (c. 1245).

> **TC/EP.** For chaplains and personal pastors, as suggested in the introduction to this chapter, the faculty should be worded: "In individual cases and for a just cause, you may dispense those entrusted to your pastoral care wherever they are staying from the obligations to attend Mass..."

Vows and Oaths (Chpl)

11.3 In the external or internal forum, you may dispense from private vows, provided the dispensation does not injure the acquired rights of others. You may dispense from promissory oaths, unless dispensation from an oath would tend to harm one or other persons who refuse to remit its obligation. You may commute the obligation of a private vow or oath to a lesser good. This faculty may be used in the external forum on behalf of parishioners wherever they are staying, and within the boundaries of the parish on behalf of visitors (cc. 1196, 1°; 1203).

PC. [See commentary above, faculty 10.8.]

CHAPTER SIX

Deacons

This chapter has five sections. The first is a list of faculties that deacons have by universal law in virtue of their ordination (powers of order of ecclesiastical law). Including such faculties on a *pagella* is unnecessary, since all deacons have them, but dioceses often list such faculties as information.

Section 2 consists of faculties that deacons have by the universal law itself, to be used only on behalf of someone in danger of death. These faculties could be integrated with those of the first section, if desired, since their source is the same. All deacons—not just those who serve in parishes—have the faculties of sections one and two.

The third section consists of several model faculties for parish deacons that the bishop may grant. A "parish deacon," in this work, is a deacon who serves in a parish, with or without a pastor. Some of these faculties are also appropriate for deacons who are in non-parochial apostolates. Deacons not assigned to a parish should be given a separate *pagella*, consisting of the faculties by law of sections one and two and the faculties of section three that are indicated for all deacons.

The fourth and fifth sections contain additional faculties and mandates for deacons who share in the pastoral care of a parish without a pastor (c. 517, §2). The universal law has no title for this office. In this work, it is called "pastoral administrator." These sections are applicable also to deacons assigned as Catholic chaplain for a military chapel or unit without a priest chaplain and for a community of the faithful (e.g., migrants) for whom a deacon is assigned as principal chaplain in the absence of a priest. The faculties of section 4 are to be granted by the bishop. The priest supervisor himself grants the three mandates of section 5.

The reader should recall that faculties are not obligations. They grant the power of governance or are authorizations for liturgical and ministerial acts and acts of administration. Thus, faculties should not be confused with a job description that lists all the rights and duties of a pastoral administrator or another office held by a deacon.

Commentaries on faculties introduced in a previous chapter are not repeated. The corresponding commentary can be found in the place indicated in the brackets at the end of the faculty. The pastoral commentary can be included on the deacon's *pagella* under the appropriate faculty, making necessary adjustments like changing "priest" to "deacon" or "pastor" to "pastoral administrator." Commentaries are unnecessary for faculties in the first section, since their use is commonplace and their meaning is well known.

Sections 1 and 2 have introductions in italics, which means they are to be included on the *pagella*. The introductions to sections 3 and 4 are not to be included on the *pagella*.

1. Faculties Granted at Ordination

You have the following faculties from the moment of your ordination. You may use them anywhere in the world with at least the presumed consent of the pastor or rector of the church.

Ministry of the Word

1.1 You may catechize and preach to the faithful apart from the liturgy (cc. 757, 762; SDO 22, 6°).

1.2 You may preside at the liturgy of the hours, celebrations of the word, and Sunday celebrations in the absence of a priest where this is permitted; you may preach at the liturgies at which you preside (GILH 254; SDO 22, nn. 7–8; DSCAP 29; c. 764).

1.3. You may proclaim the gospel at Mass; you may give the homily at Mass, at the discretion of the priest celebrant (GIRM 175, 171c).

Sacraments

1.4 You may administer baptism to infants—those under seven and those lacking the use of reason (cc. 861, §1).

1.5 You may assist the presiding priest at Mass and other liturgical celebrations as indicated in the rites (SDO 22, 1°).

1.6 You may administer the blood of Christ at Mass or, when communion is given only under the species bread, the body of Christ (c. 910, §1; GIRM 182).

1.7 You may preside at the Rite of Distributing Holy Communion Outside Mass, and you may bring holy communion to the sick and infirm (HCWE 17, 26; PCS 81–96).

Sacramentals

1.8 You may preside at benediction and give the blessing with the reserved Eucharist (c. 943).

1.9 You may celebrate the minor exorcisms and blessings of catechumens (RCIA 91, 96; OICA 109, 119).

1.10 You may give the blessings of the rites at which you preside; you may preside at other blessings in accord with the *Book of Blessings* (DB/BB 18c).

1.11 You may preside at penitential celebrations when the sacrament of penance is not celebrated (RP 36–37).

1.12 You may celebrate the rites for visits to the sick and the prayers on the occasion of death (OUI 138, 151; PCS 212, 221).

1.13 When a priest is unavailable, you may preside at funeral rites—the vigil, funeral liturgy outside Mass, and committal (OE 19; OCF 14).

1.14 You may celebrate or impart other sacramentals in accord with the law (cc. 1168; 1169, §3).

2. Faculties for Use in Danger of Death

You also have the following faculties from the moment of your ordination, but they may be used only if someone is in danger of death. These faculties may be used anywhere in the world with at least the presumed consent of the pastor.

Baptism

2.1 If a priest is unavailable, you may baptize anyone not yet validly baptized, including a fetus, provided the person is alive (cc. 861, §2; 868, §2; 871). Those who had the use of reason at any time during their life may not be baptized without having manifested this intention; they must also have some knowledge of the principal truths of the faith and must promise to observe the commandments of the Christian religion (c. 865, §2). [Commentary, faculty 5.1, p. 122]

> **PC.** [The following sentence should be added at the beginning of the pastoral commentary from faculty 5.1, p. 122.]: Normally, a priest should baptize in danger of death so that he may confirm the person immediately afterward, even if an infant (c. 866). Thus, this faculty should be used only if no priest who has the sacred chrism is available. [Continue with the rest of the pastoral commentary, omitting the parts on confirmation.]

Viaticum

2.2 You may celebrate the Rite of Viaticum Outside Mass (PCS 197–211), except the apostolic pardon *(formula indulgentiae plenariae),* with at least the presumed permission of the pastor, chaplain, or superior, who must be notified afterwards (c. 911, §2; PCS 197–211). You may also give Viaticum to a baptized non-Catholic who is in danger of death, in accord with the law (c. 844, §§ 3–4). [Commentary, faculty 5.3, p. 123]

> **PC.** The dying person must request the sacrament and be properly disposed. To ensure the proper disposition, if the person has not had an opportunity to confess, you should ask him or her to make an act of perfect contrition, that is, to be sorry for all grave sins committed after baptism, which have not yet been confessed, with the intention of sinning no more. This requirement applies both to Catholics and baptized non-Catholics. A Catholic, moreover, should be exhorted to intend to confess any serious sins later in individual confession.
>
> In addition to the request for the sacrament and the proper disposition, members of ecclesial communities (Anglicans and Protestants) must be unable to approach a minister of their own community, and they must manifest Catholic faith in the sacrament. A suitable manifestation of faith would be an affirmative answer to the question: "Do you accept the faith in the sacrament of the Eucharist as Christ instituted it and as the Catholic Church has handed it down?" (See SPCU, instruction *In quibus rerum circumstantiis,* no. 5, June 1, 1972.)

Commendation of the Dying

2.3 You may celebrate the Rite of Commendation of the Dying (OUI 142; PCS 165, 212–222).

Marriage Dispensations

2.4 Even if you lack the faculty to assist at marriage, when one or both parties is in danger of death and when the local ordinary cannot be reached, you may dispense the parties to marriage both from the form to be observed in the celebration of marriage and from every impediment of ecclesiastical law, whether public or occult, except the impediment arising from the sacred order of the presbyterate (c. 1079, §2). [Commentary, faculty 5.7, pp. 125–126]

3. Faculties Granted by the Bishop for Parish Deacons

The bishop may grant the following faculties to deacons who minister in parishes (or who are chaplains in like communities for the military, migrants, etc.). Those faculties appropriate for all deacons, including those who serve in non-parochial apostolates, are indicated by the word "All" in parentheses following the heading for the faculty. Note that the sample grant of faculties (Appendix II, 6) says that these faculties may be used within the territory of the diocese unless otherwise specified.

Baptism in a Private Home

3.1 You may confer infant baptism in a private house for a grave reason that makes it difficult or dangerous for the infant to be brought to the church (c. 860, §1; RBC 12). This faculty may be used only within the territory of the parish [within the limits of your pastoral charge] except in danger of death. [Commentary, faculty 1.6, p. 134]

Participation of Christian Minister in Baptism

3.2 For pastoral reasons, in particular circumstances, you may invite a minister of another church or ecclesial community to take part in the celebration of baptism by reading a lesson, offering a prayer, or the like. The actual baptism is to be celebrated by the Catholic minister alone (DAPNE 97). [Commentary, faculty 1.7, p. 135]

Sacramental Sharing in Cases of Grave Need (All)

3.3 Observing the conditions of canon 844, §4, you may administer holy communion to validly baptized persons who are in danger of death or who live in areas or institutions where they do not have regular access to a minister of their own. [Additional cases can be listed here as determined by the conference of bishops and/or the diocesan bishop.]

> **TC/Au.** The pastoral commentary (on faculty 3.2, pp. 116–117) should be modified when included here to eliminate mention of penance and anointing of the sick.

Faculty to Assist at Marriage

3.4 Within the territory of the parish, you may validly assist at marriages involving at least one party who is a Catholic of the Latin church (cc. 1108, 1111). This faculty may be used only within the territory of the parish [within the limits of your pastoral charge].

> **TC/Au.** In some dioceses, the pastor rather than the local ordinary gives the faculty. The determination as to whether the faculty is given by the local ordinary or the pastor depends in part on the formation of deacons in the diocese and their readiness and aptitude for this function. [Additional commentary may be added from faculty 11.1, p. 155.]

Dispensation from Impediments

3.5 Whenever an impediment is discovered after everything has already been prepared for the wedding, and the marriage cannot be delayed without probable danger of grave harm until a dispensation is obtained from the competent authority, you may dispense in occult cases from all impediments except prior bond, impotence, consanguinity in the direct line and the second degree of the collateral line, sacred orders, and a public perpetual vow of chastity in a religious institute of pontifical right (c. 1080, §1). You may dispense either Catholic party, even if they live outside the parish territory, provided the marriage takes place in the parish, and you may dispense parishioners even if the marriage is lawfully celebrated outside the parish territory.

> **TC/EP**. This is a faculty granted to deacons by law, provided they have the faculty to assist at marriage. Thus, it is not a faculty granted by law at ordination. It is listed here because it follows logically from the grant of the faculty to assist at marriage. Additional pastoral commentary is found at faculty 10.5, pp. 152–153. The first paragraph of that pastoral commentary should be dropped here and replaced with the following paragraph:

> **PC**. This is a faculty you have by law provided you have the faculty to assist at marriage. This faculty is intended for a marriage at which you will assist according to the canonical form, not the extraordinary form of canon 1116. When a marriage is celebrated according to the extraordinary form, all deacons have this faculty, not just those who have the faculty to assist at marriage.

> [Add here the second and third paragraphs of the commentary at faculty 10.5, pp. 152–153.]

Permission for Mixed Marriage

3.6 After the conditions of canon 1125 have been fulfilled, you may, for a just and reasonable cause, permit a mixed marriage between a Latin Catholic and a baptized non-Catholic to be celebrated in the parish, provided there is no doubt about the validity of the baptism of the Catholic party (c. 1124). [Commentary, faculty 7.1, pp. 142–143]

Participation of Non-Catholic Minister (All)

3.7 Upon the request of the couple, and if you have the faculty to assist at marriage, even by special delegation, you may invite the minister of the party of the other church or ecclesial community to participate in the celebration of the marriage by reading from scripture, giving a brief exhortation, and/or blessing the couple (DAPNE 158). [Commentary, faculty 3.4, p. 118]

Funerals with Cremated Remains Present

3.8 When a priest is unavailable, you may celebrate the funeral liturgy in the presence of the cremated remains of a deceased person, taking into account the concrete circumstances in each individual case, and always observing the following conditions: (1) There is no anti-Christian motive for choosing cremation (c. 1176, §3). (2) The cremated remains will be handled with respect and buried or entombed in a place reserved for this purpose. (3) There is no other canonical prohibition of a funeral liturgy, namely, for notorious apostates, heretics, and schismatics and other manifest sinners for whom ecclesiastical funerals cannot be granted without public scandal to the faithful (c. 1184). Doubtful cases are to be referred to the bishop [or delegate, named here]. [Commentary, faculty 8.4, p. 146]

Ecumenical Meetings (All)

3.9 You may take part in meetings with other Christians aimed at improving ecumenical relations and resolving pastoral problems in common (DAPNE 91b). [Commentary, faculty 3.5, p. 118]

4. Faculties Granted by the Bishop for Pastoral Administrators

Deacon pastoral administrators are to be granted two *pagellae*, that given to all deacons and parish deacons (sections 1–3 above) and some or all of the additional faculties below. A sample grant of faculties is given in Appendix II, 7. Note that the sample says these faculties may only be used in the territory of the parish (or within the limits of the pastoral charge in a personal jurisdiction).

The faculties of section 4 may be granted or not, depending on the circumstances. One such circumstance is the canonical education of the deacon. Faculties requiring more specialized knowledge of canon law should not be granted unless the deacon understands the meaning and use of the faculty.

The most important consideration in granting special faculties to deacon pastoral administrators is the involvement of the priest who supervises the pastoral care of the parish (priest supervisor). Sometimes, the priest supervisor is a retired priest or a priest who has one or more apostolates elsewhere; he has responsibility for only minimal pastoral care in the parish. Mainly, he celebrates the sacraments that require presbyteral orders, but he does little else that could be done by the deacon administrator. In that case, the faculties granted the deacon should be as wide as possible, matching those that would be given to the pastor of a parish, to the extent permitted by law and the ability of the deacon. However, if the priest supervisor has greater time to devote to overseeing the pastoral care of the parish, even if not resident there, the need for some faculties in section 4 will be less.

Deputation of Catechists

4.1 You may depute catechists, truly worthy and properly prepared, to celebrate the minor exorcisms of the catechumenate and the blessings of the catechumens when a priest or deacon cannot be present (OICA 44, 48, 109, 119; RCIA 12, 16, 91, 97). [Commentary, faculty 1.1, p. 132]

Abbreviated Catechumenate in Exceptional Circumstances

4.2 You have the faculty to permit the simple rite for the initiation of an adult in the exceptional circumstances envisioned in the law, namely, sickness, old age, change of residence, long absence for travel, or a depth of Christian conversion and a degree of religious maturity in the catechumen. In all other cases, the permission of the diocesan bishop is necessary to use the abbreviated rite (c. 851, 1°; OICA 240, 274; RCIA USA 331–332, Canada 307–308). [Commentary, faculty 1.2, p. 132]

Dispensation from Scrutinies

4.3 You may dispense from one scrutiny for a serious reason or, in extraordinary circumstances, even from two. The extraordinary circumstances for granting the dispensation from two scrutinies are those mentioned in faculty 4.2 (OICA 52, 66, §3; RCIA 20, 34, §3). [Commentary, faculty 1.3, p. 133]

Sunday Celebrations Without a Priest

4.4 When no priest is available to celebrate Mass, and neither you nor another deacon is available for the Sunday celebration of the word or liturgy of the hours, you may appoint a suitably instructed lay minister, approved by the bishop for this function, to take your place, using the appropriate rite (DSCAP 24; EDM art. 7). [Commentary, faculty 9.1, p. 147]

Designation of Eucharistic Minister

4.5 You may appoint a qualified person to distribute holy communion for single occasions when you are presiding at a communion service and there are too many communicants and insufficient ordinary and extraordinary ministers of communion, or when bringing Viaticum to a dying person is necessary and no ordinary or extraordinary minister is available (c. 230, §3; EDM art. 8, §1). [Commentary, faculty 4.2, p. 119]

> **TC/EP.** The first faculty may be needed if the deacon has a large congregation and occasionally there are insufficient eucharistic ministers.

Lay Minister of Exposition

4.6 In the absence of a priest, deacon, acolyte, or extraordinary minister of communion, you may, in individual instances, appoint a lay person to expose publicly the Eucharist for the adoration of the faithful and afterward to repose it (HCWE 91–92). [Commentary, faculty 4.2, p. 139]

Permissions to Marry

4.7 You may permit: (1) the marriage of transients *(vagi),* provided the diocesan marriage preparation program is observed to the extent possible, and baptismal certificates or sworn affidavits show they are free to marry; (2) the marriage of a person who is bound by natural obligations toward another party or children arising from a previous union, provided these obligations are being fulfilled; and (3) the marriage of a Catholic with another Catholic who has notoriously rejected the faith, provided the norms of canon 1125 have been observed (c. 1071, §1, nn. 1, 3, 4; §2). [Commentary, faculty 7.4, p. 144]

Permission to Marry in Another Catholic Church

4.8 You may permit a parishioner to be married in another Catholic church or oratory (c. 1118, §1).

> **PC/EP**. The permission should be granted in writing, retaining one copy for the archives.

Delegation of Faculty to Lay Minister

4.9 In a case of necessity when you are unable to assist at a marriage, if no other cleric is available, you may grant special delegation to a lay substitute, previously approved by the bishop, or to a lay minister from another parish who has been appointed by the diocesan bishop for this ministry.

> **TC/EP.** This is not a case of necessity for the extraordinary form of marriage (c. 1116). Rather, the necessity here is on the part of the administrator who unexpectedly is unable to assist at a scheduled wedding due to illness, an emergency, etc. If, in this situation, no other cleric is available for the marriage, the deacon pastoral administrator may grant special delegation to a lay minister. Since only the diocesan bishop (or someone mandated by him) can grant the faculty to assist to a lay person, and since this faculty is normally restricted territorially to the lay minister's own parish, the bishop himself must be reached in this urgent situation (unless he has delegated someone else).

> **PC.** In necessity, when you are unexpectedly impeded from assisting at a scheduled marriage, you may use this faculty provided no cleric is available to take your place. You may grant special delegation to a lay person whom the diocesan bishop has approved as your substitute, or to one who exercises this ministry in another parish. If you have general delegation to assist at marriages, you already have the power by law to subdelegate the faculty to another cleric in individual instances.

> To grant the faculty, whether to a cleric or a lay minister, you should write on parish stationery or another sheet of paper: "I grant you, N., the faculty to assist at the marriage of N. and N. on [date] at [name and place of parish]." You must sign and date the document of delegation and keep a copy of it in the marriage file.

Blessings

4.10 You may permit competent lay ministers and catechists to celebrate blessings from the *Book of Blessings* that are not reserved to a priest or deacon, provided sufficient clergy [or instituted acolytes and readers] are unavailable (DB/BB 18d). [Commentary, faculty 8.1, p. 145]

Funeral of Unbaptized Children

4.11 You may permit church funeral rites for children who died before baptism, provided their parents had intended to have them baptized (c. 1183, §2) [Commentary, faculty 8.2, p. 145]

Funeral of Baptized Non-Catholic

4.12 You may celebrate the Church's funeral rites for a validly baptized member of another church or ecclesial community, provided this would not be contrary to the wishes of the deceased person and provided the minister of the deceased person is unavailable (c. 1183, §3; DAPNE 120). [Commentary, faculty 8.3, pp. 145–146]

> **TC/Au**. The first paragraph of the commentary on faculty 8.3, p. 145, on the funeral Mass, should not be included in the pastoral commentary.

Feast Days and Days of Penance

4.13 In individual cases and for a just cause, you may dispense parishioners anywhere they are and others who are in the parish territory from the obligations to attend Mass and abstain from work on Sundays and holy days of obligation, or you may commute the obligation to another pious work. Under the same conditions, you may dispense from or commute the obligations of fast and abstinence on a day of penance (c. 1245). [Commentary, faculty 11.2, p. 155]

Vows and Oaths

4.14 You may dispense from private vows, provided the dispensation does not injure the acquired rights of others. You may dispense from promissory oaths, unless dispensation from an oath would tend to harm one or other persons who refuse to remit its obligation. You may commute the obligation of a private vow or oath to a lesser good. This faculty may be used on behalf of parishioners wherever they are staying and within the boundaries of the parish on behalf of visitors (cc. 1196, 1°; 1203). [Commentary, faculty 10.8, p. 154]

5. Mandates Granted by Priest Supervisors for Pastoral Administrators

The priest supervisor of canon 517, §2 is not the pastor of the parish he supervises. Nevertheless, he is endowed with all the faculties and powers of a pastor. As explained in chapter 5, pages 129–130, these are the ordinary powers and faculties of office, not the delegated faculties additionally granted by the bishop. The executive power of governance for various acts that a pastor may perform by law is ordinary power, so the supervisor can give general delegation for any such acts to the deacon pastoral administrator, as appropriate, unless he already has these faculties from the bishop.

This section refers to "mandates" rather than to the delegation of faculties. A mandate, in this context, means that the priest supervisor assigns to the deacon pastoral administrator spheres of responsibility in the parish and assures that he has the legal competence to fulfill his duties within those areas. The mandate is a sharing in the supervisor's canonical authority, not a faculty that the deacon exercises in his own right.

Several important mandates generally needed by pastoral administrators should come from the priest supervisor because they are proper to him, not to the bishop. Unless the priest supervisor wishes to assume the duties of administering the parish himself, he should grant the three mandates of this section to the pastoral administrator. A sample grant is provided in Appendix II, 9, page 248. The original document is given to the pastoral administrator, with copies for the files of the parish, the priest supervisor, and the diocesan curia.

The technical commentaries in this section are intended not only for diocesan authorities but also for the priest supervisor. The pastoral commentary is for the pastoral administrator.

Legal Representation of the Parish

5.1 You may act in my name as the legal representative of the parish in accord with the pertinent laws of Church and State and within the limits of your job description (c. 532).

> **TC.** This mandate presumes the pastoral administrator has a job description that specifies the duties and competencies of the office, particularly concerning financial administration.[1] With this mandate, the pastoral administrator could act in the name of the priest supervisor with the authority to administer the parish goods in specified areas of competence, and he would have the obligations that go with this authority (cc. 1282–1283). The job description should cover the acts of ordinary administration that the pastoral administrator may authorize, such as purchasing supplies, routine maintenance, paying bills, paying salaries of parish employees, etc.
>
> As the priest supervisor's delegate in legal affairs, the deacon could represent the parish in matters of the civil law such as making reports, applying for tax exemptions, signing documents, etc. The pastoral administrator would also have the authority of a pastor in certain juridic affairs in canon law that are not duties but could be categorized as "competencies."[2] Such matters could be listed on the job description, except for those the priest supervisor wishes to reserve to himself. Other competencies and duties could be added.[3]

---

1. The job description should be supplied by the diocese for use in all parishes without a resident pastor. However, it may be tailored to the needs of individual parishes in keeping with the abilities and interests of the pastoral administrator and the extent of involvement of the priest supervisor in the parish. Many of the duties of a pastor could be included in the job description, e.g., cc. 528; 529; 531; 535, §§ 1, 4; 757; 767, §4; 770; 771; 773; 776; 777; 794, §2; 843, §2; 847, §2; 851, 2°; 855; 861, §2 (the duty of instructing the faithful on the correct way to baptize in emergency); 877, §1; 890; 895; 898; 914; 958, §1; 1001; 1063; 1067; 1072; 1128; 1307, §2; 1054; 1121, §1; 1122, §2; 1123; 1252; 1267; 1280-1289; 1298; 1706.

2. See cc. 535, §3; 858, §2; 867, §1; 874, §1, 1°, 2°; 877, §§ 1, 2; 878; 896; 1043; 1069; 1070; 1114; 1121, §§ 2, 3; 1123; 1285; 1706.

3. For suggestions in this regard, see Barbara Anne Cusack and Therese Guerin Sullivan, *Pastoral Care in Parishes Without a Pastor: Applications of Canon 517, §2* (Washington, D.C.: Canon Law Society of America, 1995).

PC. With this mandate, you may act in the name of the priest supervisor as the representative of the parish in routine legal matters, in both canon law and civil law. This applies especially to the area of financial administration. You are bound not only to the civil laws on contracts, taxation, etc., but to all the laws of the Church, both universal and particular. As delegated legal representative, you have the duties of a financial administrator in canon law and must administer the parish's finances in keeping with Book V of the Code of Canon Law, especially canons 1281–1288.

For the precise areas of responsibility in which you can use this mandate, you must consult your job description. In any doubt as to whether you have the power to act, you must consult the priest supervisor unless the matter is urgent and you cannot reach him.

Pastoral and Finance Councils

5.2 In my absence, you may preside at meetings of the parish pastoral council and finance council (cc. 536 and 537).

TC. The words "in my absence" should be retained, even if the priest supervisor has no intention of presiding at the meetings. This will enable him to preside in an unforeseen situation without suspending or removing the mandate. If he is present at a meeting but prefers the pastoral administrator to conduct the meeting, he can appoint the deacon as moderator of the meeting, leaving the mandate intact.

Decisions

5.3 You may make decisions necessary for the fulfillment of the duties enumerated in your job description and for implementing an approved pastoral plan or project. The more important decisions, as determined by the priest supervisor, and all decisions adversely affecting the rights of persons, require the prior consent of the priest supervisor; but if he cannot be reached, you may decide the matter, which decision must be confirmed by him or the local ordinary.

TC. This mandate allows the pastoral administrator to make every-day decisions necessary for fulfilling the tasks of the office while requiring consultation with and the consent of the priest supervisor for decisions of greater importance. Unless the priest supervisor is fully involved in the operations of the parish and can make all decisions himself, he should give this mandate to the pastoral administrator. It contains sufficient safeguards to protect the rights of persons and uphold the proper authority of both the pastoral administrator and the priest supervisor.

PC. This mandate gives you the canonical authority necessary to decide matters within your areas of competence, which authority is subject to that of the priest supervisor and the local ordinary. The priest supervisor determines what constitutes a major decision, so he can revoke a decision made by you if he was not first consulted on an important matter. The "rights of persons" refers mainly to their canonical rights, especially the right to the sacraments (c. 213). Doubtful matters must be resolved in favor of the rights of persons. Doubts could arise, for example, regarding whether a person is really ineligible to receive a sacrament (cc. 843, §1; 851, 2°; 868, §1, 2°; 913, §1; 914; 915; 1125), have a funeral (cc. 1183, §§ 2, 3; 1184), or be a godparent (c. 874, §1, 3°). Contractual rights and civil rights must also be honored.

CHAPTER SEVEN

Lay Ministers

The paradigmatic lay minister for this chapter is the pastoral administrator. By "pastoral administrator" is meant a lay religious or other lay person who participates in the exercise of the pastoral care of a parish without a pastor under the supervision of a priest (the "priest supervisor") who has the powers and faculties of a pastor (c. 517, §2), as discussed above (pp. 129–130). The lay pastoral administrator has a broad participation in the pastoral care of a parish, as does a deacon pastoral administrator, so more faculties are needed for this lay ministry than for any other. Any or all of the faculties of this chapter may be granted to lay pastoral administrators and certain other lay ministers, such as some military chaplains, missionaries, catechists in mission territories (c. 785), and others who serve a Catholic community that lacks a resident pastor. Some faculties may also be given to other lay ministers, such as pastoral associates, lay chaplains, and catechists in the RCIA, depending on their responsibilities and their abilities.

As explained in chapter 5, the term "pastoral administrator" is not in the code. The 1997 Instruction on Certain Questions Concerning the Collaboration of the Lay Faithful in the Ministry of Priests cautioned that the titles for lay ministries should not cause confusion with that of "pastor," who can only be a priest.[1] In current canon law,

---

1. EDM art. 1, §3 says the laity may not "assume for themselves" any such confusing titles. The instruction gives several examples: "pastor," "chaplain," "coordinator," and "moderator." The term "lay chaplain" is customary in the English-

the diocesan bishop is competent to decide what to call this office within the diocese.

No faculties are given for ministries or works of the apostolate that lay persons exercise in their own right, such as catechetical instruction; social and charitable assistance; the ministries of reader, altar server, commentator, cantor, or usher at Mass; etc. The faculties of this chapter require deputation by the diocesan bishop or other competent authority. Most are authorizations for extraordinary ministries, indicated by the abbreviation "ExM." Two faculties grant executive power of governance for specified acts. Regarding faculties for the exercise of either an extraordinary ministry or executive power, lay persons have the basic juridic capacity for such functions in virtue of their baptism, but they are functions that pertain by legal right to the clergy. However, the bishop may grant a competent lay person the faculties for certain acts of this nature when the needs of the Church require it. (See above, pp. 33–35.) Since nearly all the faculties are authorizations, only those involving the grant of executive power will be indicated by the abbreviation "EP".

The faculties in sections 1–6 are granted by the diocesan bishop or his delegate. The priest supervisor grants the mandates in section 7, as discussed in chapter 6.

The faculties below are suggestions. They are faculties the bishop could grant to lay ministers, depending on the needs and circumstances of the diocese, parish, or other community. The most important consideration with respect to the pastoral administrator's faculties is the extent of involvement of the actual priest supervisor in the pastoral care of the parish. Sometimes, the priest supervisor is a retired priest who assumes responsibility only for the minimum of the pastoral care, namely, the celebration of those sacraments requiring presbyteral orders, but he does little else that could be done by the pastoral administrator. Or the supervisor may be a priest who is a pastor in another parish or who has significant responsibilities elsewhere; he has little time for involvement in the priestless parish and

---

speaking world for lay ministers who serve in the military, in hospitals, etc. The title is legitimate by custom and by the fact that the laity did not assume this title for themselves.

must rely extensively on the pastoral administrator. In such cases, the faculties granted the lay minister should be as wide as feasible, approximating those given to the pastor of a parish, to the extent allowed by law. If the priest supervisor assumes greater, direct responsibility for the regular pastoral care of the parish, the need for the faculties of this chapter will be less.

In a few cases, a model faculty is presented below that enables pastoral administrators to subdelegate a certain faculty when they cannot be present for a scheduled liturgical celebration. Instead of granting the faculty to subdelegate, the diocesan bishop could appoint another person or persons from the parish, or even a neighboring pastoral administrator, as substitutes when the pastoral administrator is absent due to illness, vacation, retreat, etc. The sample grant of faculties (Appendix II, 8) states that the faculties may not be subdelegated unless otherwise noted.

Besides certain faculties on this list that are unique to lay ministers, other faculties are the same or nearly the same as those given to priests and deacons. Granting such faculties is appropriate, depending on the needs and circumstances of the diocese and parish. Generally, faculties that grant executive power on the *pagellae* of priests and deacons are reworded in this chapter so that they are authorizations by the bishop.

The bishop should ensure that lay ministers have sufficient knowledge, particularly of canon law and liturgy, to understand their faculties, and that they have acquired the pastoral skills necessary to use them properly under the guidance of the priest supervisor (c. 231, §1; EDM art. 13). This is especially necessary regarding the marriage faculties of sections 4 and 6, which should not be given if there is any doubt about the adequacy of the minister's formation. Optimally, every pastoral administrator should have a master of divinity or equivalent professional degree from a Catholic university, school of ministry, or seminary.

Commentaries on faculties introduced in a previous chapter are not repeated. The corresponding commentary can be found in the place indicated in the brackets at the end of the faculty. The pastoral commentary can be included on the minister's *pagella* under the appropriate faculty, making necessary adjustments like changing "priest" or "deacon" to "minister" or changing "pastor" to "pastoral administrator."

1. Ministry of the Word

Liturgies of the Word and Hours (ExM)

1.1 You may preside at liturgies of the word apart from the eucharistic celebration, penitential celebrations apart from the sacrament of penance, and the liturgy of the hours. If you will be absent, you may subdelegate this faculty to another suitably instructed lay person (cc. 230, §3 and 1174, §2; GILH 258).

> **PC.** These celebrations should normally be conducted on weekdays, but may be carried out on Sundays provided they do not compete with the Sunday Eucharist or the liturgy celebrated in the absence of a priest.

Sunday Celebrations (ExM)

1.2 On Sundays and holy days of obligation, you may preside at the liturgy of the word, morning prayer, or evening prayer at which holy communion is distributed in accord with the approved rite. This may be done only for the benefit of the faithful who are unable to go to another church for the Eucharist; it may not be done more than once a day in any one place or when Mass is celebrated there that day (DSCAP 24; EDM art. 7). With the permission of the priest supervisor, you may subdelegate this faculty when you are absent or impeded, but only to a person who has been suitably instructed.

> **TC.** This faculty fulfills the requirement of the 1997 Instruction: "A special mandate of the bishop is necessary for the non-ordained members of the faithful to lead such celebrations. This mandate should contain specific instructions with regard to its duration, the place and conditions in which it is operative, as well as indicate the presbyter responsible for overseeing these celebrations" (EDM

7, §1). The duration of the faculty and the place of its exercise are indicated in the document granting the faculties (Appendix II, 8). The conditions for its use are the absence of a priest or deacon and the permission of the priest supervisor. This priest is responsible for overseeing the celebrations.

It belongs to the diocesan bishop, after hearing the presbyteral council, to decide whether Sunday assemblies without the celebration of the Eucharist should be held regularly in his diocese (DSCAP 24).

In the USA, the approved ritual book is *Sunday Celebrations in the Absence of a Priest: Leader's Edition* (New York: The Catholic Book Publishing Company, 1994). In Canada, the approved rites are found in *Sunday Celebration of the Word and Hours* (Ottawa: CCCB, 1995).

PC. A Sunday celebration of this nature may be conducted only for the benefit of the faithful who are unable to go to another church for the Eucharist; this may not be done more than once a day in any one place or when Mass is also scheduled that day. These restrictions on this faculty are from the Directory for Sunday Celebrations in the Absence of a Priest. In necessity, when one of these restrictions cannot be observed, you may request a dispensation from the bishop [or priest supervisor, if delegated by the bishop].

You may subdelegate this faculty only when you are unable to preside and only to someone who has been instructed on the proper celebration of the liturgy in question. You may presume the priest supervisor's permission to subdelegate when he cannot be reached; otherwise, his permission must be express.

Preaching (ExM)

1.3 You may preach in the parish church [in keeping with the policy on lay preaching of the conference of bishops and/or the diocese] and at all liturgical celebrations at which you lawfully preside (c. 766; EDM art. 2).

TC. Pertinent conditions of particular law may be included in the faculty or in the pastoral commentary following the faculty.

PC. You may preach at all liturgical services at which you preside, including Sunday celebrations in the absence of a priest, or you may read a homily prepared by the priest supervisor (DSCAP 43). You may also preach the word of God apart from the liturgy. Preaching outside a church or oratory requires no faculty. You may not preach the homily at Mass. However, occasionally you may, with the permission of the presiding priest, give a brief instruction or personal testimony by way of explanation of the homily given by the priest or speak as part of a dialogue homily. (See EDM art. 3, §§ 2–3.)

2. The Catechumenate and Baptism

Minor Exorcism and Blessings (ExM)

2.1 You may celebrate the minor exorcisms of the catechumenate and the blessings of catechumens (OICA 44, 48, 109, 119; RCIA 12, 16, 91, 97).

PC. The minor exorcisms and blessings are found in OICA 109–124, 374; RCIA 90–97.

Abbreviated Catechumenate in Exceptional Circumstances

2.2 You may use the abbreviated catechumenate in the exceptional circumstances envisioned in the law, namely, sickness, old age, change of residence, long absence for travel, or a depth of Christian conversion and a degree of religious maturity in the catechumen. In all other cases, the permission of the diocesan bishop is necessary to use the abbreviated process (c. 851, 1°; OICA 240, 274; RCIA USA 331–332, Canada 307–308). [Commentary, faculty 1.2, p. 132]

Infant Baptism (ExM)

2.3 Apart from danger of death, in individual instances, you may celebrate infant baptism only if one of the following conditions applies: (1) a priest or deacon has already scheduled the baptism, but he is unable to come and another priest or deacon is not available; or (2) no priest or deacon can celebrate the baptism within four weeks after the child's birth (cf. EDM art. 11).

> **TC.** The faculty granted to a lay person for celebrating baptism may not be granted habitually, according to EDM, article 11. Although this faculty is granted with other habitual faculties, it is not a faculty for general use, as is clear from the words, "in individual instances," and from the restrictive conditions for its use. The faculty, in effect, is a determination by the diocesan bishop of the circumstances in which he would grant permission for the lay minister to baptize in an individual instance. It also upholds the right and duty of the parents to have their child baptized "in the first few weeks" after birth (c. 867, §1).

> **PC.** Canon 867, §1 says that an infant is to be baptized "in the first few weeks" after birth. If serious reasons prevent a priest or deacon from celebrating the baptism within this time, the faculty may be used. If the parents request that a priest or deacon celebrate the baptism, and they are willing to delay the baptism until this is possible, you should respect their wishes, unless the infant is in danger of death. An infant in danger of death should be baptized immediately. You may not celebrate the baptism of anyone seven years of age or older with the use of reason, except in danger of death when a priest is unavailable, since the presbyter who baptizes must administer confirmation at the time of adult baptism.

Baptism in a Private Home (ExM)

2.4 Under the same circumstances in faculty 2.3, you may confer infant baptism in a private house for a grave reason that makes it difficult or dangerous for the infant to be brought to the church (c. 860, §1; RBC 12). [Commentary, faculty 1.6, p. 134]

PC. This faculty may be used if (1) a priest or deacon has already scheduled the baptism, but he is unable to come and another priest or deacon is not available; or (2) no priest or deacon can come for the baptism within four weeks after birth.

Participation of Christian Minister

2.5 For pastoral reasons, in particular circumstances, you may sometimes invite a minister of another church or ecclesial community to take part in the celebration of baptism by reading a lesson, offering a prayer, or the like (DAPNE 97). The actual baptism is to be celebrated by the Catholic minister alone. [Commentary, faculty 1.7, p. 135]

> **PC**. This faculty may be used only with the consent of the priest or deacon who celebrates baptism, unless you are using faculties 2.3 or 2.4.

3. Eucharist

Extraordinary Minister of Holy Communion (ExM)

3.1 You may distribute holy communion outside Mass to the sick, infirm, and aged who cannot come to church. Whenever Mass cannot be celebrated on a weekday or Sunday, you may distribute holy communion at the liturgy of the word or the liturgy of the hours. You may distribute holy communion under either species during Mass when necessary (cc. 230, §3; 910, §2; EDM art. 8).

> **PC**. The Rite of Distributing Holy Communion Outside Mass (HCWE 13–53) is to be observed for a weekday celebration of the word or the liturgy of the hours. For the administration of holy communion to the sick, infirm, and aged, you must observe the Rite of Administration of Communion and Viaticum to the Sick by an Extraordinary Minister (HCWE 54–78). You may distribute holy communion during Mass when there are too many communi-

cants for the priest to do it by himself, or if you are administering the chalice. (See EDM art. 8, §2.)

Cases of necessity for subdelegation of the faculty include an unexpectedly large number of communicants and occasions when you are impeded or will be absent.

Exposition of the Eucharist (ExM)

3.2 In the absence of a priest or deacon, you may expose publicly the Eucharist for the adoration of the faithful and repose it afterwards (HCWE 91–92; c. 943).

> **PC.** Only a priest or deacon may give the benediction.

4. Marriage

Faculty to Assist at Marriage (ExM)

4.1 You may assist at marriages, provided at least one party is a Latin Catholic or is a catechumen who intends to become a Catholic of the Latin church. This faculty may be licitly used with at least the presumed permission of the priest supervisor (c. 1112, §1; EDM art. 10).

> **TC.** This faculty may be granted in dioceses where this is permitted in accord with canon 1112, §1. For validity, the faculty must be delegated by the diocesan bishop or by someone to whom he has delegated the power to grant the faculty. The grant of this faculty requires that the pastoral administrator will have had sufficient formation in canon law and liturgy, and that all the other norms of universal and particular law be observed regarding the preparation, celebration, and recording of marriages.
>
> **PC.** The priest supervisor may give the pastoral administrator general permission to use the faculty for all marriages or for specified

marriages. At times, this permission may be presumed, for example, if the priest supervisor is away and no other minister has been assigned to assist at a scheduled marriage. The priest supervisor's permission is for liceity only, as the diocesan bishop grants the faculty itself.

If the marriage is between two Catholics, or a Catholic and a baptized non-Catholic, you are to observe the Rite of Celebrating Marriage Before a Lay Minister. If the marriage involves a non-baptized person, you are to use the Rite of Celebrating Marriage Between a Catholic and a Catechumen or a Non-Christian. Although catechumens are not obliged to celebrate their marriage in the Church, they have the right to do so, whether they marry a Catholic or a non-Catholic (OCM 152).

If neither party is a parishioner, you may not celebrate the marriage rite without the permission of the (Catholic) pastor of either of them or of the local ordinary, also observing canon 1070 (cc. 1115; 1118, §1; 1114).

Delegation of Faculty

4.2 In individual cases, when the local ordinary or priest supervisor cannot be reached, you may grant special delegation to another priest or deacon to assist at marriage. In necessity, when you are unable to be present and no cleric is available, and when you are unable to reach the diocesan bishop [or the priest supervisor], you may grant special delegation to a lay substitute, previously approved by the bishop, or to a lay minister from another parish whom the diocesan bishop has appointed for this ministry.

> **TC/EP**. This faculty is intended for two urgent situations. The first is when a marriage is soon to take place, but the pastoral administrator is unable to reach the priest supervisor or the local ordinary to request special delegation for a visiting cleric. The pastoral administrator can then grant the special delegation. The commentary for the second situation is found in chapter 6, faculty 4.9, page 169. If the bishop delegates the priest supervisor to grant the fac-

ulty to assist at marriage to a lay substitute, then the words in brackets, "or the priest supervisor," should be included in the wording of the faculty.

PC. It may happen that a visiting priest is to assist at a marriage, but the priest supervisor neglected to give him special delegation. In a case like this, you may grant him the special delegation, after attempting without success to reach the priest supervisor or local ordinary if there is time. Similarly, if you are impeded from celebrating the marriage rite, you may grant special delegation to another priest or deacon who can take your place. [Continue with the pastoral commentary, 4.9, p. 169, omitting the sentence that refers to the deacon having the power to subdelegate the faculty to another cleric.]

Participation of Non-Catholic Minister

4.3 At mixed marriages in the parish church, when the couple requests it, you may invite the minister of the party of the other church or ecclesial community to participate in the celebration of marriage, to read from the scriptures, to give a brief exhortation, and/or to bless the couple (DAPNE 158). [Commentary, faculty 3.4, p. 118]

5. Other Acts of Divine Worship

Blessings

5.1 You may celebrate blessings from the *Book of Blessings* that are not reserved to a priest or deacon.

TC. The *Book of Blessings* 18d says the local ordinary may grant this faculty to lay persons after ascertaining their proper pastoral formation and prudence in the apostolate. Lay persons who may celebrate blessings in virtue of their office (e.g., parents on behalf of their children) do not require a faculty.

Penitential Celebrations (ExM)

5.2 You may preside at penitential celebrations when the sacrament of penance is not celebrated (RP 36–37).

> **TC**. It would be helpful for the diocesan worship office to offer several model penitential services.

Other Sacramentals (ExM)

5.3 You may celebrate the rites for visits to the sick and say the prayers on the occasion of death (OUI 138, 151; PCS 212, 221). On Ash Wednesday, you may administer ashes previously blessed by the priest supervisor or another priest or deacon (BB 1659). You may celebrate other sacramentals in accord with canon law (c. 1168).

Funeral Liturgy (ExM)

5.4 You may celebrate the funeral rites of the Church—the vigil, the funeral liturgy outside Mass, and the rite of committal—for deceased parishioners, including a catechumen, and for non-parishioners, if this was requested by them before death or by the person in charge of the funeral arrangements (OCF 14; OE 19; EDM art. 12; c. 1177, §2).

> **TC**. This faculty may be granted by the diocesan bishop where this is permitted by decree of the conference of bishops or by indult of the Holy See.

> **PC**. A parishioner is any Catholic living within the boundaries of the parish. If funeral rites are requested for a non-parishioner, the pastor of the deceased must be notified, but his permission is not necessary. For those excluded from funeral rites, see canon 1184.

Funeral of Unbaptized Children (ExM)

5.5 You may celebrate funeral rites for children who died before baptism, provided their parents had intended to have them baptized (c. 1183, §2).

> **PC.** It suffices that one parent had intended to have the child baptized.

Funeral of Baptized Non-Catholic (ExM)

5.6 You may celebrate the Church's funeral rites for a validly baptized member of another church or ecclesial community, provided this would not be contrary to the wishes of the deceased person and provided the minister of the deceased person is unavailable (c. 1183, §3; DAPNE 120). [Commentary, faculty 8.3, pp. 145–146]

> **TC.** The first paragraph of the commentary on faculty 8.3, p. 145, on the funeral Mass, should not be included in the pastoral commentary.

Funerals with Cremated Remains Present (ExM)

5.7 You may celebrate the funeral liturgy in the presence of the cremated remains of a deceased person, taking into account the concrete circumstances in each individual case, and always observing the following conditions: (1) There is no anti-Christian motive for choosing cremation (c. 1176, §3). (2) The cremated remains will be handled with respect and buried or entombed in a place reserved for this purpose. (3) There is no other canonical prohibition of a funeral liturgy, namely, for notorious apostates, heretics, and schismatics and other manifest sinners for whom ecclesiastical funerals cannot be granted without public scandal to the faithful (c. 1184). Doubtful cases are to be referred to the bishop [or delegate, named here].

TC. See NCCB, *Order of Christian Funerals*, Appendix: Cremation, 426; CCCB, *Order of Christian Funerals*, Appendix IV: Cremation, in *National Bulletin on Liturgy* 26 (1993) 29.

6. Select Faculties in Danger of Death

The first faculty is granted by law but may be listed for information.
The other faculties require delegation from the local ordinary.

Baptism (ExM)

6.1 If a priest or deacon is unavailable, you may baptize anyone not
yet validly baptized, including a fetus, provided the person is alive
(cc. 861, §2; 868, §2; 871). Those who had the use of reason at any
time during their life may not be baptized without having manifested
this intention; they must also have some knowledge of the principal
truths of the faith and must promise to observe the commandments of
the Christian religion (c. 865, §2). [Commentary, faculty 5.1, p. 122]

> **PC.** [The following sentence should be added at the beginning of
> the pastoral commentary on faculty 5.1, p. 122]: Normally, a priest
> should baptize in danger of death so that he may confirm the per-
> son immediately afterward, even if an infant (c. 866). [Continue
> with the rest of the pastoral commentary.]

Viaticum (ExM)

6.2 You may celebrate the Rite of Viaticum Outside Mass, except the
parts reserved to a priest or deacon, with at least the presumed permission of the pastor, chaplain, or superior, who must be notified
afterwards (c. 911, §2; PCS 197–211). You may also give Viaticum
to a baptized non-Catholic who is in danger of death, in accord with
the law (c. 844, §§ 3–4). [Commentary, chapter 6, faculty 2.2, p.
161]

Commendation of the Dying (ExM)

6.3 You may celebrate the Rite of Commendation of the Dying (OUI 142; PCS 165, 212–222).

Dispensation from Form and Marriage Impediments

6.4 When one or both parties to a marriage is in urgent danger of death and there is no time to get a dispensation by mail from the local ordinary or from the priest supervisor [even by telephone], you may dispense the parties to marriage both from the form to be observed in the celebration of marriage and from every impediment of ecclesiastical law, whether public or occult, except the impediment arising from the sacred order of the presbyterate. This faculty may be used: (1) for a marriage in the territory of the parish; (2) outside the parish, when either party is a parishioner (c. 1079).

> **TC/EP.** This faculty is based on canon 1079, §2, but here it is a delegated faculty from the local ordinary (c. 1079, §1). The faculty is more restrictive than that given to priests and deacons in canon 1079, §2, since it requires that both the local ordinary and the priest supervisor cannot be reached. This could be made even more restrictive by including the words "even by telephone" in the place indicated, which is recommended. The faculty applies to a marriage of a parishioner or a marriage to be celebrated in the territory of the parish, unlike canon 1079, §2 where it also applies to the priest or deacon who may be summoned to any marriage celebrated according to the extraordinary form of canon 1116.
>
> This faculty is intended only for an emergency so that a member of the faithful may die in peace in a valid marriage. The granting of this faculty is, in a real sense, a matter of justice, lest the faithful who lack a resident pastor also lack the pastoral care and benefits of the law that other Catholics enjoy.
>
> **PC.** [Pastoral commentary, faculty 5.7, pp. 125–126]

7. Mandates Granted by the Priest Supervisor

The introduction and commentaries for this section are the same as those for deacon pastoral administrators, pages 171–174. Only the mandates themselves are given here.

Legal Representation of the Parish

7.1 You may act in my name as the legal representative of the parish in accord with the pertinent laws of Church and State and within the limits of your job description (c. 532).

Pastoral and Finance Councils

7.2 In my absence, you may preside at meetings of the parish pastoral council and finance council (cc. 536 and 537).

Decisions

7.3 You may make decisions necessary for the fulfillment of the duties enumerated in your job description and for implementing an approved pastoral plan or project. The more important decisions, as determined by the priest supervisor, and all decisions adversely affecting the rights of persons require the prior consent of the priest supervisor; but if he cannot be reached, you may decide the matter, which decision must be confirmed by him or the local ordinary.

CHAPTER EIGHT

Offices of the Diocesan Curia

The faculties in this chapter are intended for officials of the diocesan curia. All the faculties may be given to the vicar general, who has many of them anyway in virtue of the law. They could also be given to an episcopal vicar, depending on the extent of his administrative responsibilities; he too has all the faculties of a local ordinary. Faculties the vicar general and episcopal vicar have by law are shown with the abbreviations "VG, EV" in brackets following the faculty. The vicar general and episcopal vicar should at least be granted the delegated faculties in sections 3–6, unless circumstances suggest otherwise.

Separate faculties are suggested for the judicial vicar, the diocesan finance officer, the director of the diocesan worship office, the director of the office for ecumenism, and the vicar for religious. Additionally, many faculties may be delegated to the chancellor or a similar official, depending on how the diocesan curia is organized and on the abilities, especially the knowledge of canon law, of these other officials.

In some dioceses, the vicar general is also a pastor or auxiliary bishop and does not work regularly in the diocesan curia. In other dioceses, the vicar general, though full-time in the curia, has major responsibilities that prevent him from handling routine permissions, dispensations, etc. In such places, the chancellor or another official may be delegated faculties that pertain to the local ordinary by law or that could be granted to him by the bishop.

Most faculties in this chapter grant executive power. These should be delegated to lay officials only when necessary, in particular, when a competent cleric is not available for a specific office in the diocesan curia that can be held by a lay person. (See the discussion on this point in chapter 1, p. 35.) The grant of faculties for diocesan administration is a way that diocesan officials, clerical and lay, cooperate in the exercise of the executive power that pertains by law to the diocesan bishop or other local ordinary.

These lists of faculties should not be confused with a job description. Job descriptions list the duties of office and the powers and rights granted by law. Special faculties granted to officeholders are powers and authorizations beyond the normal faculties of office granted by the law.

Some faculties, which could be delegated, are not on these lists. They are not recommended for delegation but should be reserved to the local ordinary and, occasionally, to the diocesan bishop himself. Some examples of matters that are not included below are permission for the alienation of church property, granting the *imprimatur*, granting the *mandatum* to a professor of theology, dispensing from public impediments and irregularities to ordination or the exercise of orders, the establishment of a juridic person, the approval of statutes of a public juridic person, approval of a diocesan shrine, and reducing a church or shrine to profane use. The bishop could grant a faculty to allow persons within their competence to issue general administrative norms (cc. 31–34). However, as a rule, it is better that binding documents be issued in the name of the bishop or other competent local ordinary rather than by a delegate, even by one who heads a diocesan agency. An exception is made below for the diocesan finance officer, since priests and bishops frequently lack the specialized knowledge required to write detailed instructions and policies on financial affairs.

Some of the following faculties, especially in the sections on the liturgy and ecumenism, were also listed in preceding chapters for priests, deacons, and lay ministers. If all these faculties are granted to these ministers, the same faculties should still be granted to the responsible diocesan officials. At times, the diocesan officials will need to grant them to visiting clergy who do not receive the diocesan *pagella* and for the benefit of the faithful when a pastor or other minister, without sufficient reason, refuses them a sacrament, sacramental, dispensation, or permission.

Commentaries on faculties listed in previous chapters are not repeated, but they are cross-referenced for inclusion on the *pagella*, as may be desired. No commentary is given when it can be presumed the official in question understands the meaning and application of the faculty.

The sample grant of faculties (Appendix II, 10, p. 249) allows the curial officials to delegate the habitual faculties of their office to the person who replaces them when they are absent or impeded. This is the grant of the bishop's *power* to delegate; without it, they could not grant a general delegation to their replacement but only special delegation for individual cases (c. 137, §3).

1. Tribunal Administration

The following list of faculties is intended for the judicial vicar and adjutant judicial vicar(s). If there is no judicial vicar or adjutant judicial vicar who serves full-time in the tribunal, delegating the faculties to the judge who directs the tribunal in their absence would be appropriate. For the adjutant judicial vicar and tribunal director, it may be desirable to condition the grant of faculties as follows: "You may validly use any of the following faculties when the judicial vicar is absent or impeded, or with his permission." This will enable the judicial vicar to exercise as much control as he wishes in keeping with the circumstances (e.g., if he is frequently absent due to other responsibilities).

Although these faculties are intended for use by judicial officials, all of them (except 1.5) are acts of executive power capable of delegation and subdelegation. Since the faculties of this section are intended only for canon lawyers who are knowledgeable about their use, the brief commentaries given elsewhere are, for the most part, unnecessary here.

1.1 You may assign officials in tribunal processes in accord with the law, in particular:

–approving qualified advocates and procurators, also from outside the diocese (c. 1483);

–appointing auditors (c. 1428, §2);

–appointing the promoter of justice in individual cases and substituting the promoter for a just cause (cc. 1430, 1435, 1436, §2);

–appointing the defender of the bond in individual cases and substituting the defender for a just cause (cc. 1432, 1435, 1436, §2);

–determining whether the promoter of justice should intervene in contentious cases (c. 1431, §1);

–appointing judges out of turn (c. 1425, §3);

–committing cases to judgment by a single clerical judge (c. 1425, §4).

1.2 You may execute sentences (c. 1653, §1).

1.3 You may impose and remove prohibitions of marriage (cc. 1077, 1684, §1), and you may grant this faculty by way of general delegation to the other judges of the tribunal [VG, EV].

> **TC.** Since the second instance court can impose the *vetitum* only by attaching it to the sentence (c. 1684, §1), the faculty allows for the imposition of a *vetitum* extrajudicially, even by the first instance court after a second affirmative judgment. This may be useful in some cases. A *vetitum* cannot be imposed by the first instance court, but only recommended. Often, however, the first instance court has a better sense of whether a *vetitum* should be imposed than the second instance court, since it has dealt with the parties and witnesses firsthand. This faculty would give the first instance court the power to impose and remove *vetita* extrajudicially, using the delegated executive power of the local ordinary.

1.4 You may permit a judge or auditor from another tribunal to acquire proofs in the territory of this diocese (c. 1469, §2).

1.5 You may respond as my delegate in a consultation on the admission to an ecclesiastical process of a civilly appointed guardian or curator (c. 1479).

Additional Faculties

Any or all of the special faculties in section 6 below may be added here, if desired.

2. Financial Administration

Any or all of the following faculties may be granted to the diocesan finance officer. Since the canons on which these faculties are based refer to the ordinary (whether diocesan or religious) and not the diocesan bishop, the vicar general and episcopal vicar can exercise them by law, except for faculty 2.7, which would require an explicit delegation unless the applicable particular law already provides for this. Including the commentaries on the list of faculties would be helpful to the financial administrator. Faculties 1, 4, and 9 are authorizations; faculty 3 is mixed; the other faculties grant executive power.

Oversight of Temporal Goods

2.1 In keeping with the directives of the local ordinary and applicable laws, diocesan policies, and customs, you may oversee the administration of all temporal goods of public juridic persons subject to this diocese, notifying the administrators of these goods of any problems, especially regarding budgets and reports, and keeping the vicar general [or bishop, or moderator of the curia] informed of any difficulties and of more important matters (cc. 1276, §1; 1278).

> **TC.** This faculty gives the finance officer the authority to act in everyday affairs, such as, for example, notifying a pastor of a discrepancy on his financial report and asking that it be remedied. The finance officer would not have the power to make a decree to compel the pastor or other administrator to take some action. That would require the intervention of the local ordinary.

Issuing Instructions

2.2 You may issue special instructions to administrators of temporal goods on matters regarding the implementation of the universal law and diocesan policies and customs affecting financial administration (c. 1276, §2).

> **PC.** The instructions (c. 34) must be in accord with the law, whether this is universal or particular law, including diocesan custom.

Presidency of Finance Council

2.3 You may convene and preside over meetings of the diocesan finance council (c. 492, §1).

> **TC.** By delegating this power, the bishop does not lose his rights to convene and preside over meetings of the finance council. Convening the meeting is an exercise of executive power (a decree); the faculty to preside is an authorization.

Trusts and Wills

2.4 You have the faculty of overseeing goods held in trust or left to the Church by will, in keeping with canons 1301 and 1302.

Appointment of Administrator

2.5 If a public juridic person does not have its own administrator, whether by law, custom, the charter of foundation, or its statutes, you may appoint a suitable administrator for a three-year term and reappoint the same person for another term (c. 1279, §2).

> **TC.** The finance officer may also serve as the administrator for the temporal goods of such a juridic person (as, for instance, a diocesan cemetery if it were given juridical personality). See canon 1278.

Lawsuits

2.6 You may grant written permission to an administrator of ecclesiastical goods to initiate or contest a lawsuit in a civil court, except permission for the initiation of a lawsuit by a parish, which is reserved to the local ordinary (c. 1288).

> **TC.** The initiation of a lawsuit by a parish is reserved for two reasons: (1) parishes are central to the identity of the local church itself, in that they are communities of the faithful established in the diocese and under the authority of the bishop (c. 515), and thus a lawsuit by one parish can affect the wider good of the diocese; (2) pastors do not always have sufficient information at hand to make informed decisions in this area. Additional restrictions could be placed on the use of this faculty according to the circumstances of the diocese.

Acts of Extraordinary Administration

2.7 You may grant written permission for acts of extraordinary administration whose value does not exceed _____ [with the exception of], and you may convene and preside over the college of consultors and the finance council, even by conference call, for the sole purpose of requesting their consent, informing the bishop of the outcome (c. 1277).

TC. The purpose of this faculty is to allow the bishop to reserve to himself only the more important acts of extraordinary administration and to allow lesser acts to be approved by the finance officer or vicar general. Exceptions for certain kinds of acts of extraordinary administration could be inserted in the brackets, depending on the desire of the bishop and the circumstances of the diocese.

The bishop could not delegate his power to permit acts of extraordinary administration without also delegating his power to convene the college of consultors and finance council for this purpose (cc. 1277; 502, §2; 492, §1). If the finance officer already has general delegation to convene and preside over meetings of the finance council, then this need not be mentioned again in the above faculty.

It is recommended that permission for an alienation be reserved to the bishop, except perhaps for movable goods whose value does not exceed a specified amount. Such a faculty could be worded: "You may grant written permission for an act of alienation of movable goods whose value does not exceed _____, and you may convene and preside over the college of consultors and finance council, even by conference call, for the sole purpose of requesting their consent, informing the bishop of the outcome (cc. 1290–1295)."

Leases

2.8 You may permit administrators to lease temporal goods belonging to the Church, but not if the annual lease income exceeds [amount in currency] or if the duration of the lease exceeds [. . .] years (c. 1297).

TC. The wording of this faculty depends on the policy of the conference of bishops. In countries where the conference of bishops has left the matter of leasing to the discretion of the diocesan bishop, or has made no policy, the bishop is free to make his own policy (e.g., England and Wales, Ireland, Scotland). For the policies of the English-speaking conferences, see CCLA, Appendix III. Note that, since the decision of the bishops of the U.S.A. on this matter did not receive the *recognitio* of the Holy See, this faculty could also be granted in the dioceses of the U.S.A.

In places where the conference policy requires a favorable vote of the finance council and college of consultors above a certain amount or over a certain number of years (e.g., in Canada), the faculty could not be given, since the finance officer cannot convene a meeting of the college of consultors. In such places, the faculty could be given only up to the maximal amount and/or number of years of the lease. An example of a faculty in accord with the policy of the Canadian bishops is: "You may permit administrators to lease temporal goods, but not if the annual lease is for more than two years." In Canada, if the lease is for more than two years, the norms of canon 1277 or 638, §1 must be applied. Of course, it is possible also to grant to the finance officer the power to convene a meeting of the college of consultors by adding this provision to the faculty: "You may convene and preside over the college of consultors and the finance council, even by conference call, for the sole purpose of requesting their consent, informing the bishop of the outcome."

Investments for Endowments

2.9 After consulting the finance council and other persons concerned, you may make investments of money and movable goods assigned to an endowment, seeing that the revenues respond to the obligations of the endowment (cc. 1304–1305).

> **TC.** This faculty does not allow the finance officer to *accept* a foundation. Since the acceptance of a foundation pertains to the mission of the local church, that should be the decision of the ordinary, whose written permission is required for the validity of acceptance. (See c. 1304, §1.)

3. Institutes of Consecrated Life and Societies of Apostolic Life

The following faculties may be granted to the vicar for religious or an equivalent diocesan official. They could also be granted to the vicar general and episcopal vicar, if they are acquainted with the laws governing institutes of consecrated life and societies of apostolic life. This list contains only *faculties*, not any duties that might be mandated to the vicar for religious, for example, protecting the autonomy of an institute (c. 586, §2) or serving as diocesan liaison with exclaustrated religious (c. 687). Duties should be enumerated in a separate job description. All the faculties grant executive power, unless otherwise specified.

Individual Apostolates

3.1 Upon the recommendation of the major superior, you may permit a member of an institute of consecrated life or society of apostolic life to undertake an apostolate in the diocese. You may also sign the contract with the major superior, without prejudice to the rights of pastors (cc. 678, §3; 713; 738, §2).

> **PC.** Taking on a corporate apostolate by an institute or society, or province or house of the same, is reserved to the bishop, as is the conferral of an ecclesiastical office (cc. 681–682). If the apostolate is to be exercised in a parish context, the pastor is the competent authority to authorize it.

Canonical Erection of Oratories

3.2 You may grant written permission to establish an oratory in the house of a community after first visiting the place and ensuring that it is suitable for the intended purposes (cc. 1224, §1). [VG, EV]

> **PC.** Only formally established houses have a right to an oratory with the reservation of the blessed sacrament (cc. 934, §1, 1°; 608–609; 733). This would not apply to members living in apartments or houses that have not been canonically established or that lack a proper oratory suitable for the celebration and reservation of the Eucharist. Clerical major superiors have the faculty by law to permit the establishment of an oratory in houses of their jurisdiction.

Reservation of the Eucharist

3.3 You may permit the Eucharist to be reserved in a second oratory of a religious house, provided at least some individuals of that house do not have access to the principal oratory (c. 936). [VG, EV]

> **PC.** There might be a second oratory for the sick and disabled, for students, etc. The major superior of a clerical institute or society has this faculty by law.

Use of Oratory

3.4 You may permit a community, in individual instances, to use its oratory or other sacred place for a purpose other than the exercise or promotion of worship, piety, or religion, provided the use is not contrary to the holiness of the place (c. 1210). [VG, EV]

> **PC.** The major superior of a clerical institute or society has this faculty by law.

Suppression of Oratory

3.5 You may issue a decree converting an oratory of a house to profane use (c. 1224, §2). [VG, EV]

> **PC.** Clerical major superiors have this faculty by law.

Confessors

3.6 After consultation with the community, you may approve confessors for monasteries of nuns, houses of formation, and the more numerous lay communities (cc. 630, §3; 734). [VG, EV]

Cloister of Nuns

3.7 For a just cause, you may enter the cloister of monasteries of nuns and, for a grave cause and with the consent of the superior, you may permit others to be admitted to the cloister and allow the nuns to leave it temporarily when it is necessary (c. 667, §4).

> **TC.** This faculty is needed only if there is at least one monastery of cloistered nuns in the diocese. The faculty to enter the cloister is an authorization; granting permission to others to enter or to the nuns to leave is an act of executive power.

Autonomous Monasteries

These faculties are needed only if there is an autonomous monastery and the diocese is the principal see for that monastery.

3.8 You may preside at elections of the superior of an autonomous monastery and confirm the election of the superior in accord with the constitutions (cc. 625, §2; 179).

> **TC.** The faculty to preside at an election is an authorization; the confirmation of the election is an act of executive power.

3.9 You may grant written consent for an act of extraordinary administration and for an alienation, the value of which does not exceed _____, excepting alienation of the monastery itself (cc. 638, §4; 741). [VG, EV]

> **TC.** The amount depends on the proper law of the institute or society and the amount that the bishop can approve in accord with the law of the conference of bishops.

3.10 You may conduct the canonical visitation and, if necessary to enforce universal, particular, or proper law or to resolve a conflict, you may issue precepts or decrees, reporting the facts of the case as soon as possible to the bishop (cc. 628, §2, 1°; 48–58).

> **TC.** A precept or decree may be needed in some situations requiring immediate solutions to correct an abuse or resolve a conflict. The bishop may confirm or revoke the decrees and precepts. The faculty to conduct the visitation is an authorization. Decrees and precepts are acts of executive power.

3.11 You may review the annual financial report of the monastery, notifying both the superior and the local ordinary of any irregularities and, if necessary to enforce universal, particular, or proper law, you may issue precepts or decrees, reporting the facts of the case as soon as possible to the bishop (c. 637). [VG, EV]

> **TC.** The bishop may confirm or revoke the precepts or decrees. The faculty to review the financial report is an authorization. Precepts and decrees are acts of executive power.

Institutes and Societies of Diocesan Right

These faculties are needed only if there is at least one house of an institute or society of diocesan right in the diocese (cc. 589, 594; 732).

3.12 For a just and reasonable cause and taking into account the gravity of the law, you may dispense from norms of the proper law (cc. 595, §2; 732).

> **TC.** Proper law includes the constitutions, directories, and other norms of the institute and its provinces. The canon mentions only the constitutions, but one who can do the greater can do the lesser.

3.13 You may preside at the election of the supreme moderator and confirm the election in accord with the constitutions (cc. 625, §2; 734; 179).

> **TC.** The faculty to preside is an authorization; confirming an election is an act of executive power.

3.14 You may conduct the canonical visitation of houses in the territory of the diocese, including the generalate [or motherhouse], in keeping with the proper law. If necessary to enforce universal, particular, or proper law or to resolve a conflict, you may issue precepts or decrees, reporting the facts of the case as soon as possible to the bishop (cc. 628, §2, 2°; 734; 48–58).

> **TC.** A precept or decree may be needed in some situations requiring immediate solutions, such as, for example, to correct an abuse or resolve a conflict. The bishop may confirm or revoke the decree. The faculty should be reworded if the generalate is not in the diocese. The faculty to conduct the visitation is an authorization; precepts and decrees are acts of executive power.

3.15 For a just cause, you may require, even by decree if necessary, that the financial reports of a house be submitted for your information (c. 637). [VG, EV]

3.16 You may grant written consent for an act of extraordinary administration and for an alienation, the value of which does not exceed _____, but permission for the alienation of a canonically erected house is reserved to the bishop (cc. 638, §4; 741, §1). [VG, EV]

> **TC.** The amount depends on the proper law of the institute or society and the amount that the bishop can approve in accord with the law of the conference of bishops.

3.17 Upon the request of a religious in perpetual vows together with the recommendation of the supreme moderator and the favorable vote of the council, you may extend an indult of exclaustration. You may also grant the indult initially if the request is for a period longer than three years (c. 686, §1).

> **PC.** It belongs to the Apostolic See alone to grant an indult of exclaustration to cloistered nuns.

3.18 You may confirm an indult permitting a religious in temporary vows to leave religious life, provided the house of assignment of the religious is in the diocese (c. 688, §2).

3.19 You may grant a religious in perpetual vows an indult to leave religious life, provided the house of assignment of the religious is in the diocese (c. 691, §2).

3.20 You may grant to a perpetually incorporated member of a society of apostolic life an indult to leave the society, in keeping with the constitutions of the society (c. 727, §1).

4. Regulation of the Sanctifying Function

The following faculties should be granted to the vicar general and episcopal vicar and, according to the circumstances and organization of the diocesan curia, to the chancellor or other responsible official who handles routine canonical matters. Many faculties could also be granted to the director of the diocesan worship office. The faculties concerning the RCIA could be given to the diocesan director of the catechumenate. All the faculties of this section grant executive power except 4.11.

A. INITIATION

Deputation of Catechists

4.1 At the request of the pastor, you may depute catechists, truly worthy and properly prepared, to celebrate the minor exorcisms of the catechumenate and the blessings of the catechumens when a priest or deacon cannot be present (OICA 44, 48, 109, 119; RCIA 12, 16, 91, 97). [Commentary, faculty 1.1, p. 132]

Abbreviated Catechumenate in Exceptional Circumstances

4.2 You may permit the abbreviated rite of initiation of an adult in exceptional circumstances, in particular, sickness, old age, change of residence, long absence for travel, or a depth of Christian conversion and a degree of religious maturity in the catechumen (c. 851, 1°; OICA 240, 274; RCIA USA 331–332, Canada 307–308). [Commentary, faculty 1.2, p. 132]

Dispensation from Scrutinies

4.3 You may dispense from one scrutiny for a serious reason or, in extraordinary circumstances, even from two. The extraordinary circumstances for granting the dispensation from two scrutinies are those mentioned in faculty 4.2 (OICA 52, 66, §3; RCIA 20, 34, §3). [Commentary, faculty 1.3, p. 133]

Rite of Election

4.4 You may permit the Rite of Election or Enrollment of Names when a catechumen or godparent is unable to participate in the rite celebrated by the bishop, to be celebrated in the parish on the first Sunday of Lent, provided it is celebrated on the Sunday before or after the first Sunday of Lent or, if that is impossible, at a weekday Mass during the week before or after the first Sunday of Lent (OICA 44, 138–139; RCIA USA 12, 125–126, Canada 12, 112–113). [Commentary, faculty 1.4, p. 133]

Baptism in a Private Home

4.5 You may permit a minister of baptism to celebrate the sacrament in a private house due to a grave cause (c. 860, §1). [Commentary, faculty 1.6, p. 134] [VG, EV]

Additional Baptismal Font

4.6 You may permit a baptismal font to be placed in another church or oratory within the parish boundaries for the sake of those distant from the parish church, provided the baptism is recorded in the register of the parish (c. 858, §2; RBC 11). [VG, EV]

Extraordinary Minister of Baptism

4.7 You may designate a lay person with the necessary formation to celebrate the rite of baptism [in urgent necessity] when an ordinary minister is absent or impeded (c. 861, §2; EDM art. 11). [VG, EV]

> **TC.** In dioceses where the faculty would not be needed apart from urgent necessity, the words in brackets should be included.

> **PC.** Besides danger of death, another case of urgent necessity is when a scheduled baptism is soon to begin, but the cleric who was supposed to celebrate it is absent or impeded and no other cleric can be found on short notice to replace him. The lay minister should be instructed on how to celebrate the entire rite of baptism, not just what is required for validity.

Faculty to Confirm

4.8 You may grant the faculty to pastors and parochial vicars [and military chaplains] to confirm baptized Catholics who are over the age when children are normally confirmed in the diocese. You may also grant the faculty to a presbyter to confirm baptized Catholic children at the age of [insert normal age or age range for confirmation in the diocese] when the [or a] bishop is unable to be present for the celebration (c. 884, §1; RC 8).

> **TC.** In this faculty, the bishop determines that a case of need arises whenever there are individuals who for one reason or another missed being confirmed when children are normally confirmed in the diocese. This faculty allows the confirmation to be celebrated by a priest in the parish after a formation appropriate to the circumstances of the individual confirmandi. [Additional commentary, faculty 3.1, p. 137]

Delay of Confirmation until After Marriage

4.9 When the preparation of baptized adults for confirmation coincides with preparation for marriage and it is foreseen that the conditions for a fruitful reception of confirmation cannot be satisfied, or if confirmation cannot be conferred without grave inconvenience, you may permit the delay of confirmation until after the marriage (RC 12; c. 1065, §1). [Commentary, faculty 3.2, pp. 137–138] [VG, EV]

Rite of Reception

4.10 You may permit the Rite of Reception into the Full Communion of the Catholic Church to be expanded or shortened to suit the particular circumstances of the persons and place involved (OA 12; RCIA USA 485, Canada 398). For the sign of welcome, you may permit another suitable gesture besides having the celebrant take the hands of the newly received person. (OA 18; RCIA USA 495, Canada 408). [VG, EV]

B. EUCHARIST

Celebret

4.11 You may issue a letter of commendation so that priests may be admitted to celebrate Mass in places where they are not known (c. 903). [VG, EV]

> **TC.** If this faculty is used by any official other than a local ordinary, he should indicate on the celebret that he has been mandated by the bishop to grant it.

Bination and Trination

4.12 For a just cause, you may permit priests to celebrate Mass twice a day and, if required by pastoral necessity, three times on Sundays and holy days of obligation (c. 905, §2). [VG, EV]

Second Mass of the Lord's Supper

4.13 You may permit a pastor to have a second evening Mass of the Lord's Supper on Holy Thursday if any of the following conditions is applicable: (1) there are too many faithful to accommodate at one Mass on Holy Thursday; (2) the pastor has the care of more than one parish, and coming together at a single church is not possible; (3) Mass is celebrated in more than one language, and having a multicultural celebration is not feasible (cf. *Roman Missal*, rubrics for Holy Thursday). You may permit one parish in each deanery to have a celebration of the Lord's Supper earlier in the day, but only if a significant number of the faithful cannot attend the celebration in the evening. [Commentary, faculty 4.3, pp. 139–140] [VG, EV]

> **TC.** In the U.S.A., a second faculty could be added here or in the section on other acts of divine worship below (beginning at 4.34), as follows: "You may permit a second celebration of the Lord's Passion on Good Friday in the same church if the size or nature of

a parish or other community indicates the pastoral need for an additional liturgical service" (*The Sacramentary*, approved for use in the U.S.A., rubrics for Good Friday).

Saturday Trination

4.14 In a case of necessity, you may dispense from canon 905 so a priest can celebrate three Masses on a Saturday, provided that only one Mass is an anticipated Mass of Sunday (c. 87, §1).

> **TC.** This faculty is the delegation of the bishop's power to dispense from a universal disciplinary law. The faculty may be needed due to a lack of priests and the demands of the apostolate, especially for the celebrations of weddings, funerals, etc. Canonically, the anticipated Mass of Sunday is celebrated on Saturday, on which only a bination may be permitted (c. 905, §2); it is not counted as one of the three Masses on Sunday that a priest may be permitted to celebrate, since the canonical day runs from midnight to midnight (c. 202, §1). The restriction on the use of the faculty (only one anticipated Mass) helps to ensure that a true pastoral necessity exists and that anticipated Masses are not being multiplied to the detriment of the Lord's day.

Masses with Children

4.15 You may permit priests to use the adaptations described in nn. 38–54 of the Directory for Masses with Children at a Mass celebrated with adults in which children also participate, if the Mass is intended primarily for the benefit of children or for families with children (Directory for Masses with Children 19). [Commentary, faculty 1.2, p. 110]

Alternate Mass Texts

4.16 In cases of serious need or pastoral advantage, you may permit a priest to celebrate an appropriate Mass other than the Mass of the day except on solemnities, the days of the Easter octave, All Souls, Ash Wednesday, during Holy Week, and on the Sundays of Advent, Lent, and Easter (GIRM 374).

Infirm Priests

4.17 You may permit an infirm or elderly priest to celebrate the Eucharist publicly while seated (c. 930, §1). [Commentary, faculty 1.4, p. 111] [VG, EV]

Communion Under Both Kinds

4.18 You may permit priests to administer communion under both kinds whenever it is appropriate (GIRM 283c). [Commentary, faculty 1.3, p. 110]

Reservation of the Eucharist

4.19 You may permit the Eucharist to be reserved in an oratory or private chapel, provided it is foreseen that Mass will be celebrated there at least twice a month (c. 934). You may permit the Eucharist to be reserved in a second oratory of a house of a religious institute or another pious house, provided at least some individuals of that house do not have access to the principal oratory (c. 936). [VG, EV]

> **PC.** There might be a second oratory for the sick and disabled, for students, etc. Only formally established houses of a religious institute or society of apostolic life have a right to an oratory with the reservation of the blessed sacrament (cc. 934, §1, 1°; 608–609; 733). This would not apply to religious or others living in houses that have not been canonically established, or to any house that lacks a proper oratory suitable for the celebration and reservation of the Eucharist.

Eucharistic Procession

4.20 You may permit a parish or other community of the faithful to have a public procession in which the Eucharist is carried through the streets solemnly with singing on the solemnity of the Body and Blood of Christ, but this may not be done unless the dignity of the procession is assured (HCWE 101–102; c. 944).

Extraordinary Ministers of Communion

4.21 You may appoint suitably instructed lay persons for a term of one to three years to serve as extraordinary ministers of holy communion, both at Mass and outside Mass, whenever it is necessary for the pastoral benefit of the faithful and sufficient ordinary ministers [or instituted acolytes] are lacking or unavailable (HCWE 17; c. 230, §3; EDM art. 8, §1). You may delegate the pastor or another priest to preside at the Rite of Commissioning Special Ministers of Holy Communion. [Commentary, faculty 4.1, pp. 138–139]

> **TC.** The diocesan bishop appoints extraordinary ministers of holy communion (EDM art. 8, §1). The Rite of Commissioning Special Ministers of Communion, no. 1, says that the local ordinary or his delegate is to preside at the rite of commissioning. The priest celebrant has the faculty by law to appoint extraordinary ministers for an individual celebration when there are not enough ordinary or extraordinary ministers (GIRM 162).

Lay Minister of Exposition

4.22 In the absence of a priest, deacon, instituted acolyte, or extraordinary minister of communion, you may appoint another person to expose publicly the Eucharist for the adoration of the faithful, and afterward to repose it (c. 943). [VG, EV]

C. PENANCE AND ANOINTING OF THE SICK

Grant of Faculty to Hear Confessions

4.23 In accord with canons 970–973, you may grant the faculty to hear confessions to priests with domicile and quasi-domicile in the diocese and to extern priests in good standing for the duration of their stay in the diocese (c. 969, §1). [VG, EV]

> **TC.** A citation or summary of canons 970–973 could be included here as a pastoral commentary, if desired. Revocation of faculties is fittingly reserved to the bishop himself.

General Absolution

4.24 After judging that the conditions of canon 961, §1, 2° are satisfied in keeping with the apostolic letter *Misericordia Dei* and diocesan policy, you may permit a priest to celebrate the Rite of Reconciliation of Several Penitents with General Confession and Absolution (c. 961, §2).

> **TC.** The cases indicated in the diocesan policy, established in accord with the criteria of the conference of bishops, could be added in a pastoral commentary. An English translation of Pope John Paul II's April 7, 2002, *motu proprio, Misericordia Dei*, may be found in *Origins* 32 (2002) 13–16.

Communal Celebration of Anointing

4.25 You may permit the celebration of the anointing of the sick for several of the sick together in a sacred place or other suitable place, provided there is previous instruction on the eligibility requirements for the sacrament, in particular, that the recipients must be seriously ill or notably weakened due to old age. You may also designate other priests to anoint at these times (PCS 108; OUI 83). [Commentary, faculty 6, pp. 141–142]

D. MARRIAGE

Permission to Marry

4.26 According to the circumstances, you may grant permission for the following marriages upon the recommendation of the pastor or the minister who will be assisting at the marriage. If the pastor or minister does not recommend that the marriage be permitted, the case must be referred to the local ordinary. [VG, EV]

> **PC.** If you judge that the marriage may be permitted but the pastor or other priest or deacon refuses to assist, or if you judge that the marriage may not be permitted, the case must be referred to the local ordinary. (This is to help ensure that the natural right to marry is not unduly restricted.) Permissions are also reserved to the local ordinary for placing a condition on consent to marry (c. 1102, §§ 2, 3) or for a secret marriage (c. 1130).

a. You may permit a mixed marriage (cc. 1124–1125), in keeping with the policy of the [name of the conference of bishops].

> **TC.** The policy of the conference of bishops could be included under the faculty. For policies in English-speaking countries, see CCLA, Appendix III.

b. You may permit a Catholic to marry a person who has notoriously rejected the Catholic faith, if canon 1125 has been observed (c. 1071, §1, 4° and §2).

> **PC.** A limitation is placed on the faculty, in that the permission may be granted only in favor of the natural right of the faithful Catholic party to marry. Permission should not be given for a mixed marriage of a non-Catholic and a Catholic who has notoriously rejected the faith, nor should it be given to two Catholics who both have notoriously rejected the Catholic faith. Doubtful cases must be referred to the local ordinary.

c. You may permit a marriage of transients, if proof of baptism is available and freedom to marry has been shown by documentary evidence or sworn affidavits (cc. 1071, §1, 1°; 876).

> **PC.** If proof of baptism or freedom to marry cannot be demonstrated, the case must be referred to the local ordinary who will determine whether the marriage can proceed or whether further investigations may be necessary.

d. You may permit a marriage that cannot be recognized or celebrated in the civil law due to [give the reason(s) for which permission may be granted, if any] (c. 1071, §1, 2°).

> **TC.** The faculty should not be delegated if there are no reasons acceptable to the local ordinary.

e. You may permit a marriage of a person who is bound by natural obligations to another party or to children of a previous union, provided there are assurances that these obligations are being observed and there is no evidence to the contrary (c. 1071, §1, 3°).

> **PC.** The case must be referred to the local ordinary if there are not sufficient assurances from the party that the obligations are being met or if there is any evidence from another source that the obligations are not being met.

f. You may permit a marriage of a person who is under a censure to another Catholic party, provided there is a serious reason for the marriage and the faith of the Catholic not under censure is protected (c. 1071, §1, 5°).

> **PC.** Since a person under censure is barred from receiving the sacraments (cc. 1331–1332), this permission should be granted only to favor the natural right to marry of the Catholic party who is not under censure. The other restrictions on the faculty are rooted in the canonical tradition. (See commentaries on c. 1066 of the 1917 code.) In doubt as to whether the conditions are met, the case

must be referred to the local ordinary. If the censure has been imposed or declared, granting the permission would not be advisable unless there is an urgent reason for celebrating the marriage before the censure can be remitted.

g. You may permit a marriage of a minor when the parents do not know about it or are reasonably opposed to it (c. 1071, §1, 6°).

h. You may permit a proxy marriage in accord with canon 1105 (c. 1071, §1, 7°).

Special Delegation to Assist at Marriage

4.27 After consulting the pastor of the territory where the marriage is to take place, you may grant special delegation for assisting at marriage (cc. 1111). [VG, EV]

> **TC.** Since the pastor, as well as other priests and deacons with general delegation in the parish, can grant special delegation, this faculty will be needed only for exceptional cases. It is recommended that the grant of *general* delegation to non-parochial ministers be reserved to the local ordinaries, as this may infringe on parochial rights.

Dispensation from Canonical Form

4.28 You may dispense from canonical form for a mixed marriage or for a marriage between a Catholic and a party who has formally defected from the Catholic faith provided grave difficulties are hindering the observance of canonical form, such as the need to maintain family harmony, to obtain parental agreement to the marriage, to recognize the religious commitment of the non-Catholic party, to recognize the relationship of the non-Catholic party with the non-Catholic minister who will do the wedding, [additional reasons from the policy of the conference of bishops should be added here] (c. 1127, §2; DAPNE 154). [VG, EV]

TC. The reasons given in the faculty are from no. 154 of the Directory for the Application of the Principles and Norms on Ecumenism. Although canon 1127 speaks only of the dispensation for a mixed marriage, the local ordinary may also dispense from the canonical form if a Catholic is marrying someone who has defected from the Catholic faith. (See Pontifical Commission for the Interpretation of the Decrees of Vatican Council II, 11 February 1972, AAS 64 (1972) 397; CLD 7:750.)

Dispensations from Impediments to Marry

4.29 You may dispense from all impediments of ecclesiastical law except those reserved to the Apostolic See (c. 1078, §1), those that may not be dispensed, and the impediments of age and consanguinity in the third degree, which are reserved solely to the diocesan bishop. [VG, EV]

TC. It is recommended that the impediments of age and consanguinity in the third degree be reserved to the bishop himself.

PC. The minimal age for valid marriage (sixteen for males and fourteen for females) is so low that only the bishop himself is to judge whether the impediment may be dispensed. The dispensation from consanguinity in the third degree (uncle marries niece or aunt marries nephew) is reserved to the bishop himself, given the potential for grave scandal and other harm. The impediments of ecclesiastical law that may be dispensed are: disparity of worship (c. 1086), abduction (c. 1089), consanguinity in the fourth degree (c. 1091, §2), affinity (1092), public propriety (c. 1093), and legal relationship (c. 1094).

Dispensations in Urgent Cases

4.30 Whenever an impediment is discovered after everything has already been prepared for the wedding, and the marriage cannot be delayed without probable danger of grave harm until a dispensation is obtained from the competent authority, you may dispense from all impediments, including those reserved to the Apostolic See, except prior bond, impotence, consanguinity in the direct line and the second degree of the collateral line, sacred orders, and a public, perpetual vow of chastity in a religious institute of pontifical right (c. 1080). [VG, EV]

Dispensations in Danger of Death

4.31 If danger of death threatens, you may dispense from the canonical form and from all impediments of the ecclesiastical law, including those reserved to the Apostolic See, except the impediment of presbyteral orders (c. 1079, §1). [VG, EV]

> **PC.** A dispensation is never given from the impediments of impotence, prior bond, or consanguinity in the direct line or the second degree of the collateral line (cc. 1078, §3; 1084; 1085; 1091, §2). The dispensation to permit a priest to marry is reserved to the Apostolic See and can be obtained by fax in danger of death through the Congregation for Divine Worship and Discipline of the Sacraments.

Place of Marriage

4.32 You may permit a marriage to be celebrated in a church or oratory other than the parish church, or you may permit it to be celebrated in another suitable place (cc. 1115, 1118, §§ 1, 2). [VG, EV]

> **PC.** No permission is necessary to celebrate a *non-sacramental* marriage in a suitable place besides a Catholic church (c. 1118, §3), nor is any permission necessary if a dispensation from canonical form has been granted.

Special Marriage Cases

4.33 [Any or all of the special faculties in section 6 below may be added here, if desired.]

E. Other Acts of Divine Worship

Blessings

4.34 You may permit competent ministers and catechists to celebrate blessings from the *Book of Blessings* that are not reserved to a priest or deacon, provided enough priests and deacons [or instituted acolytes or readers] are unavailable (DB and BB 18d). [Commentary, faculty 8.1, p. 145] [VG, EV]

Exorcism

4.35 In the absence of the bishop and in an urgent case, you may permit an approved priest to perform an exorcism. (Cf. c. 1172; nn. 13–19 of *De Exorcismis et supplicationibus quibusdam*).

> **TC.** Although canon 1172 allows the local ordinary to give this faculty, *De Exorcismis et supplicationibus quibusdam*, no. 13, says that the diocesan bishop himself, as a rule, should grant the faculty. The priest who is granted the permission in an individual instance should be approved by the bishop for this ministry and have the necessary qualities and formation required by law.

Funeral of Unbaptized Children

4.36 You may permit church funeral rites for children who died before baptism, provided at least one parent had intended to have them baptized (c. 1183, §2). [VG, EV]

Funeral of Baptized Non-Catholic

4.37 You may permit the celebration of the Church's funeral rites for a validly baptized member of another church or ecclesial community, provided this would not be contrary to the wishes of the deceased person and provided the minister of the deceased person is unavailable (c. 1183, §3, DAPNE 120). [Commentary, faculty 8.3, pp. 145–146] [VG, EV]

Funeral with Cremated Remains

4.38 You may permit a priest or deacon [or lay minister, where permitted] to celebrate the funeral liturgy in the presence of the cremated remains of a deceased person, taking into account the concrete circumstances in each individual case, and always observing the following conditions: (1) There is no anti-Christian motive for choosing cremation (c. 1176, §3). (2) The cremated remains will be handled with respect and buried or entombed in a place reserved for this purpose. (3) There is no other canonical prohibition of a funeral liturgy, namely, for notorious apostates, heretics, and schismatics and other manifest sinners for whom ecclesiastical funerals cannot be granted without public scandal to the faithful (c. 1184). [Commentary, faculty 8.4, p. 146]

Dispensation from the Obligation of the Divine Office

4.39 In particular cases and for a just cause, you may dispense a cleric from the obligation of reciting the divine office either in whole or in part, or you may commute it to another obligation. (*Sacrosanctum Concilium* 97; c. 87, §1). [VG, EV]

Sunday Celebrations Without a Priest

4.40 You may appoint a deacon or, if there is no deacon, a lay minister who has had the necessary formation to preside at the liturgy of the word, morning prayer, or evening prayer at which holy communion is distributed in accord with the approved rite when no priest is available to celebrate Mass. This may be done only for the benefit of the faithful who are unable to go to another church for the Eucharist; it may not be done more than once a day in any one place, or when there is another Mass scheduled that day (DSCAP 24; EDM art. 7; c. 1248, §2) [Commentary, faculty 9.1, p. 147]

Vows and Oaths

4.41 You may dispense from private vows, provided the dispensation does not injure the acquired rights of others. You may dispense from promissory oaths, unless dispensation from an oath would tend to harm one or other persons who refuse to remit its obligation. You may commute the obligation of a private vow or oath to a lesser good (cc. 1196, 1°; 1203). [VG, EV]

F. SACRED PLACES AND TIMES

Restoration of Precious Images

4.42 After consulting experts, you may grant permission for the restoration of precious images exhibited in churches or oratories for the reverence of the faithful (c. 1189). [VG, EV]

Delegation to Bless a Sacred Place

4.43 You may delegate a presbyter to bless a sacred place, except for churches and altars in churches, including shrine churches (c. 1207). [VG, EV]

> **PC.** The blessing or dedication of a church and its altar is reserved to the bishop.

Establishment of an Oratory

4.44 After inspecting the place and finding it suitable for worship, you may grant written permission for the establishment of an oratory with the condition that it may not be used for any rites of the RCIA, infant baptism, confirmation, reception into full communion of the

Catholic Church, first holy communion, and, unless permitted by the proper pastor or local ordinary, marriages and funerals (cc. 1224, §1; 1225). [VG, EV]

Establishment of a Private Chapel

4.45 After inspecting the place and finding it suitable for its intended purposes, you may grant permission for the establishment of a private chapel and for the celebration of Mass and other liturgical celebrations there, except all rites of the RCIA, infant baptism, confirmation, reception into full communion of the Catholic Church, first holy communion, marriages, and funerals (c. 1226). [VG, EV]

Use of Sacred Places

4.46 You may permit, in individual instances, that a sacred place may be used for a purpose other than the exercise or promotion of worship, piety, or religion, provided the use is not contrary to the holiness of the place (c. 1210). [VG, EV]

Blessing of Cemetery

4.47 You may permit a priest to bless the cemetery of a juridic person or a family (c. 1241, §2).

> **PC.** No permission is needed if the cemetery belongs to a parish or a religious institute.

Desecration of a Sacred Place

4.48 If the local ordinary is absent or impeded, you may judge whether gravely harmful actions have violated a sacred place with scandal to the faithful, observing canon 1211. [VG, EV]

Reduction to Profane Use

4.49 Upon the request of the competent person and for a just cause, you may decree that an oratory or a private chapel and the altars in them be converted to profane use (cc. 1224, §2; 1212); you may decree the same for a cemetery belonging to a family or to a juridic person other than the diocese or a parish. [VG, EV]

> **PC.** The competent person is the representative of the juridic person that has ownership or canonical control of the oratory, or the physical or juridic person with ownership or juridical control of the private chapel or cemetery. A decree against the will of such persons is reserved to the local ordinary, as are cases involving churches, shrines, the altars in them, and cemeteries belonging to the diocese or to a parish.

Feast Days and Days of Penance

4.50 In particular cases and for a just cause, you may dispense residents of the diocese anywhere they are, and others who are in the parish territory, from the obligations to attend Mass and abstain from work on Sundays and holy days of obligation, or you may commute the obligation to another pious work. Under the same conditions, you may dispense from or commute the obligations of fast and abstinence on a day of penance (c. 1245).

5. Ecumenism

These faculties are intended for the vicar general, episcopal vicar, and the director of the diocesan office for ecumenism. If appropriate, faculties related to liturgical matters could be given to the director of the liturgy office. These faculties may also be given to the chancellor or another official, in keeping with local circumstances and the organization of the curia. A few faculties from section 4 are repeated here, as they are ecumenical in nature. All the faculties of this section grant executive power.

Delegates to Ecumenical Dialogues

5.1 You may give a mandate to a competent Catholic theologian to represent the Catholic Church in an official ecumenical dialogue (DAPNE 175). [VG, EV]

Ecumenical Meetings

5.2 (1) You may permit Catholic clergy and those with pastoral responsibility in the diocese to take part in inter-confessional meetings aimed at improving reciprocal relationships and at trying to resolve pastoral problems together (DAPNE 91b). (2) You may determine which other kinds of ecumenical meetings are suitable for Catholic participation (DAPNE 164). (3) You may authorize Catholics to participate in ecumenical exchanges or dialogues arranged by groups of lay people, clergy, professional theologians, or by various combinations of these (DAPNE 174).

Use of Church, Liturgical Items, Cemetery

5.3 If priests, ministers, or communities not in full communion with the Catholic Church do not have a place or the liturgical objects necessary for celebrating worthily their religious ceremonies, you may allow them the temporary use of the church and lend them what may be necessary. Permission for long-term use beyond a year is reserved to the bishop. In similar circumstances, you may give them permission for internment or for the celebration of services in a Catholic cemetery (DAPNE 137).

Use of Catholic Schools

5.4 With the consent of the school principal or other competent administrator, you may permit the clergy of other Christian denominations to use a Catholic school or other facilities, including the church or chapel, for spiritual and sacramental ministration to their own faithful who attend such schools or institutions (DAPNE 142).

Participation of Christian Minister at Catholic Baptism

5.5 For pastoral reasons, in particular circumstances, you may permit a Catholic minister to invite a minister of another church or ecclesial community to take part in the celebration of baptism by reading a lesson, offering a prayer, or the like. The actual baptism is to be celebrated by the Catholic minister alone (DAPNE 97). [Commentary, faculty 1.7, p. 135] [VG, EV]

Conditional Baptism

5.6 You may determine, in individual cases, what rites are to be included or excluded in conditional baptism (OA 7, RCIA USA 480, Canada 393). [Commentary, faculty 2.1, pp. 135–136] [VG, EV]

Reader at Mass

5.7 On exceptional occasions and for a just cause, you may permit a Catholic minister to invite a member of another church or ecclesial community to be a reader at the Eucharist (DAPNE 133). [Commentary, faculty 3.1, p. 116]

Mass in a Church of Another Denomination

5.8 For a just cause, you may permit a priest to celebrate the Eucharist in the church of another Christian denomination, provided there is no scandal (c. 933). [VG, EV]

> **PC.** Since the canon speaks only of permitting Mass in the place of worship of another church or ecclesial community, it excludes

non-Christian places of worship. Permission is not needed for a nondenominational chapel in the military, in a hospital, etc.

Sacramental Sharing in Cases of Grave Need

5.9 Observing the conditions of canon 844, §4, you may permit Catholic ministers to administer the sacraments of penance, Eucharist, and anointing of the sick to validly baptized persons who live in areas or institutions where they do not have regular access to a minister of their own. [Additional cases can be listed here as determined by the conference of bishops or diocesan bishop.] [Commentary, faculty 3.2, pp. 116–117]

Permission for Mixed Marriage

5.10 After the conditions of canon 1125 have been fulfilled, you may, for a just and reasonable cause, permit a mixed marriage between a Latin Catholic and a baptized non-Catholic (c. 1124). [Commentary, faculty 7.1, pp. 142–143] [VG, EV]

Participation of Non-Catholic Minister at Wedding

5.11 Upon the request of the couple, you may permit the minister who assists at a mixed marriage in the Catholic church to invite the minister of the party of the other church or ecclesial community to participate in the celebration of marriage, to read from the scriptures, to give a brief exhortation, and/or to bless the couple (DAPNE 158).

Mixed Marriage at Eucharist

5.12 Because of problems concerning eucharistic sharing that may arise from the presence of non-Catholic witnesses and guests, a mixed marriage between a Catholic and an Anglican [Episcopalian] or

Protestant ordinarily should not take place during the eucharistic liturgy. For a just cause, however, you may permit the celebration of the Eucharist, provided the non-Catholic party comes from a eucharistic tradition and truly agrees to it, after being informed that the non-Catholic guests may not be invited to holy communion. When the conditions of canon 844, §4 are fulfilled, however, you may permit the Anglican or Protestant party to receive holy communion (OCM 36; DAPNE 159). [Commentary, faculty 7.3, pp. 143–144]

Mixed Marriage Outside Church or Oratory

5.13 You may permit a marriage to be celebrated outside the parish church of either party in another church or oratory or another suitable place. This faculty can be used only if the marriage takes place in the territory of the diocese (c. 1118, §§ 1, 2). [VG, EV]

Dispensation from Disparity of Worship

5.14 Provided the conditions of canons 1125 and 1126 have been fulfilled, you may dispense from the impediment of disparity of worship. [VG, EV]

Dispensation from Canonical Form

5.15 [Insert faculty 4.28 above.] [VG, EV]

Participation of Catholic Minister in Wedding at Non-Catholic Church

5.16 You may permit a Catholic priest or deacon to attend or participate in some way in the celebration of a mixed marriage in another Christian church, provided a dispensation from canonical form is also granted (DAPNE 157). [VG, EV]

PC. The priest or deacon may offer appropriate prayers, read from the scriptures, give a brief exhortation, and/or bless the couple. However, he may not receive the consent of the parties.

Funeral of Baptized Non-Catholic

5.17 You may permit the celebration of the Church's funeral rites for a validly baptized member of another church or ecclesial community, provided this would not be contrary to the wishes of the deceased person and provided the minister of the deceased person is unavailable (c. 1183, §3; DAPNE 120). [Commentary, faculty 8.3, pp. 145–146] [VG, EV]

6. Special Marriage Cases

The following faculties require specialized canonical knowledge, so they should be granted only to a canonist or a person who is otherwise expert in the law and procedures. Given the complexity of these matters, no brief commentary is offered. Faculties 1, 5, and 6 are authorizations; the other faculties grant executive power.

6.1 You may process cases for the Pauline Privilege, including making the interpellation (cc. 1143–1147). [VG, EV]

6.2 For a grave cause, you may dispense from the interpellation in accord with canon 1144, §2. [VG, EV]

6.3 For a grave cause, you may permit the converted party who uses the Pauline Privilege to marry a non-Catholic (c. 1147). [VG, EV]

6.4 You may issue a declaration of presumed death of a spouse (c. 1707).

6.5 You may process *ratum et non consummatum* cases (c. 1700).

6.6 You may instruct the process for the dissolution of marriage in favor of the faith (CDF Norms, April 30, 2001, arts. 3, 11).

6.7 In the absence of the bishop, you may grant a *sanatio in radice* in accord with canon 1165, §2.

7. Additional Faculties

The following faculties may be delegated to the vicar general, episcopal vicar, and/or various other diocesan officials according to the nature of the faculty and the customs and needs of the diocese. The canons are clustered according to the book of the code to which they pertain. All the faculties of this section except faculty 7.21 grant executive power.

Book I: General Norms

7.1 You may grant diocesan faculties to visiting clergy in good standing for no more than three months. Regarding those who have domicile or quasi-domicile in the diocese, when the bishop is absent or impeded, you may grant the habitual faculties on the respective diocesan *pagellae* to priests, pastors, parochial vicars, chaplains, rectors of churches, deacons, lay ministers, and [name additional offices or ministries] (c. 137, §1).

> **TC.** With respect to clerics with domicile or quasi-domicile in the diocese, it is better that the bishop personally signs the grant of faculties, as explained in chapter 2. However, delegating another person for those occasions when he is absent or impeded would be useful.
>
> **PC.** You may grant the diocesan faculties to clerics who are *peregrini*, that is, who intend to stay in the diocese for less than three

months. For those who intend to establish domicile or quasi-domicile, you may grant the faculties only when the bishop is absent or impeded, informing him afterward.

7.2 Besides the dispensations you may grant in virtue of this *pagella* of faculties, when the bishop is absent or impeded, or in an urgent case, you may dispense from other universal disciplinary laws for a just and reasonable cause after taking into account the circumstances of the case and the gravity of the law. If the dispensation is reserved, you may dispense only if recourse to the Holy See is difficult and there would be grave harm in delay, provided that the Holy See is accustomed to granting the dispensation under the same circumstances (cc. 87, 90).

7.3 You may dispense from diocesan laws and, as often as you judge that a dispensation will contribute to the good of the faithful, from laws passed by a plenary or provincial council or by the conference of bishops, observing canon 90 (c. 88). [VG, EV]

7.4 You may execute rescripts for which the local ordinary is the executor (c. 68). [VG, EV]

7.5 You may extend for three months, but only once, any rescripts granted by the Apostolic See that have expired (c. 72).

7.6 You may grant permission for persons to transfer their church *sui iuris*, provided the Eastern Catholic church *sui iuris* (the one from which or to which a person is transferring) has an eparchial bishop in the territory, who also must grant his permission to effect the transfer. (CCEO, c. 32, §2, which also applies in the Latin Church; see AAS 85 [1993] 81.)

TC. If this faculty is given, a list of Eastern churches that have an eparchy in the territory should be appended. Even if there is only one eparch (or equivalent) in the entire country, he has jurisdiction over all the Eastern faithful of his church *sui iuris* in that country. The official using this faculty should mention in the grant of permission that he is acting as the bishop's delegate.

Book II: The People of God

7.7 You may appoint spiritual directors for the seminarians of the diocese (c. 239, §2).

7.8 You may admit qualified candidates to the seminary (c. 241, §1).

7.9 During the academic year of the seminary and especially during vacation periods, you may determine suitable pastoral activities for the seminarians, adapted to the age of the students and to local conditions and under the supervision of a skilled priest (c. 258). [VG, EV]

7.10 You may decide the place and manner of the retreat for candidates for holy orders (c. 1039).

TC. The above four faculties could be granted to the rector of the seminary, if desired, or to someone in a similar position.

No model faculties are given for dispensing intervals between ministries and orders and for dispensing from impediments and irregularities to ordination or the exercise of orders. These matters should be reserved to the diocesan bishop (or major superior), since they involve judgments about the suitability of a man for the ordained ministry.

Although faculty 7.10 is based on a canon of Book IV of the code, its placement here together with faculties 7.7 to 7.9 is more logical than in the faculties for the sanctifying function.

7.11 In keeping with the statutes of a diocesan public association of the faithful, you may confirm as moderator the person elected by the association, or you may install the one presented, or you may appoint the moderator. You may also appoint the chaplain or ecclesiastical assistant, having heard the major officials of the association when this is expedient (c. 317, §1).

7.12 In special circumstances, where grave reasons require it, you may designate a trustee for a diocesan public association of the faithful (c. 318, §1).

7.13 You may approve the statutes, or amendments to them, of a diocesan private association of the faithful (c. 322, §2).

7.14 You may confirm the choice of a priest as spiritual advisor chosen by a diocesan private association of the faithful (c. 324, §2). [VG, EV]

7.15 You may appoint notaries and [name other lesser offices] for the diocesan curia (cc. 470, 157).

> TC. This faculty would be limited to the offices in the "executive branch" of the curia if a comparable faculty is granted to the judicial vicar to appoint notaries and lesser officials for the tribunal.

7.16 In the absence of the bishop, you may install pastors in office; for a just cause, you may dispense from the installation (c. 527, §2). [VG, EV]

7.17 You may appoint chaplains for [hospitals, nursing homes, migrants, sea journeys, houses of lay institutes of consecrated life and societies of apostolic life, associations of the faithful, etc.] (cc. 565–568). [VG, EV]

> **TC.** The wording of this faculty depends on the apostolates in the diocese for which chaplains are appointed by the local ordinary.

Book III: The Teaching Function of the Church

7.18 You may grant to a competent lay person, including lay members of institutes of consecrated life and societies of apostolic life, the faculty to preach in churches and oratories in accord with the law (c. 766).

> **TC.** Pertinent provisions of the diocesan policy and/or the policy of the conference of bishops may be inserted with this faculty as commentary.

7.19 You may appoint teachers of religion in Catholic schools (c. 805). [VG, EV]

7.20 If the bishop is absent or impeded for more than a month, you may grant the *mandatum* to a professor to teach the sacred sciences in institutes of higher studies and ecclesiastical universities and faculties; the *mandatum* must be confirmed by the bishop to remain valid (cc. 812, 818, 229, §3).

> **TC.** Normally, the bishop himself should grant the *mandatum*. This faculty allows for temporary provision to be made if the bishop is absent or impeded for more than a month. After the bishop confirms the decree granting the *mandatum*, it remains valid for the rest of the professor's career, unless revoked by the competent authority.

7.21 In the absence of the bishop or other responsible official, you may administer the profession of faith and oath of fidelity to all those mentioned in canon 833, nn. 4–6. [VG, EV]

Book VI: Sanctions in the Church

7.22 Unless it is reserved to the Apostolic See, you may remit a non-declared, *latae sententiae* penalty incurred by a subject of the diocese and anyone who committed the offense in the territory of the diocese (c. 1355, §2). [VG, EV]

> **TC.** It is recommended that the remission of penalties that have been declared or imposed be reserved to the bishop himself.

> **PC.** Subjects of the diocese are those with domicile or quasi-domicile in the diocese as well as transients *(vagi)* present in the diocese. The remission of penalties that have been imposed or declared is reserved to the bishop.

APPENDICES

Authorizations in Canon Law

An authorization is a category for any faculty other than a faculty for the exercise of the power of governance. The list below demonstrates that a variety of terms are used in canon law to indicate an authorization. The words are in the promulgated version of a law, usually in Latin. The promulgated version of the Directory for the Application of the Principles and Norms on Ecumenism is in French. After each word is an English translation, followed on the next line by the canon number or number of another document in which the word is found. The cited norms are taken from those used in this book in the various lists of faculties; there are many other examples of these and similar words elsewhere in the Code of Canon Law and in other sources of law.

While canon law uses a variety of words to indicate the grant of a faculty that is an authorization, these same words can be used for other kinds of juridic acts. The word "to permit," for example, can sometimes indicate a singular administrative act granting a faculty that is an authorization, or it could be one that grants a favor. Sometimes, a permission can be granted by a general act (a law or a general executory decree). Or it could even be a judicial act, a permission granted by a judge in a church tribunal. Consequently, the words on the list below are not used exclusively for the grant of a faculty that is an authorization, but they are used this way in the sources cited. When used elsewhere in canon law, the act indicated by these words can be determined only by examining the original law in which the word is found and identifying the nature of the act by which the permission is being granted.

It should also be noted that many of these same words, used from a different viewpoint, can indicate executive power of governance. It depends on who is the subject of the verb. For example, with the word "to permit," if the bishop is permitting a minister to do something, he is authorizing the minister to perform an act. The one who does the permitting (the bishop) is exercising executive power of governance. In other words, the act of granting the permission is an act of executive power; the use of the authorization for some ministerial, liturgical, or other act is not an act of power of governance.

Diocesan faculties that are authorizations may not be subdelegated to others, with the notable exception of the faculty to assist at marriage. Faculties that are for the executive power of governance may be delegated and subdelegated, unless the one delegating the faculty has excluded subdelegation.

admittere, to admit, permit, allow
    Canon 766

autorisation, authorization
    DAPNE 157

concedere, to grant, to allow, to permit
    Canons 884; 905, §2; 970; 971; 972; 973; 1125; EDM art. 10, §§ 1, 3

conferre, to grant, to confer
    Canon 969

concessio, grant, concession
    Canon 967, §3

consentement, consent, approval
    DAPNE 91b

consensus, consent, permission
    OCM 36

delegare, to delegate
    Canons 1111, 1112, §1; EDM arts. 8, §1; 10, §1

delegatio, delegation
    Canon 1113; EDM art. 8, §§ 1, 2

deputare, to depute
    Canon 910, §2; 943; HCWE 91; OICA 48, 109; OE 19

deputatio, deputation
    Canon 230, §2; OICA 44

designare, to designate
    EDM art. 11

donare, to give, to grant
    Canon 966, §2

licentia, permission, authorization
    Canons 930, §1; 933; 1071, §§ 1, 2; 1118, §1; 1124; 1125

mandatum, mandate
    EDM art. 7, §1

permettre, to permit, to allow
    DAPNE 97, 158, 159

permissio, permission
    OICA 274

permittere, to permit, to allow
    Canons 858, §2; 860, §1; 1118, §2; 1183, §2; Directory for Children's
    Masses 19; OICA 240

tribuere, to grant, allow, concede
    DB 18d

Sample Documents

1. GRANT OF FACULTIES TO PRIESTS

See chapter 4 for the faculties that are to accompany this document.

I have the pleasure of granting to you, [name of the priest], the enclosed faculties for priests and confessors in the Diocese of [name of the diocese]. This list of faculties replaces any previous list of diocesan faculties for priests granted by me, my predecessors, or any other diocesan official.

1. Unless otherwise noted, you may **not** validly subdelegate these faculties.

2. Unless otherwise noted, you may use these faculties only within the territory of the diocese.

3. These faculties remain in force as long as you retain your domicile or quasi-domicile in this diocese, unless they are expressly revoked.

Given at _____ this .... day of .... [year].

_____
Signature of Bishop or Delegate

Seal of Diocese

_____
Signature of Chancellor or other Notary

2. Grant of Faculties to Pastors of Territorial Parishes

This document may also be used for the priest supervisor of a parish without a pastor, since he is to have the powers and faculties of a pastor (c. 517, §2). See chapter 5 for the faculties.

I have the pleasure of granting to you, N., the enclosed faculties of a pastor in the Diocese of N. This list of faculties replaces any previous list of diocesan faculties granted to pastors [priest supervisors] by me, my predecessors, or any other diocesan official.

1. Unless otherwise noted, these faculties may be validly used only within the territory of the parish of N.

2. These faculties remain in force as long as you hold office, unless they are expressly revoked.

3. Unless otherwise noted, you may subdelegate any of these faculties, in individual cases, to another priest in good standing or to a deacon, if permitted by canon law.

4. When you are on vacation or otherwise legitimately absent, you may grant to the priest who replaces you all the faculties on the diocesan *pagellae* for priests and pastors, including those faculties that otherwise may not be validly subdelegated. The delegation must be in writing, dated, and signed by you, with a copy retained in the parish archives. It should be worded as follows:

   I, [name of pastor], hereby grant to you, [name of visiting priest], all the faculties of the diocese for priests and pastors as indicated on these *pagellae*, which faculties are valid until [give the date of your return, which may not be more than a month without permission of the bishop].

A copy of the pagellae *for priests and pastors should be attached to the document of delegation.*

If applicable:
5. You may also grant to a priest who replaces the parochial vicar the faculties on the diocesan *pagellae* for priests and parochial vicars, using the same procedure as in no. 4.

Given at _____ this .... day of .... [year].

_____
Signature of Bishop or Delegate

Seal of Diocese

_____
Signature of Chancellor or other Notary

3. GRANT OF FACULTIES TO PASTORS OF PERSONAL PARISHES, RECTORS OF CHURCHES, MILITARY CHAPLAINS, AND LIKE CHAPLAINS

This document must be adjusted according to whether the priest is a pastor of a personal parish, a rector of a church, a military chaplain, or another chaplain who has the full pastoral care of a community of the faithful. See chapter 5 for the faculties, noting especially the limited faculties for rectors of churches (indicated by the abbreviation "R").

I have the pleasure of granting to you, N., the enclosed faculties of [a pastor of a personal parish, a rector of a church, a military chaplain, or other chaplain] in the Diocese [or in the Military Ordinariate] of N. This list of faculties replaces any previous list of diocesan faculties for pastors [or other office] granted by me, my predecessors, or any other diocesan official.

1. Unless otherwise noted, these faculties may be validly used only within the limits of your pastoral charge and for those persons entrusted to you for pastoral care.

2. These faculties remain in force as long as you hold office, unless they are expressly revoked.

3. Unless otherwise noted, you may subdelegate any of these faculties, in individual cases, to another priest in good standing or to a deacon, if permitted by canon law.

4. When you are on vacation or otherwise legitimately absent, you may grant to the priest who replaces you all the faculties on the diocesan *pagellae* for priests and [pastors, rectors, or chaplains], including those faculties that otherwise may not be validly subdelegated. The delegation must be in writing, dated, and signed by you, with a copy retained in the archives. It should be worded as follows:

> I, [name of pastor/rector/chaplain], hereby grant to you, [name of visiting priest], all the faculties of the diocese for priests and [pastors, rectors, or chaplains] as indicated on these *pagellae*, which faculties are valid until [give the date of your return, which may not be more than a month without permission of the bishop].

A copy of the pagellae *for priests and [pastors, rectors, or chaplains] should be attached to the document of delegation.*

If applicable:
5. You may also grant to a priest who replaces the parochial vicar the faculties on the diocesan *pagellae* for priests and parochial vicars, using the same procedure as in no. 4.

Given at _____ this .... day of .... [year].

_____
Signature of Bishop or Delegate

Seal of Diocese

_____
Signature of Chancellor or other Notary

4. Grant of Faculties to Parochial Vicars

See chapter 5 for the faculties appropriate to the office of parochial vicar (indicated by the abbreviation "PV").

I have the pleasure of granting to you, N., the enclosed faculties of a parochial vicar in the Diocese of N. This list of faculties replaces any previous list of diocesan faculties granted to parochial vicars by me, my predecessors, or any other diocesan official.

1. Unless otherwise noted, these faculties may be validly used only within the territory of the parish of N.

   Alternate for a personal parish:
   [1. Unless otherwise noted, these faculties may be validly used only for parishioners within the limits of your pastoral charge.]

2. These faculties remain in force as long as you hold office, unless they are expressly revoked.

3. Unless otherwise noted and with at least the presumed permission of the pastor, you may subdelegate any of these faculties, in individual cases, to another priest in good standing or to a deacon, if permitted by canon law.

Given at _____ this .... day of .... [year].

_____
Signature of Bishop or Delegate

                                                            Seal of Diocese

_____
Signature of Chancellor or other Notary

5. GRANT OF FACULTIES TO PRIEST CHAPLAINS WITHOUT THE FULL PASTORAL CARE OF A COMMUNITY

*This document is intended for chaplains of health care institutions, educational institutions, convents of lay religious, etc. It is **not** intended for chaplains who have the full pastoral care of a community (those who may celebrate adult initiation, reception into full communion, and funerals and assist at marriages). See chapter 5 for the appropriate faculties of such chaplains (indicated by the abbreviation "Chpl").*

I have the pleasure of granting to you, N., the enclosed faculties of a chaplain in the Diocese of N. This list of faculties replaces any previous list of diocesan faculties granted to chaplains by me, my predecessors, or any other diocesan official.

1. Unless otherwise noted, these faculties may be validly used only within the limits of your pastoral charge and for those persons entrusted to you for pastoral care.

2. These faculties remain in force as long as you hold office, unless they are expressly revoked.

3. Unless otherwise noted, you may subdelegate any of these faculties, in individual cases, to another priest in good standing or to a deacon, if permitted by canon law.

Given at _____ this .... day of .... [year].

_____
Signature of Bishop or Delegate

Seal of Diocese

_____
Signature of Chancellor or other Notary

6. Grant of Faculties to Deacons

See chapter 6, sections 1–3, for the faculties to accompany this document.

I have the pleasure of granting to you, [name of deacon], the enclosed faculties for deacons in the Diocese of N. This list of faculties replaces any previous list of diocesan faculties granted to deacons by me, my predecessors, or any other diocesan official.

1. Unless otherwise noted, you may validly use these faculties within the territory of the diocese.

2. These faculties remain in force as long as you retain your domicile or quasi-domicile in this diocese, unless they are expressly revoked.

3. Unless otherwise noted and with at least the presumed permission of the pastor or other rector of the church, you may subdelegate any of the faculties granted by the bishop [section 3], in individual cases, to another deacon or priest in good standing.

Given at _____ this .... day of .... [year].

_____
Signature of Bishop or Delegate

Seal of Diocese

_____
Signature of Chancellor or other Notary

7. Grant of Faculties to Deacon Pastoral Administrators

See chapter 6, section 4 for the faculties to accompany this document.

I have the pleasure of granting to you, N., the enclosed faculties for a pastoral administrator in the Diocese of N. This list of faculties replaces any previous list of diocesan faculties granted to deacon pastoral administrators by me, my predecessors, or any other diocesan official.

1. Unless otherwise noted, you may validly use these faculties only within the territory of the parish of N.

   Alternate for deacons in personal parishes or equivalent personal jurisdictions:
   [1. Unless otherwise noted, these faculties may be validly used only within the limits of your pastoral charge and for those persons entrusted to you for pastoral care.]

2. These faculties remain in force as long as you hold the office of pastoral administrator.

3. Unless otherwise noted, you may subdelegate any of these faculties in individual cases to another deacon or priest in good standing.

Given at _____ this .... day of .... [year].

_____
Signature of Bishop or Delegate

                                                          Seal of Diocese
_____
Signature of Chancellor or other Notary

8. Grant of Faculties to Lay Pastoral Administrators

See chapter 7 for the faculties that are to accompany this document.

In order that you may exercise the ministry of pastoral administrator in the Diocese of N., I have the pleasure of granting to you, [name of minister], the enclosed faculties. This list of faculties replaces any previous list of diocesan faculties granted to lay pastoral administrators by me, my predecessors, or any other diocesan official.

1. Unless otherwise noted, you may not validly subdelegate these faculties.

2. Unless otherwise noted, you may validly use these faculties only within the territory of the parish of N.

3. Unless otherwise noted, you may use the faculties for extraordinary ministries (ExM) only if an ordinary minister is unavailable or if ordinary ministers are not available in sufficient numbers.

4. Unless these faculties are expressly revoked, they remain in force as long as you hold the office of lay pastoral administrator.

Given at _____ this .... day of .... [year].

_____
Signature of Bishop or Delegate

Seal of Diocese

_____
Signature of Chancellor or other Notary

9. Grant of Mandates from the Priest Supervisor to the Pastoral Administrator

See chapter 6, section 5 (deacons) and chapter 7, section 7 (lay ministers) for the mandates that are to accompany this document.

I grant you, N., the following mandates, to be fulfilled in accord with canon law and civil law. These mandates are in effect for the duration of your office as pastoral administrator of [name of parish] unless they are legitimately amended or revoked.

Given at _____ on [date].

_____
Signature of Priest Supervisor

_____
Signature of Notary or Witness

Copies: [The bishop of the diocese]
         [Parish archives of the pastoral administrator]

10. Grant of Faculties to Officials of the Diocesan Curia

See chapter 8 for faculties specific to various officials of the diocesan curia.

To facilitate the functioning of your office of [name of office] in the Diocese of N., I have the pleasure of granting to you, N., the enclosed faculties.

1. Unless otherwise noted, you may delegate any of these faculties, in writing, to another competent official of the diocese whenever you will be absent or impeded, either for all cases or for individual cases, using these or similar words: "I delegate you, N., all the faculties of my office, except those that may not be delegated, which you may use for all cases that arise [during my absence] or [whenever I am absent]." The delegation must be signed and dated, with a copy retained in the archives.

2. Unless otherwise noted, these faculties may be used on behalf of those who are in the territory of the diocese, including transients *(vagi)* and visitors *(peregrini),* and they may be used on behalf of persons who have domicile or quasi-domicile in the diocese even if you or they are outside the diocese.

3. These faculties remain in force as long as you hold office, unless they are expressly revoked.

Given at _____ this .... day of .... [year].

_____
Signature of Bishop or Delegate

                                                        Seal of Diocese

_____
Signature of Chancellor or other Notary

Select Bibliography

English Titles

Beal, John P. "The Exercise of the Power of Governance by Lay People: State of the Question." *The Jurist* 55 (1995) 1–92.

The Canon Law: Letter and Spirit. Prepared by the Canon Law Society of Great Britain and Ireland in association with the Canadian Canon Law Society. Collegeville, Minn.: The Liturgical Press, 1995.

Chyang, Peter B. *Decennial Faculties for Ordinaries in Quasi-Dioceses.* Canon Law Studies, no. 402. Washington, D.C.: The Catholic University of America, 1961.

Clergy Procedural Handbook. Edited by Randolph R. Calvo and Nevin J. Klinger. Washington, D.C.: Canon Law Society of America, 1992.

Code of Canon Law Annotated. Translation of the fifth Spanish-language edition of the commentary prepared under the responsibility of the Instituto Martín de Azpilcueta. Edited by E. Caparros, M. Thériault, and J. Thorn. Montréal: Wilson & Lafleur Limitée, 1993.

Coriden, James A. *An Introduction to Canon Law.* New York/Mahwah, N.J.: Paulist Press, 1991.

Cusack, Barbara Anne, and Therese Guerin Sullivan. *Pastoral Care in Parishes Without a Pastor: Applications of Canon 517, §2.* Washington, D.C.: Canon Law Society of America, 1995.

Eagleton, George. *The Diocesan Quinquennial Faculties Formula IV: A Historical Synopsis and Commentary.* Canon Law Studies, no. 248. Washington, D.C.: The Catholic University of America, 1948.

Euart, Sharon A. "Parishes Without a Resident Pastor: Reflections on the Provisions and Conditions of Canon 517, §2 and Its Implications." *The Jurist* 54 (1994) 369–386.

Groves, Richard. "Priestless Parishes: Exploring Future Possibilities." *CLSA Proceedings* 48 (1986) 54–60.

Huels, John M. *The Catechumenate and the Law: A Pastoral and Canonical Commentary for the Church in the United States.* Chicago: Liturgy Training Publications, 1994.

————. "Interpreting an Instruction Approved *in forma specifica.*" *Studia Canonica* 32 (1998) 5–46.

————. *The Pastoral Companion: A Canon Law Handbook for Catholic Ministry.* Third ed., revised and updated. Quincy, Ill.: Franciscan Press, 2002.

————. "Permissions, Authorizations and Faculties in Canon Law." *Studia Canonica* 36 (2002) 25–58.

————. "The Power of Governance and Its Exercise by Lay Persons: A Juridical Approach." *Studia Canonica* 35 (2001) 59–96.

————. "A Theory of Juridical Documents Based on Canons 29–34." *Studia Canonica* 32 (1998) 337–370.

Kearney, Raymond A. *The Principles of Delegation.* Canon Law Studies, no. 55. Washington, D.C.: The Catholic University of America, 1929.

McCormack, Alan. *The Term "Privilege": A Textual Study of Its Meaning and Use in the 1983 Code of Canon Law.* Serie Diritto Canonico, no. 23. Roma: Editrice Pontifice Università Gregoriana, 1997.

Matthews, Kevin. "Faculties Revisited for the New Millennium." *Canon Law Society of Australia and New Zealand Newsletter*, no. 1 (1999) 21–34.

The Ministry of Governance. Edited by James K. Mallett. Washington, D.C.: Canon Law Society of America, 1986.

Motry, Hubert L. *Diocesan Faculties According to the Code of Canon Law.* Canon Law Studies, no. 16. Washington, D.C.: The Catholic University of America, 1922.

A New Commentary on the Code of Canon Law. Commissioned by the CLSA. Edited by John P. Beal, James A. Coriden, and Thomas J. Green. New York/Mahwah, N.J.: Paulist Press, 2000.

Provost, James H. "The Participation of the Laity in the Governance of the Church." *Studia Canonica* 17 (1983) 417–448.

————. "Permanent Deacons in the 1983 Code." *CLSA Proceedings* 46 (1984) 175–191.

Renken, John A. "The Canonical Implications of Canon 517 §2: Parishes Without Resident Pastors?" *CLSA Proceedings* 50 (1988) 249–263.

Roelker, Edward G. *Principles of Privilege According to the Code of Canon Law*. Canon Law Studies, no. 35. Washington, D.C.: The Catholic University of America, 1926.

Smith, Rosemary. "Lay Persons in the Diocesan Curia: Legal Structures and Practical Issues." *CLSA Proceedings* 49 (1987) 35–44.

Torfs, Rik. "Auctoritas-potestas-iurisdictio-facultas-officium-munus: A Conceptual Analysis." *Concilium*, no. 197: *Power in the Church*. Edited by James H. Provost and Knut Walf. Pages 63–73. Edinburgh: T & T Clark, 1988.

Woestman, William H. *Sacraments: Initiation, Penance, Anointing of the Sick. Commentary on Canons 840–1007*. Ottawa: St. Paul University, Faculty of Canon Law, 1996.

Titles in Other Languages

Amann, Thomas A. *Der Verwaltungsakt für Einzelfälle: Eine Untersuchung aufgrund des Codex Iuris Canonici*. Erzabtei St. Ottilien: EOS Verlag, 1997.

Aymans, Winfried. *Kanonisches Recht: Lehrbuch aufgrund des Codex Iuris Canonici*, initiated by Eduard Eichmann, continued by Klaus Mörsdorf, and updated by Winfried Aymans. Paderborn: Ferdinand Schöningh, vols. 1 (1991) and 2 (1996).

Belluco, Bartholomaeus I. *Novissimae Ordinariorum locorum facultates: Commentarium in motu-proprio «Pastorale munus»*. Romae: Pontificium Athenaeum Antonianum, 1964.

Buijs, Ludovicus. *Facultates et privilegia episcoporum concessa motu proprio «Pastorale munus»*. Second ed. Romae: Apud Aedes Universitatis Gregorianae, 1964.

Canosa, Javier. "De rescriptis," in *Comentario exegético al Código de Derecho Canónico*. Edited by Angel Marzoa, Jorge Mira, and Rafael Rodríguez-Ocaña. Pamplona: EUNSA, 1996.

D'Ostilio, Franceso. *Il diritto amministrativo della Chiesa*. Studi Giuridici, no. 37. Città del Vaticano: Libreria Editrice Vaticana, 1995.

————. "Tipologia ed esecuzione degli atti amministrativi." *Apollinaris* 45 (1972) 261–289.

García Martín, Julio. "Facultades concedidas a los legados pontificios por la Congregación para la Evangelización de los Pueblos." *Commentarium pro Religiosis et Missionariis* 82 (2001) 317–343.

Gefaell Chamochin, Pablo. *El régimen de la potestad delegada de jurisdicción en la codificación de 1917*. Roma: Centro Accademico Romano della Santa Croce, 1991.

González Ayesta, Juan. *La naturaleza jurídica de las "facultades habituales" en la codificación de 1917*. Berriozar: Navarra Gráfica Ediciones, 2000.

————. "La noción jurídica de «facultad» en los comentadores del Código de 1917." *Ius Canonicum* 40 (2000) 99–123.

Juen, Walter H. *Kirchliches "Management by Delegation" aufgrund can. 131*. Rom: Päpstliche Universität Urbaniana, 1996.

Labandeira, Eduardo. *Cuestiones de derecho administrativo canónico*. Pamplona: Universidad de Navarra, 1992.

————. "Naturaleza jurídica del poder de absolver los pecados desde la perspectiva del Vatican II y del nuevo Código." In *Reconciliación y penitencia: V simposio internacional de teología de la Universidad de Navarra*. Edited by Jesús Sancho et al. Pages 957–981. Pamplona: Universidad de Navarra, 1983.

————. *Tratado de derecho administrativo canónico*. Second ed., rev. Pamplona: Universidad de Navarra, 1993.

López-Illana, Francisco. "La suplencia de la facultad de asistir al matrimonio." *Ius Canonicum* 37 (1997) 73–122.

Naz, Raoul. "Facultés." *Dictionnaire de droit canonique*, tome 5, cols. 800–802. Paris: Letouzey et Ané, 1953.

Peeters, Hermes. *Facultates quas Ordinarii et missionarii habere solent cum brevi commentario*. Third ed., revised. Romae: Pontificium Athenaeum Antonianum, 1960.

Politi, Vincenzo. *La giurisdizione ecclesiastica e la sua delegazione*. Milano: La Tradizione Editrice, 1937.

Tessier, Maxime. *Juridiction déléguée «ab homine»*. Rome: L'Institut Pontifical International "Angelicum," 1936.

Wernz, Franciscus X., and Petrus Vidal. *Ius Canonicum ad Codicis normam exactum*, tomus 1: *Normae generales*. Romae: Apud Aedes Universitatis Gregorianae, 1938.

Glossary

The following is a list of terms that are used in this book and that may not be familiar to all readers. The citation of a canon number following a definition does not mean that the definition is taken directly from the code. Rather, it is usually only a reference to one or more of the places in the law where the term is treated, mentioned, or exemplified.

Abrogation. The revocation of a law in its totality (cc. 6, 20).

Act of administration. Any juridic act performed in the administration of a parish, diocese, or other juridic person, e.g., singular administrative acts and contracts.

Administrative act, singular. A formal act given in writing by an executive authority that makes some determination, whether favorable or unfavorable, for an individual or individuals, e.g., an individual decree, a precept, or a rescript (cc. 35–47).

Administrator. (1) An official of the church who is responsible for administrative tasks in general, including planning, organization, leadership of groups, finances, etc. (2) A person responsible for financial administration.

Adult. A person who is at least eighteen years of age (c. 97, §1); for the RCIA, one who is seven years old and has the use of reason (c. 852).

Alienation. The transfer of ownership of property that is part of the stable patrimony of a juridic person (cc. 1291–1296).

Apostasy. The total repudiation of the Christian faith after the reception of baptism (c. 751).

Apostolic constitution. A formal, solemn document issued by the pope on matters of doctrinal or juridical importance for the universal Church.

Apostolic See. The archdiocese of Rome, also called the Holy See. In canon law it is a generic term that includes the pope, the secretariat of state, and the dicasteries of the Roman curia (c. 361).

Assist at marriages. See Canonical form.

Association of the faithful. A group of the faithful, distinct from institutes of consecrated life and societies of apostolic life, whether of a private or public nature, organized for a spiritual, charitable, or apostolic purpose (cc. 298–329).

Attempted marriage. A marriage that is manifestly null due to lack of legal form or a diriment impediment (cc. 694, §1, 2°; 1041, 3°; 1085).

Auditor. A tribunal official who assists the judge in the collection of proofs (c. 1428).

Authentic interpretation. An interpretation of the law given by the legislator or by the one to whom he has given the power to interpret his laws authoritatively. Authentic interpretations have the force of law (c. 16).

Authorization. A juridic empowerment, granted by means of an administrative act of the competent authority, which enables a person to perform lawfully an act of ministry or administration other than an act of the power of governance; a non-jurisdictional faculty.

Bination. The celebration and/or concelebration of two Masses by a priest on a single day. The verb form is "to binate" (c. 905, §2).

Canon law. (1) All the laws, both divine and ecclesiastical, universal and particular, of the Roman Catholic Church. (2) The laws that appear as canons in the Code of Canon Law and the Code of Canons of the Eastern Churches. (3) The scholarly discipline whose subject matter is the laws of the Church.

Canon penitentiary. The priest appointed as confessor with habitual faculties to remit automatic censures that have not been declared and are not reserved to the Apostolic See. In dioceses where there is no chapter of canons, he is called the priest penitentiary or penitentiary (cc. 508, 968).

Canonical form. The requirement that the marriage of a Catholic be celebrated before two witnesses and a priest or deacon who has the faculty to assist at marriages (c. 1108).

Catechist (general). One who assists the pastor or local ordinary in the religious formation of children and adults (cc. 776, 780).

Catechist (mission). A duly instructed lay person devoted to spreading the gospel and organizing liturgical functions and works of charity under the moderation of a missionary (c. 785).

Censure. A penalty of excommunication, interdict, or suspension (cc. 1331–1338).

Chancellor. An official whose principal task is to oversee the diocesan archives. Frequently chancellors are delegated other specific powers by the diocesan bishop (c. 482).

Chaplain. A priest to whom is entrusted in a stable manner the pastoral care, at least in part, of some community or particular group of the faithful (c. 564). By custom, any minister assigned to a share in the pastoral care of certain non-parochial communities and institutions, including deacons and lay ministers.

Chapter. An official, formal meeting of religious, whether at the general, provincial, or conventual level (cc. 631–633).

Chrism, sacred. The oil consecrated by a bishop for use in baptism, confirmation, holy orders, and the dedication of a church and an altar (c. 880, §2).

Christian faithful *(Christifidelis)*. A person validly baptized. Collectively, the Christian faithful make up the Church, the community of baptized believers in Christ (c. 204).

Church (building). A building designated for divine worship to which the faithful have a right to go, especially for the celebration of the liturgy (c. 1214).

Church (community). A community of the baptized faithful of Christ that has maintained the substance of Christian doctrine, valid sacraments, and a hierarchy in apostolic succession, e.g., the Roman Catholic Church, the Russian Orthodox Church, the Polish National Church (c. 844, §3). See Ecclesial community.

Church *sui iuris*. A community of the faithful united by its own hierarchy in communion with the pope that is expressly or tacitly recognized by the supreme authority of the Church as autonomous, e.g., Latin, Ruthenian, Ukrainian, Maronite, Melkite, etc. (CCEO, c. 27). There are twenty-two such churches in the Roman Catholic Church.

Civil law. The laws of the secular state, as opposed to canon law (c. 22). The term may also refer to the legal system based on Roman law, as in continental Europe.

College of bishops. All the bishops in communion with the pope (c. 336).

College of consultors. A group of six to twelve priests selected by the bishop from among the members of the presbyteral council to advise him on certain matters determined in the law (c. 502).

Common error. The mistaken judgment of a community that a minister or administrator has a power or faculty when he does not have it (c. 144).

Commutation. The substitution by the competent authority of one legal obligation for another one that the subject of the law can more easily satisfy (c. 1245).

Consecrated life. Life consecrated by the profession of the evangelical counsels. Those in consecrated life include hermits, virgins, people in religious institutes, secular institutes, and other forms recognized by the Apostolic See (cc. 573, 605).

Consent (marital). The essence of marriage; the free choice between a man and a woman to marry each other (c. 1057).

Consummation. The first act of sexual intercourse, open to procreation, between a man and a woman, performed willingly and mutually, after entering a valid marriage (c. 1061).

Convalidation. A legal remedy by which a couple's invalid marriage consent is subsequently made valid (c. 1156).

Crime. An impediment to marriage that arises when a person kills his or her spouse to marry another, or when a man and a woman have caused the death of the spouse of either of them by physical or moral cooperation to be free to marry each other (c. 1090).

Curia. Institutions and persons who furnish assistance to an ecclesiastical authority, especially the pope, Eastern patriarchs, and major archbishops, and all diocesan bishops and eparchs and their canonical equivalents. Diocesan and papal curias have pastoral, administrative, and judicial functions (c. 469).

Custom. A practice of a community that the community considers normative; it can have the force of law in accord with canons 24–26.

Danger of death. The condition of being at risk of dying due to illness, injury, warfare, execution, or other cause (c. 1079).

Days of penance. Days on which acts of penance are required or recommended, especially Ash Wednesday and Good Friday and all Fridays that are not solemnities (cc. 1249–1253).

Dean. Also called the vicar forane or archpriest, a priest in charge of a deanery (vicariate forane), which is a grouping of parishes in territorial proximity within a diocese (c. 553).

Declaration of invalidity (or nullity) of marriage. The authoritative judgment by a judicial tribunal, following procedures established in canon law, that a marriage is invalid (cc. 1671–1691).

Decree (executory). Similar to a general decree, but issued by an executive rather than a legislative authority. Executory decrees are not laws, but are binding administrative norms that determine more precisely the methods to be observed in applying the law or themselves urge the observance of laws (cc. 31–33).

Decree (general). An act that is properly speaking a law, issued by a competent legislator for a community capable of receiving laws (cc. 29–30).

Decree (judicial). An act of a judge that makes a binding determination on a matter concerning a trial (c. 1629).

Decree (singular). An administrative act issued by a competent executive authority in which a decision is given or provision is made in a particular case (c. 48).

Defender of the bond. A judicial official whose function is to propose and clarify everything that can be reasonably adduced against the nullity or dissolution of the bond of marriage (c. 1432).

Delegation by law *(a iure)*. The grant of a faculty by the law (e.g., c. 883, 3°).

Delegation, personal *(ab homine)*. The act of granting a faculty to a person by another person who has the power to grant it (c. 137). See also Subdelegation.

Delict. A crime; an offense for which a canonical punishment has been established in the law (cc. 1364–1399).

Derogation. The revocation of part of a law; an alteration in the law that does not change or abolish it completely (c. 20).

Dicastery. A generic term for any of the departments of the Roman curia, including congregations, tribunals, pontifical councils, offices (cc. 64, 354).

Dimissorial. A letter written by one's ordinary to the ordaining bishop attesting that a candidate for holy orders has met all the requirements for ordination (cc. 1050–1052).

Diocesan bishop. A bishop in charge of a diocese. Equated in the law with diocesan bishops ordinarily are the heads of other particular churches, namely, territorial prelatures, territorial abbacies, apostolic vicariates, apostolic prefectures, and apostolic administrations erected on a stable basis (c. 368).

Diocesan faculties. Habitual faculties granted by the diocesan bishop or his delegate to those who exercise offices and functions of ministry and diocesan and parochial administration.

Diocesan right. A kind of institute of consecrated life whose immediate ecclesiastical superior is the bishop of a diocese where, in general, the institute has its mother house or where it was founded (c. 594). See Pontifical right.

Diocesan synod. An assembly of priests and other members of the faithful from a particular church, convoked by the diocesan bishop, generally to enact diocesan laws and policies on various matters (c. 460).

Diriment impediment. Some fact, state, or condition that renders a person incapable of marrying validly in the Catholic Church (c. 1073).

Dismissal. A penalty which, for clerics, results in the loss of the clerical state and, for members of institutes of consecrated life and societies of apostolic life, results in loss of membership in their institute or society (cc. 290, 2°; 694; 729; 746).

Disparity of worship. An impediment to marriage between a Catholic and a non-baptized person (c. 1086).

Dispensation. A relaxation of a merely ecclesiastical law in a particular case given by someone who has the power to dispense (c. 85).

Dissolution. The act of legally terminating the bond of marriage in non-consummation and privilege of the faith cases (cc. 1141–1150).

Divine law. The law of God, whether positive or natural, that is binding on all human beings. See also Natural law, Positive law, and Ecclesiastical law.

Domicile. Permanent residence, established by residence with intent to remain in a place permanently unless called away, or by staying there five years (c. 102, §1).

Doubt. A state of mind that withholds assent between two contradictory propositions (c. 14).

Doubt of fact. The state of uncertainty arising when some fact is not conclusively proven, e.g., a doubt about someone's age, or a doubt about the fact of baptism or its valid administration (c. 14).

Doubt of law. The state of uncertainty arising when the meaning of a law is uncertain due, not to ignorance of the law's meaning, but to a defect in the law itself that allows more than one interpretation; the doubt can also pertain to an essential element of the law's effectiveness, e.g., its lawful promulgation, its binding force, its extension. Doubtful laws are not binding (c. 14).

Ecclesial community. A Christian denomination that the Roman Catholic Church does not recognize as having all the essential criteria to constitute it as a church; a Protestant denomination (c. 844). See Church (community).

Ecclesiastical law. A human law of the Church, as opposed to a divine law (c. 11).

Eparch. In the Eastern Catholic churches, the equivalent of a diocesan bishop.

Episcopal vicar. A priest appointed by the diocesan bishop with the same powers as a vicar general but limited to a determined part of the diocese, or to a specific type of business, or to a specified group of persons (c. 476).

Error. Mistaken judgment (cc. 15, 126).

Evangelical counsels. The generic term for poverty, chastity, and obedience that hermits and all members of religious and secular institutes profess (c. 573).

Excardination. The process by which a cleric relinquishes his juridic attachment to a diocese, an institute of consecrated life, or another society of clerics to incardinate in another (cc. 267–272).

Exclaustration. An indult granted to a religious in perpetual vows permitting him or her to live outside a house of the institute.

Excommunication. A censure that forbids a person from having any ministerial participation in the celebration of the liturgy; receiving the sacraments; discharging any ecclesiastical offices, ministries, or functions; and placing acts of governance. There are further effects if the excommunication has been imposed or declared (c. 1331).

Executive power. The power of governance, granted by law or delegation, needed for a capable person to perform validly a general act of canons 31–34 and 94–95 or a singular administrative act of canons 35–93 (cc. 136–144).

Expiatory penalty. A type of penalty, different from a censure; expiatory penalties may be inflicted perpetually, temporarily, or indefinitely (c. 1336).

Extern. A priest or deacon who is staying in the diocese temporarily, whether as a traveler *(peregrinus)* or with quasi-domicile, and who is not incardinated in that diocese.

External forum. As opposed to the internal forum, it is the forum of proofs, the public realm of observable, verifiable acts in which canon law generally operates and in which it can be enforced.

Extraordinary form. Marriage before two witnesses, without the active assistance of a priest or deacon who has the faculty to assist at marriage, which may lawfully be celebrated in danger of death or outside the danger of death when it is foreseen that a qualified priest or deacon will be absent for a month (c. 1116).

Extraordinary minister. A minister of a sacrament or other liturgical rite who functions when the number of ordinary ministers is insufficient for pastoral needs (c. 230, §3).

Faculty. An ecclesiastical power or authorization necessary for performing lawfully an act of ministry or administration in the name of the Church. See also Habitual faculty.

Favor. An exception to the law, such as a dispensation, privilege, or indult, granted to a physical or juridic person by the competent authority.

Feast days. Sundays and holy days of obligation (cc. 1246–1248).

Finance council. A group of the faithful at the diocesan or parish level who advise the bishop or pastor on financial matters (cc. 492, 537, 1280).

Form (canonical). The requirement that, for validity, a Catholic must be married in the presence of a priest or deacon who has the faculty to assist at marriages and two witnesses (c. 1108).

Form (sacramental). The essential words or formula necessary for the validity of a sacrament (c. 841).

General delegation. The act of granting a habitual faculty for all cases (c. 137); used as a synonym for a habitual faculty. See also Special delegation and Habitual faculty.

General instruction *(Institutio generalis).* A text of liturgical law, also containing doctrinal and pastoral orientations, which introduces the *Roman Missal* and the *Liturgy of the Hours.*

Habitual faculty. A faculty that may be used repeatedly on an ongoing basis, whether for a determined or indeterminate period (c. 132). See also General delegation.

Heresy. The obstinate denial after the reception of baptism of some truth that is to be believed as being of divine and catholic faith, or an obstinate doubt concerning the same (c. 751).

Hierarch. In Eastern law, a term roughly equivalent to an ordinary.

Holy See. See Apostolic See.

Homily. The form of preaching done by a cleric at liturgy (c. 767, §1).

House, religious. The lawfully erected place of residence of a religious community under the authority of a superior with a church or oratory in which the Eucharist is celebrated and reserved (c. 608).

Ignorance. Lack of knowledge; also, grounds for marital nullity if the ignorance concerns essential aspects of the nature of marriage (cc. 15, 126, 1096).

Impediment (marital). See Diriment impediment.

Impediment to orders. Some fact or condition that prohibits a man from being licitly ordained (cc. 1040–1049).

Imprimatur. Permission of the local ordinary to publish certain kinds of religious books; from the Latin, "it may be printed" (cc. 824–829).

Incardination. A cleric's juridical attachment to a diocese, an institute of consecrated life, or another clerical society; incardination occurs when one becomes a cleric at ordination to the diaconate, and later by incardinating elsewhere according to the norm of law (cc. 265–272).

Indissolubility. An essential property of marriage requiring a permanent commitment of the spouses and no remarriage except after the death of the spouse (c. 1056).

Individual case(s). A specified case or specified cases for which a faculty can be delegated or subdelegated (c. 137).

Indulgence. The remission before God of the temporal punishment for sins already forgiven, which a member of the faithful obtains under the conditions specified in the List of Indulgences (c. 992).

Indult. (1) A general term for a temporary privilege or other favor granted to someone by competent authority. (2) A specific kind of favor, such as an indult of departure from religious life.

Indult of departure. A rescript granted by the competent authority that permits a perpetually professed or perpetually incorporated member of an institute of consecrated life or a definitively incorporated member of a society of apostolic life to leave the institute or society and cease being a member (cc. 691, 727, 743).

Infant. A person under the age of seven or one who habitually lacks the use of reason (cc. 97, §2; 99).

Institute of consecrated life. The generic term for a religious or secular institute (c. 573).

Instructions *(instructiones).* Norms of executive power that clarify or elaborate on laws and determine the approach to be followed in implementing them (c. 34).

Interdict. A censure that prohibits a person from having any ministerial participation in the liturgy or receiving the sacraments (c. 1332).

Internal forum. The forum of conscience, the private realm of a person's thoughts, sins, and actions that are not publicly known, the confidentiality and privacy of which confessors and spiritual directors must strictly respect (cc. 240, 630, 983–985, 1388).

Invalid. Legally inefficacious.

Irregularity. A perpetual impediment to ordination (c. 1041).

Judicial vicar. Also known as the officialis, the priest who has ordinary power to judge cases in a diocese; he is typically the chief administrator of the tribunal (c. 1420).

Juridic act. An intentional act, performed by a capable person and which, when all requirements for performing the act validly have been observed, has juridic effects specified in the law.

Juridic person. Aggregates of persons or things, whether public or private, established by law or by a competent ecclesiastical authority and ordered toward a purpose congruent with the mission of the Church and transcending the purpose of the individuals who comprise it; a canonically established church corporation, e.g., a diocese, a province of a religious institute, a Catholic hospital, a charitable foundation (cc. 113–123).

Jurisdiction. (1) The extent of an official's competence, whether by territory, persons, or tasks. (2) A synonym for power of governance.

Laicization. The loss of the clerical state by means of a rescript from the Holy See (c. 290, 3°).

Latae sententiae **penalty.** A censure of excommunication, interdict, or suspension incurred automatically upon the commission of a canonical crime (c. 1314).

Legal relationship. The relationship arising through legal adoption; it is an impediment to marriage in the direct line or in the second degree of the collateral line (c. 1094).

Legate (papal). A representative of the pope to a nation and conference of bishops (a nuncio) or to the conference alone (an apostolic delegate) (cc. 362–367).

Legislative power. The power of governance exercised by an authority who is competent to enact laws, e.g., the pope, the diocesan bishop, an ecumenical or particular council (c. 135, §2).

Liceity. Lawfulness, licitness; generally used of a law whose observance is not necessary for the validity of a legal act.

Liturgy. Worship carried out in the name of the Church by persons lawfully deputed and through acts approved by the authority of the Church (c. 834, §2).

Local ordinary. Also called "ordinary of the place"; a generic term for the pope, diocesan bishops, those equivalent to diocesan bishops in law (c. 368), vicars general, and episcopal vicars (c. 134, §2).

Major superiors. Those who govern a religious institute, a province of an institute, a part equivalent to a province, an autonomous house, and their vicars (c. 620).

Minor. A person under eighteen years of age; also a person who habitually lacks the use of reason (cc. 97, 99).

Mixed marriage. A marriage between a Catholic and a non-Catholic, especially a baptized non-Catholic (c. 1124).

Motu proprio. Literally, "on his own initiative"; a term used for a document when it is issued on the legislator's or administrator's own initiative and not at the request of another, as in a rescript granted *motu proprio* (c. 63, §1).

Natural law. The body of laws and principles known by human reason as emanating from God and binding on all human beings.

Non-consummated marriage *(matrimonium non consummatum).* A presumably valid marriage in which the parties never freely and mutually have sexual intercourse, open to procreation, after exchanging marital consent (cc. 1061, §§ 1, 2; 1697–1706).

Non-jurisdictional act. An act that is not an act of the power of governance. See Power of governance.

Notary. An official appointed to authenticate official documents in the administrative or judicial arena (cc. 483, 1437).

Nuncio (papal). The ambassador of the pope to a country that has formal diplomatic relations with the Holy See (c. 365).

Oath. The invocation of the divine name as a witness to the truth; an oath cannot be taken unless in behalf of truth, judgment, and justice (c. 1199).

Oath of fidelity. A formula to be said after the profession of faith by the faithful mentioned in canon 833, nn. 5–8 (c. 833).

Occult cases. Cases of impediments to holy orders or marriage that are not publicly known, whether or not they are incapable of proof in the external forum.

Occult impediment. An impediment to ordination or marriage that is not provable in the external forum (c. 1074). See Occult cases.

Office. A stable function established by divine or ecclesiastical law to be exercised for a spiritual purpose, e.g., the office of pope, diocesan bishop, major superior, vicar general, pastor (c. 145).

Oil of catechumens. The holy oil used to anoint adult catechumens during the catechumenate or infants during the celebration of baptism.

Oil of the sick. The holy oil used in the sacrament of the anointing of the sick; it is blessed by the bishop or, in case of necessity, by a priest during the celebration of the rite (c. 999).

Oratory. A place designated for worship with the permission of the ordinary for the benefit of some community or assembly of the faithful who gather there. Other members of the faithful may also have access to it with the consent of the competent superior (c. 1223).

Ordinary. A generic term that includes all local ordinaries and major superiors of clerical religious institutes of pontifical right and of clerical societies of apostolic life of pontifical right (c. 134, §1).

Ordinary power. The power of governance that the law itself joins to a certain office (c. 131, §1).

Pagella. A list of faculties.

Parochial vicar. Also called an associate pastor or curate, a priest who assists the pastor in the pastoral ministry of a parish (c. 545).

Particular church. A generic term for the territorial units of the Latin church, namely, dioceses, territorial prelatures, territorial abbacies, apostolic vicariates, apostolic prefectures, and apostolic administrations erected on a stable basis (c. 368).

Particular law. As opposed to universal law, a law made for a particular territory or for a particular group of the faithful (c. 13).

Pastor *(parochus).* Also called "parish priest"; the priest who is entrusted with the pastoral care of a parish (c. 519).

Pastoral administrator. One of several unofficial titles for a deacon or lay minister who has a share in the exercise of the pastoral care of a parish in accord with canon 517, §2.

Pastoral council. A group of the faithful at the diocesan or parish level who assist and advise the bishop or pastor, especially in matters relating to pastoral work (cc. 511, 536).

Pastors of souls, or pastors *(pastores).* A generic term referring to bishops and presbyters who exercise the pastoral ministry.

Pauline privilege. The dissolution of a marriage between two unbaptized parties, one of whom is later baptized, provided the non-baptized party departs (cc. 1143–1147).

Penal precept. A precept that threatens to impose a penalty (c. 1319). See Precept.

Penal remedy. A warning from the ordinary to a person who is in the proximate occasion of committing an offense or who is suspected of having committed an offense, or a rebuke by the ordinary to a person from whose behavior there arises scandal or serious disturbance of order (c. 1339).

Penance (penal). Some work of religion, piety, or charity imposed by an ordinary on a person who has committed some offense (c. 1340).

Personal parish. A non-territorial parish established for a homogeneous group of persons, usually on the basis of language and/or ethnicity.

Petitioner. The party who brings a case before a church tribunal, e.g., a spouse seeking a declaration of invalidity of marriage (cc. 1476–1480).

Petrine privilege. The dissolution of a marriage between a baptized and an unbaptized party given by the pope in favor of the faith of one party.

Pious foundation. A trust or endowment established for a specific religious purpose, e.g., the celebration of Masses for a deceased person (cc. 1303–1307).

Plenary council. A particular council, generally convoked to enact particular laws, for all the particular churches belonging to the same conference of bishops (c. 439).

Pontifical right. A kind of institute of consecrated life whose immediate ecclesiastical superior is the Apostolic See (c. 593).

Positive law (divine). The truths of the faith revealed in sacred scripture and proclaimed in the dogmas of the Church.

Power of governance. Also known as jurisdiction, the power connected with ecclesiastical offices or granted to persons for the performance of specific juridic acts. It is divided into legislative, executive, and judicial power of governance (cc. 129–144).

Precept. An individual decree by which a direct and legitimate injunction is placed upon a determined person or upon determined persons to do or to omit something, especially urging the observance of a law (c. 49).

Presbyter. The second rank of the clergy; a priest who is not a bishop. See Priest.

Presbyteral council. A group of priests chosen to represent all the priests of a diocese to aid the bishop in the governance of the diocese (c. 495).

Presumed permission. The tacit permission of competent authority for a ministerial act; a permission that may be supposed unless there is evidence to the contrary.

Priest *(sacerdos).* A generic term for both presbyters and bishops.

Priest supervisor. An unofficial title for the priest, endowed with the powers and faculties of a pastor, who oversees the pastoral care exercised by a pastoral administrator in a parish without a resident pastor (c. 517, §2).

Prior bond. An impediment to marriage due to one or more previous marriages when the spouse(s) from that marriage is (are) still alive (c. 1085).

Private chapel. A place designated for divine cult for the advantage of one or more physical persons, established with permission of the local ordinary (c. 1226).

Privation. Removal from office as a penalty for an offense (c. 196).

Privilege. A favor for a physical or juridic person that grants a right in perpetuity, unless it is specified as temporary. A privilege can be granted by rescript of the competent legislator and by an executive authority to which the legislator has granted this power (c. 76).

Procurator. Similar to an advocate, someone appointed to perform judicial business for a party in an ecclesiastical proceeding (c. 1481).

Profession. The act, whether by vow or other sacred bond, of a person assuming a life of poverty, chastity, and obedience in a religious or secular institute (cc. 573, 654, 712).

Profession of faith. A formula, approved by the Apostolic See, which must be uttered by certain officials and professors at the beginning of their term of office or appointment (c. 833).

Prohibition. See *Vetitum.*

Promoter of justice. A diocesan judicial official appointed by the bishop for contentious cases in which the public good could be at stake and for penal cases (c. 1430).

Promulgation. The official act by which a new law or general executory decree is published (cc. 7–8; 31, §2).

Proper power. The ordinary power of governance exercised in one's own name, e.g., the power exercised by a diocesan bishop or a major superior (c. 131).

Province (ecclesiastical). A territorial unit consisting of all the particular churches in one area, namely, the metropolitan see and its suffragan sees (c. 431).

Provincial council. A particular council, generally held to enact particular laws for all the particular churches of a province (c. 440).

Proxy marriage. The exchange of marital consent given by one party who is present and by someone mandated by the absent party to represent him or her (c. 1105).

Public propriety. A relationship that arises from an invalid marriage after common life has been established or from notorious and public concubinage; it is an impediment to marriage in the first degree of the direct line between a man and the blood relatives of the woman, and vice-versa (c. 1093).

Quasi-domicile. Temporary residence, acquired by intent to stay in a certain place at least three months unless called away, or by staying there for three months (c. 102, §2).

Radical sanation *(sanatio in radice).* The convalidation of an invalid marriage without the renewal of consent (c. 1161).

Ratified marriage *(matrimonium ratum).* A valid marriage of two baptized persons; a sacramental marriage (c. 1061).

Recourse. An appeal against a decision made by a church authority through an administrative, rather than a judicial, process (cc. 1734 ff.).

Rector (of a church). (1) The priest in charge of any church (pastor, religious superior, etc.). (2). A priest to whom is given the care of some church that is not parochial, capitular, or connected with a house of a religious community or a society of apostolic life (c. 556).

Region (ecclesiastical). A grouping of neighboring provinces, e.g., all the provinces of a nation (c. 433).

Religious institute. The generic term for a religious order, congregation, or society. Religious institutes are characterized by members who take public vows of poverty, chastity, and obedience and live in common as brothers or sisters (c. 607).

Removal. The involuntary loss of office for grave reasons according to the procedures determined in law (cc. 192–195).

Rescript. An administrative act given in writing by a competent executive authority by which there is granted to someone requesting it a privilege, dispensation, or another favor (c. 59).

Resignation. The voluntary renunciation of office by an officeholder for a just and proportionate reason (cc. 187–189).

Respondent. In a church trial, the party who is the defendant and responds to the charges made by the petitioner (cc. 1476–1480).

Rite. The liturgical, theological, spiritual, and disciplinary patrimony, culture, and heritage of a church *sui iuris* that originated and developed in the ancient centers of Christendom. These rites are the Roman, Constantinopolitan (Byzantine), Alexandrian, Antiochene, Armenian, and Chaldean (CCEO, c. 28).

Rules of order. Rules or norms to be observed in assemblies of persons defining the constitution, moderation, and procedures of assemblies (c. 95).

Sanatio in radice. See Radical sanation.

Schism. The refusal of submission to the pope or of communion with the members of the Church subject to him (c. 751).

Secular institute. An institute of consecrated life, akin to a religious institute, in which the members' proper canonical state as clerics or lay persons is unchanged (c. 711).

See. A diocese or archdiocese.

Shrine. A church or other sacred place to which the faithful, with the approval of the local ordinary, make pilgrimages for a particular pious reason (c. 1230).

Society of apostolic life. A group of the faithful organized for an apostolic purpose who, like religious, live in common as brothers or sisters but without taking religious vows (c. 731).

Special delegation. The act of granting a faculty for one or several specified cases (c. 137).

Statutes. The bylaws of a juridic person, by which their purpose, constitution, government, and operation are defined (c. 94).

Subdelegation. The act of further granting to another a faculty that one has been delegated (c. 137, §§ 2–4). See also Delegation, personal.

Sui iuris. See Church *sui iuris.*

Supreme authority. The pope and the college of bishops.

Supreme moderator. A major superior of a religious institute who has power over the entire institute (c. 622).

Suspension. A censure affecting only clergy that forbids the exercise of one or more of their powers, rights, or functions (c. 1333).

Taxative. Complete, total, allowing of no other possibilities or options.

Transfer. (1) The act of a competent authority that effects an officeholder's change from one office to another one (cc. 190–191). (2) The movement of a member of an institute of consecrated life or society of apostolic life to another such institute or society (cc. 684, 730, 744).

Transient *(vagus).* A person who lacks any domicile or quasi-domicile (c. 100).

Traveler *(peregrinus).* A person who is outside the place of domicile or quasi-domicile (c. 100).

Tribunal. A church court, especially for the processing of cases of marital nullity (cc. 1417–1445).

Trination. The celebration by one priest of three Masses on a single day. The verb form is "to trinate" (c. 905, §2).

Universal law. A law binding everyone for whom it was made in the entire Latin Catholic church (c. 12, §§ 1, 2).

Use of reason. The intellectual and volitional capacity necessary to be subject to canon law, presumed to be attained at age seven (c. 11).

Validity. Legal efficacy. Laws affecting the validity of a legal act must be observed for the act to be juridically recognized as effective.

Vetitum. A prohibition on a person from marrying in the Catholic Church that the local ordinary or a tribunal imposes for a time (cc. 1077; 1684, §1).

Viaticum. Holy communion given to a person in danger of death (c. 921).

Vicar forane. See Dean.

Vicar general. A priest appointed by the diocesan bishop to assist him in the governance of the diocese; a vicar general is a local ordinary and has executive power of governance for the entire diocese.

Vicarious power. Ordinary power of governance exercised in the name of another, e.g., the power of a vicar general or judicial vicar exercised in the name of the diocesan bishop (c. 131).

Visitation. The official visit of a diocesan bishop, major superior, or other official to institutions and persons subject to them at the time, conducted in the manner prescribed by law (cc. 396–398; 436; 628; 683; 806; 1301, §2).

Vow. A deliberate and free promise made to God concerning a possible or better good that must be fulfilled in virtue of religion (c. 1191).

INDICES

Index of Canons

The canons cited are from the 1983 Code of Canon Law.

Index of Faculties

This index is divided into two sections: faculties that are acts of executive power of governance and faculties that are authorizations. In searching for a specific faculty, it will often be necessary to consult both sections.

Acts of Executive Power

Acts of extraordinary administration, permission for, 197
Administrator of juridic person, appointment of, 197
Anointing of the sick, permission for communal celebration of, 141, 213
Assistance at marriage, delegation of faculty for, 32, 34, 89–95, 168, 216

Baptism
  additional font of, permission for, 207
  appointment of extraordinary minister of, 207
  conditional, determination of rites for, 225
  participation in by non-Catholic minister, permission for, 225
  in a private home, permission for, 207
Bination and trination, permission for, 209
Blessing
  of a cemetery of a juridic person or family, permission for, 222
  of a sacred place, delegation of a presbyter for, 221
Blessings, designation of lay minister of, 144, 169, 219

Canonical form of marriage, dispensation from, 25, 125, 189, 216, 218, 227
Catechists, deputation of, 131, 166, 206
Catechumenate, abbreviated, permission for, 132, 166, 206
Celebration of Mass while seated, permission for, 211
Censures, remission of, 75, 87, 112, 119, 123
Chaplains, appointment of, 233
Communion under both kinds, permission for, 46, 211
Confessions, hearing
  grant of faculty for, 21, 26, 44, 53, 96, 115, 140, 213
  revocation of faculty for, 72, 73

Authorizations